INERT AMERICA

CROSSROADS TO THE FUTURE

GARY W. GRIFFIN, PH.D.

ISBN: 145159528X
ISBN-13: 9781451595284

Library of Congress Control Number: 2010904972

TABLE OF FIGURES

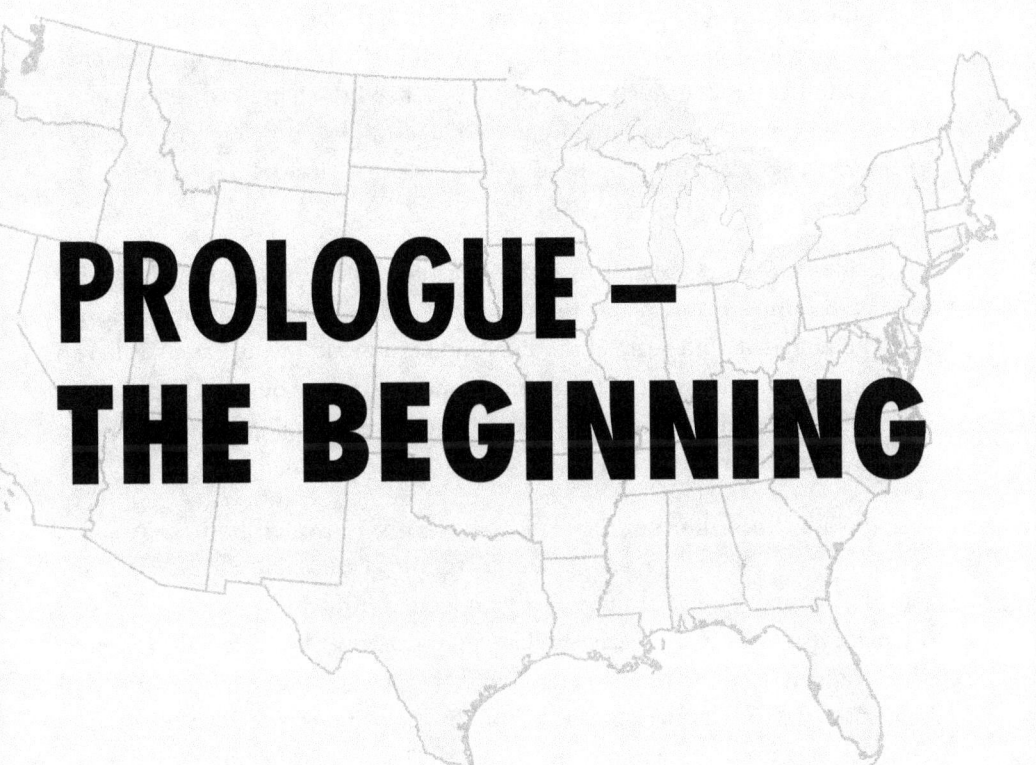

PROLOGUE – THE BEGINNING

I thought I should start with a brief description of my journey. Most, I think, would find it interesting to know that at the end of 2007, I had no intention of writing this book. It wasn't even a thought in my head. So, how did I arrive at the idea for this book?

The year is 2007. I had spent seven years sacrificing, investing, and building a small company. It embodied my hopes, dreams, and my ambitions for a bright future for me and for my family. I was very busy working hard to build my piece of the "American dream."

At the end of 2006 and the beginning of 2007, things were tough financially. I was running low on cash, and I thought I would sell my small company and live to fight another day. The company was sold—or so I thought. At the last minute the deal fell through, and to my disgust and agony, I had no choice but to close the doors and declare bankruptcy as 2007 came to a close. I did everything in my power to no avail.

Besides the very stressful financial situation with the company, I had my own personal finances to deal with that year. I had put everything into the company, thinking that with years of sacrifice and hard work, I would one day have a big company that had created thousands of jobs and put thousands of people to work. As this American dream came crashing down around me, I was forced to take a hard look at reality. I had never felt more disillusioned.

I thought I had done all the right things. I had invested in my education, earning three college degrees—one a doctorate. I had built a small company from the ground up and always tried to operate with honesty and integrity. I had many years of work experience that could scarcely be covered in a ten-page vita. I thought I had surrounded myself with all the right skills and credentials. I thought I had done all the right things. But by the beginning of 2008, I had gone almost eighteen months without any income. That's right, I couldn't find a job; I couldn't find a contract; I couldn't sell my company; I could not get my hands on a single buck. I just couldn't understand that reality. On more than one occasion, I thought, "Isn't this the land of opportunity? Isn't this America where anyone who wants to work, can work?" I had never felt more disillusioned. Of course, I was also mad as hell—who wouldn't be?

I am man of faith, and this challenged my faith. I couldn't understand how a loving God could lead me down such a road. Was I being punished for some crime that I had committed? These thoughts and many others played over and over in my mind.

As someone who has never been able to accept things unquestioningly, I just couldn't accept my situation. I couldn't reconcile the reality with what I believed about God, about myself, and about America. This led me on a thirty-month journey. This book is dedicated to a search for the truth. The more I sought out and understood the truth of my situation, the more I began to understand what truth is—what it looks like, what it tastes like, what it feels like, what it smells like, and what it sounds like. I learned that truth is multifaceted, and that it has characteristics that define it just as much as any science and scientific endeavor can define anything.

When you arrive at the knowledge of the truth, you just know it. If you don't know it, then it's not truth. There is only one truth. There may be many different beliefs people have about what they believe to be true, but a close inspection of those beliefs will reveal that it is something they believe based on a TV broadcast, a newspaper article, a talk show host, or a blog on the Internet. It is rarely thought out, wrestled with, analyzed with a critical eye, or questioned with an analytical mind. It's a belief, and beliefs can be either true or false. If you want to know the truth, you and only you can find it. It takes a lot of hard work, though, and a great deal of hard thinking.

The words I write in this book are the knowledge I've discovered on my journey as I searched for the truth. I'm not trying to convince you that it's the truth—this is a point that you have to arrive at all by yourself. However, I am challenging you to not simply believe everything you hear or read. Do your own thorough investigation; you'll be surprised at what you find.

Here's the knowledge I've obtained, and the truth I've discovered. I now wish to share it with you in hopes that it will enlighten you and change your thinking. I'll see you on the other side.

CHAPTER 1: AMERICA AT A CROSSROADS

The future is not known, but the path we must take toward that future is clear.

Gary W. Griffin

INTRODUCTION

Powerlessness in the most powerful nation on planet Earth is the state of affairs in America today. America is approaching a grinding halt and everything is slowing down. "All stop," has been the command of the ship's captain. We're sitting at a four-way stop, and even if we haven't come to a full stop the car is slowing down, and the brakes are being applied. "These are uncertain times," said President George W. Bush in a press conference in early 2008. My response is these are not uncertain times—we can be very certain that to continue on the same course is not the right answer. America has to move forward instead of taking a left or a right at this crossroads in its history. There are no easy answers, but there are answers, or at the very least, clear indicators of the right direction for America in the twenty-first century. That direction is straight ahead. America must move forward, but it currently lacks the power to do so. Through both quantitative and qualitative means, I provide readers of this book with simple and straightforward answers to the complexities that have become a twenty-first century America as we explore the *Inert America* condition.

THE CURRENT STATE OF AFFAIRS

I begin this chapter with the use of two analogies—America as a ship commanded by a captain and American society as a car sitting at a four-way stop, where the driver has to make a decision about the direction to take. Both of these analogies aptly describe the current state of America on a number of different levels.

First, both a ship and a car are born out of the mind of a man, perhaps the mind of multiple men, or women for that matter. The main point here that both of these, a car and a ship, were once only ideas in someone's brain that became a reality in our experience here on planet Earth. We created both as a means of transportation to move us through space from one point to another. Both of these artifacts of American civilization are creations that originated in the mind. They were once only ideas, but now they have become a part of everyday experience. Everyone knows what they are, and on some level, they can be used as a point of reference in communication between two people.

Second, while both the car and the ship are powerful, they both require the mind of a human being to function. That is to say, a ship moves across the Atlantic by means of the interaction of people like the captain who makes the decisions that guide it across the ocean. Similarly, the automobile can't move forward through the intersection of the crossroads without a decision from the man or woman who is driving the car. On some level, both the car and the ship are technological innovations that aid humans in the everyday chores of life. They are tools, but no matter how sophisticated, they can't work by themselves. They require the mind of a man or woman to work.

We've entered the twenty-first century, and the years that have passed since the turn of the century have been anything but uneventful. There's something special about this century and this particular time in human history, some would say; we are embarking on an entirely new journey. Things seem different now, but are they really? Has human kind entered a new plane of existence? Does the twenty-first century offer something new that we've never seen before? Those who are more optimistic would say absolutely. As for me, I perceive that things are the same. There's a lot of truth in the old saying the more things change, the more they stay the same.

Certainly technology has improved, but the human condition remains the same. We've witnessed some spectacular things and new inventions have appeared almost daily, but neither the human experience nor the human condition has changed. We who are alive today are experiencing something that is new to us, but it's not a new experience.

We began this century with both a boom and a bust. The beginning of the century started with the bust of dot-com bubble that began in 1995 and spanned approximately six years through 2001. That same year, America experienced a tragedy that most never thought would occur on American soil—we were attacked on September 11, 2001. For the first time since the attack on Pearl Harbor that marked our entry into World War II, we became a nation at war in response to an attack on our home soil.

The focus of this book is on America and Americans in the twenty-first century. Few would argue that America is not the most powerful nation on the face of planet Earth. That's a status we have enjoyed for quite some time. Why then does it seem as though America is slowing down—almost as if there's a sense of powerlessness to move forward. It is as the ship's captain has said, "All stop." The car is rolling to the stop sign, and if we haven't stopped, we're at least beginning to apply the brakes. There's no way forward—the road ends here.

Political parties pretend that we have to take a left or a right. Their arguments assume that their philosophical ideals are the right ones for America. I agree that it's time for a decision for America, and all must make it. We must make it as individuals first and as a nation second. We must find the will to change because it is only then that we will be able to push forward through this crossroads in America's history. We've been down the road to the right, and we've traveled down the road to the left. Neither road leads us to prosperity; in fact, the opposite seems to be truer. We don't need another pendulum swing to the left or right. What we need is to move straight ahead because to move to the left or to the right does not move our nation forward.

The purpose of this book is to challenge your beliefs—all the beliefs that form your individual belief system. This belief system forms the basis for your choices and ensuing actions. It is only through action that work gets done; it is the end result, the output. Here's the problem—beliefs can be either true or false but not both. False beliefs that form the basis of action often yield unintended consequences. These unintended consequences of false beliefs are one of the reasons America is inert, that is, lacks the power to move forward. The American ideal so often referred to as the American dream is such a belief system.[1]

In order for America to return to a state of prosperity, we must once again become a nation of producers. Our action must be directed toward an ideal that is based on true beliefs—or more specifically, on knowledge that is truth. The current social structures of our society—political, economic, social, and philosophical—do not allow the working population of America to be productive. The production system is broken. The social structure no longer meets the needs of the mass of the population. This is the reason for the economic crises[2] in 2008 and 2009 that likely will continue and worsen through the next decade. Before we can be restored to a prosperous nation, we must make drastic changes to our ideal or our current belief system to be more specific. Through these changes, we can then alter the social fabric of our society.

As stated previously, it's my intention that this book will challenge your beliefs. It is only through challenging your beliefs that your beliefs can change. The measurement of success of this endeavor will be your acceptance of the truth that is the reality of our society in the twenty-first century. It is my belief that if you know the truth, that you will alter your belief system to align with the reality. My main reason for this exercise is to move America toward prosperity and away from poverty. I wish to spare Americans the pain and suffering that are inevitable if we do not make the systemic changes we need to make in our society. So, if you don't want to have your beliefs challenged, you should stop reading right here.

Although not an exhaustive list, the following compose the primary set of beliefs that I will challenge in this book either explicitly or implicitly.

1. There is a God, and he is in control.
2. There is no God.
3. Man has free will.
4. Man evolved from apes.
5. Every American is free.
6. We have the inalienable rights of life, liberty, and the pursuit of happiness.
7. Our system of government is a democracy.
8. The actions of the American government always represent the best interests of the people.
9. All social policy is informed and intended for the good of the U.S. population.
10. All laws are applied equally—justice is blind.
11. Our elected officials only serve the interests of the voters who put them into office.
12. There are two major political parties in the United States.
13. The Federal Reserve is a part of the American government.
14. Our currency is based on the gold standard.
15. The American dollar has value.
16. Capitalism is the only economic system that works.
17. The current economic crisis was unavoidable.
18. People who know what they are doing set economic policy and monetary policy.
19. Government is the solution to all our problems.

SIGNIFICANT EVENTS OF THE TWENTY-FIRST CENTURY

This century began with a boom and bust. We were faced with the Millennium Bug.[3] While companies were busy trying to fix this bug, the Internet evolution/revolution exploded into our lives and in our homes. These major technological innovations saw the end of the twentieth century and the beginning of the twenty-first century with what we now call the dot-com bust. As is usual, the stock market had major gains, but then with sudden, unstoppable forces, wealth was washed away; there were many losers and a few winners as the technology stocks that had propped up the dot-com boom lost their favor.

As quickly as it began, the information revolution came to a grinding halt, at least on Wall Street, and technology was no longer the answer for all that ails us.

With hanging chads and months of controversy over the counting of our votes, Americans elected a new Republican president—George W. Bush. On September 11, 2001, we were attacked by terrorists, and, with less than a year in office, the president had to declare war; the war on terror campaign had begun. As the details of the attack unfolded, America went to war with the Taliban in Afghanistan and Al-Qaeda and Osama bin Laden's network of terrorists. With admirable precision, our armed forces, along with NATO allies, quickly mobilized and overthrew the Taliban regime and reduced both the Taliban and Al-Qaeda to hiding in caves. The war should've been over quickly, but at the close of 2009, American forces are still in Afghanistan hunting and fighting the Taliban. Osama bin Laden still has not been brought to justice for the atrocity that was 9/11.

With war on our minds and terror, pain, and sadness in our hearts, we were told by our president that there were others out to get us—the axis of evil that included Iraq, Iran, and North Korea. In his State of the Union address on January 29, 2009, President Bush told the nation that we must defend our national security interests. With the war on terror, we couldn't afford to ignore these nations and the threat they posed to the United States and its citizens.

Iraq continues to flaunt its hostility toward America and to support terror. The Iraqi regime has plotted to develop anthrax, nerve gas, and nuclear weapons for over a decade. This is a regime that agreed to international inspections and then kicked out inspectors. This is a regime that has something to hide from the civilized world. By seeking weapons of mass destruction, these regimes (Iran, Iraq, and North Korea) pose a grave and growing danger. They could provide these arms to terrorists, giving them the means to match their hatred. [4]

And so, we invaded another country on March 20, 2003. Again our armed forces responded admirably, and they did as our leaders and country asked. We overthrew the government of Iraq and Saddam Hussein. The war should've been over quickly, but at the end of 2009 we still had about 115,000 troops in Iraq; we're spending about $7.3 billion per month with a total estimate of about $800 billion spent thus far. We never found those weapons of mass destruction, and we never tied the attacks of 9/11 to Saddam Hussein and his government. In short, this war really had no justification based on these arguments. [5] The fact is that there is evidence to support that George W. Bush and several of his top advisers took office with the intent of invading Iraq, as demonstrated by a letter sent to Bill Clinton in 1998 encouraging invasion of Iraq and drafted by Neo-conservatives.[6] The American people may never know the truth of the Iraq invasion—at least not until long after it matters.

Of course, we can't forget about the forces of nature and the devastation wrought by Hurricane Katrina as it made landfall on August 29, 2005. This hurricane was one of the five deadliest ever to be witnessed in the United States. It wreaked havoc from central Florida to Texas, with the worst devastation in New Orleans, Louisiana. When the levee system in New Orleans catastrophically failed, 80 percent of the city became flooded, resulting in severe loss of property and life. The total loss of life was 1,836 souls and an estimated cost of damage of over $100 billion. This storm was by far one of the worst in recorded history, and the country will feel its mark for many years.

Let's also not forget the economic crises of 2008 brought on by the bursting of the housing bubble in the United States. Hailed as the worst economic crisis since the Great Depression, the crisis left the nation's largest banks teetering on the verge of bankruptcy; to avoid the complete collapse of the banking system, the U.S. government and the Federal Reserve had to step in and loan banks billions of taxpayer dollars. Scholars will debate the factors that caused the calamity for years to come, but the major contributing factors were as follows:

- The unprecedented rise in home prices from the mid 90s until about 2005.

- The low interest rates and easy terms that allowed home owners to get huge amounts of equity out their homes while refinancing.

- The downturn in the economy coupled with the maturation of many subprime mortgages to a level beyond home owners' means to pay.

- The sudden drop in home valuations that left owners owing far more on their mortgages than their home's value.

- The default on an unprecedented number of home loans.

- The over-valuation of credit derivatives guaranteed by default swaps that came due as a result of the loan defaults.

These factors culminated in the perfect economic doomsday machine at the end of 2008, as Congress and the Senate passed the huge bank bailout legislation known as the Emergency Economic Stabilization Act of 2008.

We also shouldn't forget the astronomical rise in the price of oil in 2008 that resulted in the energy crisis. With the price of a barrel of oil reaching an all-time high of $147.30 in July 2008, most Americans were forced to pay $4.00 or more at the pump for each gallon of gas. This crisis stemmed from the estimates of low petroleum reserves, tensions in the Middle East, and oil price speculation.

With all these crises fresh in their minds, voters entered the voting booths for what would be an historic election in the United States—an African American was elected president. On January 20, 2009, Barrack Hussein Obama became the forty-fourth president of the United States of America. While many factors contributed to his election, most scholars and commentators would conclude that his promise of change tapped into the hearts and minds of the voting population who were ready for something different. After the turmoil of the last eight years, the last thing the vast majority of Americans wanted was more of the same. Although it was mentioned, who else but the son of a white woman and a Kenyan could come along at this point in our history to finish the healing process we so desperately needed in the U.S? Racism didn't die with his election, but we took a step forward to unite the country at a time when we need all Americans working together regardless of the color of their skin.

THE NEED FOR REFORM EVERYWHERE

With all that the American public has experienced during the first decade of the twenty-first century; it's not hard to understand the need for change. A common theme often discussed in the debates among candidates from both parties was the need for reform. With wars in two countries, economic conditions squeezing families beyond belief, and government bailouts to top it off, it really wasn't hard to predict a shift in political power as we elected a Democrat president and Democrat majorities in both houses. Similar events have happened in the history of the United States; the stock market crash of 1929 and the subsequent election of Franklin Delano Roosevelt (FDR) in 1932, for example. FDR took over leadership from Hubert Hoover during a time of transition for America when the country was embroiled in chaos that included economic calamity and a world war.

In metaphysics, there are three dimensions of space—length, width, and depth—and one dimension of time. Taken together these represent the time-space continuum. Within the time- space continuum, time is constant. It is ever changing in a forward motion. When an object occupies space (length, width, and depth) at a given point in time, it is an event. As events flow throughout the passage of time, they often seem disconnected, but they are not. Events are connected by that thin string that is a constant—time. When events define a specific object, it persists through time until it is destroyed. In other words, the event creates an object that occupies space. It persists and occupies that space until it is destroyed. Perhaps *destroyed* is too strong a word here. As with all of the life, it dies. It is born (created), it lives (persists), and then it dies. How does this apply to twenty-first-century America and our current situation?

Let's examine a specific event to help illustrate how this applies specifically to our physical world and society. In the 1930s during the Great Depression, Franklin Delano Roosevelt (FDR) created a program called Social Security.[7] That social policy put into place (it created) an object called social security. The purpose of the object or structure was to assist struggling Americans, who were without a source of income, especially those in old age. That object was created on August 14, 1935 when FDR signed the act into law. When the policy was put into place, there were slightly more than 127 million people in the United States.

The basic idea was that you would work, pay income to the government, and the government would manage and preserve for you until retirement. The government would then return that money to you as a source of income until your death. It was an idea, and on paper, it even had a sound purpose. So this object called social security was created along with a huge bureaucracy to support its implementation. It has persisted for almost 100 years. Over the course of time, money was collected through income to be held in trust by the U.S. government until retirement.

After the social security system was instituted, the nation experienced another unplanned event—the baby boom. Once the baby boom generation came into being, the system should've been changed. The fact that it wasn't shows how poor a job the government does in planning anything. After all, this source of money was useful for politicians who wanted to spend on specialty projects by borrowing from social security. It became a part of budgets and budget planning. We sent elected officials to Washington to watch the treasure chest, but they realized that no one was watching them, so they took from the chest (*borrowed* is the term they prefer) called social security.[8] We'll pay it back later, they said, but later never came. They kept borrowing, and now there's nothing left in the treasure chest.

Here's the dilemma. The first waves of baby boomers are now ready to retire. They've paid into the system throughout their working lives, yet there's nothing there in the system for them at retirement. Where did all the money go? Who has stolen our treasure? Why am I still paying into a system that is bankrupt? Why aren't these thieves in jail? Well, because it is a *loan*. It's going to be paid back. When? How? These are the types of questions that should get asked but never do.

If we could only pinpoint the culprit, we could bring him/her to justice. But under our current system, no responsibility is assigned for these acts, and no one accepts blame. The money is just gone. We are told, "We must get over it and move ahead." Hmm, that sounds like a good plan for the people who stole the money but not so well for the people who paid into the system. Why can't we bring responsibility and accountability to our government?[9]

Wait. There is another solution. Let's just call up the Treasury Department and have them print up a few trillion dollars worth of security bonds. Then the Federal Reserve can print up a few trillion dollars of money and put it back into the treasure chest, with interest, of course. Who will know the difference? If questions are asked, just say it's a loan that will be repaid. We'll be dead and gone by the time it comes to the attention of taxpayers. It won't matter. Guess what? It matters!

Our children's future is at risk. Baby boomers are starting to retire, and they want their money. Where will it come from? Perhaps the next generation can work and pay for it? Wrong. Mathematically, it is impossible for our children to work and produce enough value in terms of goods and services to ever pay off the debt. Politicians have literally sold our children into debt slavery. Those chains get tighter with each passing year. Soon, there will be no escape.

We could resort to the same old tired ideas that have already been tried and tested. We did that already. Look around at 12 trillion in debt with trillions more likely over the next decade. Isn't it accurate to say that those ideas are bankrupt, and our current economic and fiscal situation demonstrates that condition? We need new ideas. We need real change, systemic change, the kind of change that has to come from each and every American.

CRISIS AS THE IMPETUS OF CHANGE

It's never been true that change, especially major social change, comes about without something pushing for that change. That is to say, people don't change when things are great; they make changes when things are not great. Crises, such as we have experienced in the twenty-first century, can also serve as an impetus to change. But why change? Aren't things great in the United States, you may ask? The answer is no. Some may think it's great but not most. With the recent economic crises, American families are having a hard time. Jobs are being lost and unemployment rates are at levels not seen since the Great Depression.[10]

I suggest that America is in the final stages of transition as a society. We've seen this type of transition before during the 1930s. This type of transition occurs when the basis of work changes. That is to say, our system of production has changed. Society is a system. When this system is broken, we, the people in that system, experience crises until the system is repaired or changed.

In the transition from an agricultural society to an industrial society, we initially experienced a period of prosperity that was a result of increased productivity followed massive unemployment as mechanization greatly reduced the need for farmers and farming. With the transition from industrialization to *informatization*, we see the same type of changes. Initially there was a period of increased productivity and prosperity, and now we are experiencing massive unemployment brought about by the increased productivity achieved by applying new technology to the old system of production. America is on the precipice of this change. Our actions will determine the short-term and long-term outcome for millions of Americans.

Currently, the major social structures—social, political, economic, and philosophical—of American society are out of alignment with the three macro-level trends that define an information society and a knowledge-based economy. Those three trends are:

1. The decentralization of production processes.
2. The elimination for the need of time and space management.
3. Individuals as the new owners of the means of production.

As long as American society continues down this road, we will continue to be in crisis. Until we make adjustments and realign our major social structures to these three trends, our prosperity is in jeopardy. With any type of social change, there is resistance. Those in power wish to maintain the status quo—it does serve their interest, after all. The risk is a continued downward spiral toward poverty—a very real social problem that continues to threaten our standard of living.

CHAPTER 2:
POVERTY AND
SOCIAL CHANGE

In a country well governed, poverty is something to be ashamed of. In a country
badly governed, wealth is something to be ashamed of.

Confucius

THE SOCIAL PROBLEM OF POVERTY

It has been said that a recession is when your neighbor loses his job, and a depression is when you lose your job. Our government finally made an official announcement that we were in a recession at the end of 2008. Economists determined that we had actually been in a recession for a year.[11] Our government seems content to downplay the economic crisis within the country. They use such words as *recession* only when it's so obvious that anyone would have to concede that a severe downturn is evident in the economy. Such wording may soften the blow of the news to those who are unaffected by the economy, but for the rest of us who have been affected, it's a depression. Poverty has found a home. In this chapter, I will present information to help you better understand how poverty in the United States is related to work, labor, and money. I will show a clear connection between government and social policies as root causes to poverty in this country.

There are at least four main elements to a social problem. Most recognized social problems have:

1. "Been perceived as having caused physical or mental damage to individuals or society.
2. Offended the values or standards of some powerful segment of society.
3. Persisted for a period of time.
4. Generated competing proposed solutions, each being evaluated differently by groups who are in different social positions within society. Disagreements delay the formation of a consensus on how to attack the problem."[12]

Poverty meets all of these criteria. Poverty is the only real social problem in America or in the world for that matter. All other social problems are nothing more than symptoms of this single problem. Put another way *poverty* is a "condition of having insufficient resources or income. In its most extreme form, poverty is a lack of basic human needs, such as adequate and nutritious food, clothing, housing, clean water, and health services." [13] In the United States, extreme poverty is defined by the Bureau of the Census as a family of four with an annual income that is less than half of the official poverty line. In short, the realization that poverty is related to the amount of income a person or persons in a household receive for work is important to understand the risk facing America. The outcome or "effects of poverty may include poor nutrition, mental illness, drug dependence, crime and high rates of disease."[14]

CHAPTER 2: POVERTY AND SOCIAL CHANGE

Poverty may simply be described as a lack of resources. When the lack of resources makes it impossible for an individual to procure even the most basic necessities required in life, that is, food, shelter, and clothing, much useless pain and suffering occurs. When those individual human beings are all added up to an aggregate number representing an entire nation, even more pain and suffering results. In the aggregate, it's no longer a personal problem; it's now a systemic problem that affects everyone within that society, that country. It's a systemic problem as evidenced by unemployment rates that currently reside around ten percent in the United States.[15] When people can't find a job, they can't earn income. Without income, poverty sets in and a whole host of other issues also begin to manifest themselves. When more people enter this category, such as when unemployment sky rockets, the entire country suffers.

Poverty as a social problem is not so easily solved, eliminated, or healed as is so often portrayed on TV by popping a little white pill. This particular problem requires something more than a drug created in a lab.

Money, many think, is such a drug. The idea that if we throw enough money at it, the problem will be solved is especially prevalent in American thinking. Wrong! On the surface, money does seem to solve certain aspects of this problem called poverty. But if you look closely, you'll realize that money only alleviates the symptoms of the problem, and the problem persists as it has throughout human history. When money is readily available to a large number of people, it masks the problem and provides temporary relief.

For America to remain a prosperous nation for all future generations, poverty must be defeated. It's often depicted as an ailment that afflicts only select people. However, if we view poverty as the inability to access the basic necessities of life, then poverty becomes systemic. It is systemic for two reasons. First, the Republicans were in control from 2000-2006, and they established social policies that made the current economic system into one that supports, enforces, and reinforces the inequality and unequal access to resources. This system puts the control of those resources into the hands of a few because it's the hands of a few who control all the money in America. These people live lavishly, and yet they don't work? How is this so in America? Who are these people? How did they get to such an exalted position? In short, the pendulum swung too far to the right.

When I first began conducting research for this book, and specifically for this chapter, I thought that the major social ill that has imprisoned America was poverty. As I dug into the issues with more analytical and discerning eyes, I realized that to understand and address poverty, we must also recognize and address the partners in crime—greed and division. It is, after all, the three of these working together in cohort that create and reinforce one another. It there was no greed, then poverty would be eliminated. If the was no poverty, greed would disappear. If there was no division such as by race, sex, morality, or so-cial class, then both poverty and greed would find no safe havens. It is through such divisions that we are made weak as a nation. We are divided and our power is transferred to political parties, the government, and the very social struc-ture that enforces and reinforces these conditions in America. It seems strange that an individual's power is transferred in such a way, but this is truly how it works.

The social contract that is represented by the U.S. Constitution supports the very social structures that make this possible. I will discuss this in more detail in chapter 5. It is through this transference of power that the political economy of the United States is created, and thereby such divisions facilitate both poverty and greed through the inequalities that persist throughout the social structure. These form the dominions of power that hold people captive. These domin-ions serve their master and their master is intent upon enslaving the population through these centralized mechanisms such as political, social, economic, and philosophical structures. I'm sorry to have to tell you this, but even in America, you are not free.

Freedom, from this perspective, in America is a false illusion. This illusion is part of our problem because we have been led to believe that it is part of the American dream. The American dream is just that—a dream based on an ideal. This ideal is a set of related ideas that serve to keep Americans working toward a goal. These ideals support capitalism as the economic system. When political parties control social policies and create those policies in forms that give control and advantage to those within certain social positions, it is an abuse and misuse of government power.

There's nothing wrong with goals, and there's certainly nothing wrong with work. Hard work is the cornerstone of what makes America tick. Work is a necessary part of life and living. It becomes a problem when only a few work to support the many in achieving that ideal. Such has become the state of affairs in America. Only certain segments of the population are working—the middle class—the rest are along for the ride.

This problem doesn't manifest itself clearly when there are many jobs and everyone is at work. However, when there's a severe downturn in the economy such as was experienced in 2008 and 2009, this problem becomes much more recognizable. Unfortunately, this problem manifests itself by putting more people into the category of poverty. Although poverty may be relative for some; it at least forces them to feel a sense of lack. When this situation occurs, there often is a transfer of political power such as witnessed in the 2008 elections with the Democrats now in control. One of the reasons that there is such drastic shift in power is because more people have moved toward the poverty line. Democrats, once in control, begin to put into place social programs to support people in times of need.[16] This may not create jobs, but it certainly addresses a lack of access to resources felt by so many in the population. These types of social policies are said to support the economic system of socialism. In short, the pendulum begins to swing back to the left. This creates the second problem—it makes people more dependent on the government, rather than fostering independence and self-sufficiency. The fiscal problem is that someone has to pay for these social programs. In the United States, these programs are paid for by the collection of taxes on income, which comes from people who are working. When unemployment is high, this places that burden squarely on the shoulders of the few who do have jobs. This solution doesn't solve the social problem of poverty. In fact it creates another whole host of problems, and the cure is almost worse than the problem. Poverty is not eliminated; it often causes the problem to persist over a longer period of time. What is this creature called poverty that has plagued man since the beginning of time? Is it just part of the human condition, and we must be content to deal with it?

In short, work is the only cure for poverty. Work is how we earn money, which represents the value of our time and labor; money is the medium we use to exchange out time and labor in order to acquire the basic necessities of life.[17] When there is no money, there is lack. In short, you've just been introduced to that social condition called *poverty*, and he is a constant companion to your pain and suffering. A simple definition, then, might be that poverty is the lack of resources to meet the basic needs for subsistence and survival. In economic terms, it is consumption. Consumption, however, is not independent of production. We must produce in order to consume. This translates into an economic system and a political system that support work for everyone in the United States population. Everyone who is capable of working must work in the twenty-first century to support and maintain the country as a prosperous nation.[18]

The total destruction of American society is at hand. Although this statement elicits stark images of devastation, it need not be so. This type of destruction won't happen in the same way a building is demolished. Nor will it happen like the explosion of a bomb. Perhaps you've seen such images on TV when a building is imploded or seen bombs dropped in a war movie. Such images are dramatic and induce fear.

I'm not talking about imploding buildings. This type of destruction is slow, subtle, and almost unnoticeable. It's social change that I am describing. The changes we are experiencing right now in America are social changes that will result in the destruction of the existing social structures of our society. America is undergoing massive social changes. These social changes are reflected in the tearing down of existing social, political, economic, and even philosophical social structures that are the essence of the American ideal. These structures are the foundation of American society.

A good analogy of this process of change is illustrated by an apple left on a table over a period of time. If left untouched, the apple eventually rots and then decays. The physical evidence that an apple once existed is no longer evident by any of the senses humans have become accustomed to relying on. You can't touch, taste, hear, smell, or see it. It's gone. At most, we can only deduce that it once existed. We know this is the truth because something is left behind—seeds. Whereas a single apple may provide a person with food for a single meal, when the seeds are planted, nurtured, and reach maturity as an apple tree, then we have many apples that can feed many people for many meals over many years. Such is the cycle of life. We are born, we live, and we die.

All things that make up our lives—our social reality—must conform to this same cycle of life. Social structures, too, are things—objects, if you will. These objects must conform to the established universal laws or the natural laws that control our universe.[19] It is unavoidable, and it cannot be violated. Social systems are objects too, and they also have a life cycle. When they cease to meet the needs of society—in this case, America—they, too, must rot, decay, and cease to exist. Here seeds are also left behind that can also be planted for a new beginning. A brighter day is dawning, and a new America will emerge if we simply plant the seeds to make it happen. While our transition period seems chaotic and random, it is not. It is all a part of the natural cycle of life controlled by universal laws.

CHAPTER 2: POVERTY AND SOCIAL CHANGE

It's a silly man who thinks anything can be created that does not have to comply with the laws of the universe that were established before the dawn of time. The laws of physics must be adhered to even within social systems. One of the laws states that no two objects can occupy the same time-space continuum or else they will collide.[20] A political system is an object. An economic system is an object. American society is an object. To replace the old object with new ones, the old one must die, decay, and cease to exist. What are left, however, are seeds. We are faced with planting new seeds for our society. These seeds of our society can be planted, and a new system can emerge to replace the old. Such a transition from the old social structures to the new and the accompanying human experience of that change is aptly termed social change.[21] What is social change?[22] Why is this important of us to understand? How is this connected to poverty?

SOCIETY AS A SYSTEM

Although most people rarely think of American society as a system, when framed from within this context, the current situation in twenty-first century America begins to make more sense. Let's define society as a first step. Society or human society is the manner or condition in which the members of a community live together for their mutual benefit. By extension, society denotes the people of a region or country, sometimes even the world, taken as a whole. Used in the sense of an association, a society is a body of individuals outlined by the bounds of functional interdependence. More broadly, a society is a political, economic, social, or philosophical infrastructure, made up of a varied collection of individuals. Human societies are often organized according to their primary means of subsistence—food, shelter, and clothing. People of many nations united by common political and cultural traditions, beliefs, or values are sometimes also said to be a society (such as Judeo-Christian, Eastern, and Western). Admittedly, a society such as American society can be all of these; it is a complex system of individuals who live, work, and play together.

A system is a set of interacting or interdependent entities forming an integrated whole. The concept of an *integrated whole* can also be stated in terms of a system embodying a set of relationships that are differentiated from relationships of the set to other elements, and from relationships between an element of the set and elements not a part of the relational regime. The scientific research field that is engaged in the study of the general properties of systems includes systems theory, cybernetics, dynamical systems, and complex systems. They investigate the abstract properties of the matter and organization, searching concepts and principles that are independent of the specific domain, substance, type, or temporal scales of existence. Most systems share common characteristics, including:

1. Systems have structure, as defined by parts and their composition;
2. Systems have behavior that involves inputs, processing, and outputs of material, energy or information;
3. Systems have interconnectivity: the various parts of a system have functional as well as structural relationships between each other.

The term *system* may also refer to a set of rules that governs behavior or structure. American society is such a system. It is dynamic, and it is deterministic. The dynamical system concept is a mathematical formalization for any fixed *rule* that describes the time dependence of a point's position in its ambient space. Examples include the mathematical models that describe the swinging of a clock pendulum, the flow of water in a pipe, and the number of fish each spring in a lake.

At any given time a dynamical system has a *state* given by a set of real numbers (a vector) that can be represented by a point in an appropriate *state space* (a geometrical manifold). Small changes in the state of the system correspond to small changes in the numbers. The *evolution rule* of the dynamical system is a fixed rule that describes what future states follow from the current state. The rule is deterministic: for a given time interval only one future state follows from the current state.[23]

A deterministic system is a conceptual model of the philosophical doctrine of determinism[24] applied to a system for understanding everything that has and will occur in the system, based on the physical outcomes of causality. In a deterministic system, every action or cause produces a reaction or effect and every reaction, in turn, becomes the cause of subsequent reactions. The totality of these cascading events can theoretically show exactly how the system will exist at any moment in time.[25]

The word *system* in its meaning here has a long history that can be traced back to Plato (*Philebus*), Aristotle (*Politics*) and Euclid (*Elements*). It had meant *total*, *crowd*, or *union* in even more ancient times, as it derives from the verb *sunistemi*, meaning uniting or putting together. In engineering and physics, a physical system is the portion of the universe that is being studied.[26] Engineering also has the concept of a system that refers to all of the parts and interactions between parts of a complex project.

In physics, *energy* comes from the Greek term *energeia* meaning *activity* or *operation* and *energos* meaning *active* or *working*; is a scalar physical quantity that describes the amount of work that can be performed by a force, an attribute of objects and systems that is subject to a conservation law. Different forms of energy include kinetic, potential, thermal, gravitational, sound, light, elastic, and electromagnetic energy. The forms of energy are often named after a related force. In American society, this force is human beings, and the energy is human creativity.

Any form of energy can be transformed into another form, but the total energy always remains the same. The conservation of energy is a consequence of the fact that the laws of physics do not change over time. Although the total energy of a system does not change with time, its value may depend on the frame of reference.

In physics, power is the rate at which work is performed or energy is converted. It is energy per unit of time. As a rate of change of work done or the energy of a subsystem, power is

$$P = \frac{W}{t}$$

where P is power, W is work and t is time. The dimension of power is energy divided by time. In American society, when human power is restricted, work goes undone.

THE CHAOS OF SOCIAL CHANGE

Chaos theory is an area of inquiry in mathematics, physics, and philosophy that studies the behavior of dynamical systems that are highly sensitive to initial conditions.[27] This sensitivity is popularly referred to as the *butterfly effect*.[28] Small differences in initial conditions (such as those due to rounding errors in numerical computation) yield widely diverging outcomes for chaotic systems, rendering long-term prediction impossible in general. This happens even though these systems are deterministic, meaning that their future dynamics are fully determined by their initial conditions, with no random elements involved. In other words, the deterministic nature of these systems does not make them predictable. This behavior is known as *deterministic chaos*, or simply *chaos*.

Social change is neither a new idea nor a new topic of discussion for social scientists. Theodore Caplow in his book *America Social Trends* provides an excellent overview of the various theories that have arisen to explain this human experience of social change.[29] He writes that nineteenth-century observers in Europe and America were interested in finding the magical key that explained unprecedented growth in population and production that was accompanied by new machines and new forms of organization. "The quest for the magic key eventually produced three influential models of social change: the linear progress model, the transformation model, and the apocalyptic model."[30]

The linear progress model presents social development as a steady upward ascent of mankind at predictable stages marked by parallel improvements in technology, social organization, and moral excellence. With this theory, social problems were expected to solve themselves. The transformation model predicted the modernization of all societies as traditional forms of social organization transitioned to modern ones.[31] Finally, the apocalyptic model describes modern societies as a change in the fundamental social fabric that would make them different, almost unrecognizable. This version is best illustrated by Marx's version of class struggles where the proletariat wins and abolishes all social classes.

Most of these grand theories have failed badly to explain social change because they have inadequately met the task for which they were designed. Namely, they failed to clearly establish the connection between scientific-technological progress and social change. This failure came in spite of the fact that clear evidence showed a direct effect of technology on social organization where technology, population, and productivity began an unmatched upward trend beginning in the middle of the seventeenth century. The easiest thing to do was to equate social progress with technological progress; however, the two don't always go hand in hand. Social progress often lags behind technological progress. A modern interpretation may be that social progress is a lagging indicator of productivity, while technological progress is a leading indicator.[32] Such indicators are easy to measure when they consist of people and things, but they're much more difficult when they deal with the invisible things such as beliefs that define the human experience. I will discuss more fully in chapter 4 how these beliefs are just as important to deal with because these beliefs form the basis of human action. It is action that is required to bring about the systemic changes we need in twenty-first century America.

Technology acts as an impetus to social change. That is not to say that all technology brings social change but to allude to the fact that when certain technology(ies) enter our society, they provide the means by which major social changes occur because they allow macro level structural changes that did not exist before their invention. When such technology influences the core essence of our society—work and productivity—the changes cut across all levels of society and all social institutions. We are now witnessing such changes in the twenty-first century.[33]

While technology is not the only means of change, it can be the catalyst for change. It performs this role by providing the capability to form new patterns of behavior. When this occurs, only a new social structure can serve the needs of the population. The new structure does not change people, but people do respond to a different social structure. The response to the structural change results in social change. At the end of the day, it's not really people who are changed, it the societal structure that has changed. When these changes directly affect the work or livelihood of citizens, the reaction is generally not positive. One famous example is that of the Luddites.[34] The Luddites were a social movement of British textile artisans in the early nineteenth century who protested— often by destroying mechanized looms—against the changes produced by the Industrial Revolution that they felt were leaving them without work and changing their entire way of life.

This English historical movement should be seen in the context of the era's harsh economic climate due to the Napoleonic Wars, and the degrading working conditions in the new textile factories. Since then, however, the term Luddite has been used derisively to describe anyone opposed to (or perceived to be opposed to) technological progress and technological change.

The Luddite movement, which began in 1811 and 1812 when mills and pieces of factory machinery were burned by handloom weavers, took its name from Ned Lud, an eighteenth-century resident of a Leicestershire village. For a short time the movement was so strong that it clashed in battles with the British army. Measures taken by the British government included a mass trial in York in 1812 that resulted in many executions and penal transportations.

The principal objection of the Luddites was against the introduction of new wide-framed automated looms that could be operated by cheap, relatively unskilled labor, resulting in the loss of jobs for many skilled textile workers. From the individual worker's perspective, the technological advancement took away jobs. I suggest that such conditions simply denote a structural systemic problem, and that the technology acted only as a catalyst. Today a Luddite would reject new technology simply because it is new; nineteenth-century Luddites were acting from a sense of self-preservation rather than merely a fear of change.

The need for change is very apparent throughout all levels of American society. Everyone is screaming for reform, as evidenced by the dominant issues in the 2008 presidential election. These reforms are needed in all areas of our society—government reform, education reform, welfare reform, etc. The list is long, and the time is short.

These reforms are needed because the current social structures don't meet the needs of a twenty-first century information society with a knowledge-based economy. These social institutions are artifacts of a bygone era and can no longer meet the needs of the population of this country. What most people don't realize and understand is the breadth and depth of these changes and how they influence social systems, and thus the very structure of American society. The cornerstone of American society is the social systems that support it. That is, the political, economic, philosophical, and social systems that makes it possible. The need to change the major systems and the human experience of that change are appropriately termed *social change* because they are fundamental to the social lives of every American.

In this chapter I wish to provide a deeper understanding of what these changes are, how they need to occur, and, most importantly, what these will mean to the structure of American society. If informed, the reader can then take appropriate steps to manage these changes in his or her day-to-day live. Changes both from a personal viewpoint as well as at a societal macro level through the use of informed social policies must become a strategy for American government.

Why is this happening in America? Social systems such as a political system or an economic system are fundamental structures that support our society. The human life is fundamentally about work. We are born, we live, and we die—in between, we work. Currently, the average workweek is forty hours. At fifty weeks a year[35] , this translates into 2,000 hours of work each year. If we start at age eighteen and work until age sixty-six, which equates to 96,000 hours of work in a single lifetime. Work is fundamental to our survival here on planet Earth. We must work to survive. As work is hard, somewhere along the way, someone had a spark of creativity and translated that idea into a tool that made the work easier, and the person more productive. At first, these were simple implements like a shovel.[36] Although it may seem like an odd thing to say today, this was new technology at one point. All of technology is but a tool that facilitates work. A shovel is a piece of technology that facilitates work—it's just not a sophisticated tool by twenty-first century standards. Examples of twenty-first century tools that fundamentally changed the nature of work are the desktop computer and the Internet. These pieces of technology also facilitate work—mental not physical work. These are much more advanced tools, but they are still tools nonetheless. No matter what the technology is, it still requires someone who knows how to use it in order for the work to get accomplished.

New technological advances do not influence the mass population of a society when the technology only is used by a few; the space shuttle is a good example of this.[37] While this type of technology is very advanced, very few people will ever take a trip to the moon. Thus, the more widely a technology influences work across the social spectrum of a society, the more deeply felt it is on an individual level. It is experienced at this level as job loss, income loss, etc. These traumatic events, of course, are very disturbing as they directly affect our ability to meet our basic needs of food, shelter, and clothing. That is, our very survival is threatened. When we experience such changes, we do so as social changes. These changes require fundamental shift in social structures—political, economic, social, and philosophical systems—to keep up and meet the new demands of our society.

These types of changes influence our style of living because they directly alter the choices we have available. That is to say, our choices become restrained in terms of how we can work to meet our needs for survival. From a human perspective, these changes seem chaotic and random. These changes have systemic meaning in that society itself is a system that requires human beings working together to accomplish common goals. When our social structures change, the social change triggers changes at all levels that the individual experiences as chaos.[38]

Social change is essentially chaos in the human system called society. It seems random, but it's not. When the way human beings must perform their work changes, the political, social, economic, and philosophical social structures must also change in order to align the accomplishment of work (production in economic terms and productivity in human capital terms) to the needs of a society. If the system does not change, a depression results (both the psychological and economic type). People can't be productive and meet their needs. Structurally this results in jobs loss and unemployment.

In recorded history, two major shifts have occurred that resulted in this type of chaotic system changes at the fundamental core of American society. The first was the 1929 stock market crash and the resulting Great Depression of the 1930s. This period marked a fundamental shift of work away from an agricultural society to an industrial society.[39] The next one we are currently experiencing as we move from an industrial society paradigm to an information society paradigm. As I will discuss in more detail in chapter 3, it's important to understand the what, why, and how of the Great Depression in order to learn the lessons of the past and not repeat them today. With sadness, I must report that the current leaders in our society haven't learned much, and we seemed destined to repeat these same mistakes.

The technology of the 1920s that influenced the work aspect of society on a wide scale was the invention of the mass transportation that was made available and affordable by Henry Ford.[40] This innovation helped bring about the great shift from an agricultural society to an industrial society. In chapter 3, I illustrate how these occurred and describe their significance.

This fundamental shift in work changed the dimensions of time and space, and it made possible mass transit, mass production, and mass consumption. Without these, the growth of the U.S. population of the baby boomers could never have been supported. Without these, World War II may have had a different outcome.

These social changes represent a forward progression of time where events are connected through time and space. Work is fundamental. Without it, depression results, and the outcome is poverty for the average American. The only road to prosperity is one where the average American can work, produce, and be productive. The factor that influences, prevents, and/or supports that ability is the very structure of society itself. We must focus on making the changes to our existing social structure that will make the next generation of Americans productive—hyperproductive to be more precise—and with that America a prosperous nation once again.

Why is it important to understand these social changes, their influence on social structures, and how this is related to work? Simply stated, work equates to value. Value is what supports our monetary system of exchange or the American dollar. More of this is covered in chapter 7 on the political economy, but suffice it to say here that if we don't make these changes the standard of living for the average America will plunge drastically. The current structures don't and won't allow it to go up.

How can we make these changes? When we examine planet Earth, and all that is on it, we can clearly see a certain cycle of life, even for human beings. We are born, we live for a short period, and then we die. This is true for all natural things on the planet. These events are controlled by the natural laws established by God himself. They are universal laws that no human being can change.

These universal laws and the cycle of life also have things to teach us about our existence on the planet. As mentioned elsewhere, human beings also have the capacity to create. The evidence of this ability is all around us in every detail that is not of natural—buildings, automobiles, telephones, computers, etc. Society and social structures are but examples of these types of manmade objects. They come from idea(s) created by a man/woman or sometimes a group. Such an idea was brought into reality and an object called America was born at the signing of the Declaration of Independence and then the framing of the U.S. Constitution. Ideas are like apples in that they, too, rot and then decay. Fortunately, they leave seeds behind that can be used for planting.

In America, we must plant the seeds left by the American ideal we call the American dream. We must plant, water, and nurture these seeds in order to have a prosperous nation once again. If we don't plant the seeds and water them, then poverty will overtake us and destroy this nation. We can't just simply replace the current existing social structures overnight. As I stated everything has a natural course—a cycle of life. Moreover, everything on the face of the planet, all objects, must comply with universal laws of physics. In this case, no two objects can occupy the same time-space continuum because they will collide. There are only two options. First, we can allow the idea of America as it exists to rot and decay, and then plant the seeds left behind. Second, we can destroy this object just as one destroys a building in order to build a new structure in its place. These are the only two options.

PEOPLE AS STRANGE ATTRACTORS

In mathematics, a nonlinear system is a system that is not linear, that is, a system that does not satisfy the superposition principle, or whose output is not proportional to its input. Less technically, a nonlinear system is any problem in which the variable(s) to be solved for cannot be written as a linear combination of independent components. A nonhomogeneous system, which is linear apart from the presence of a function of the independent variables, is nonlinear according to a strict definition, but such systems are usually studied alongside linear systems because they can be transformed to a linear system of multiple variables.

Nonlinear problems are of interest to physicists and mathematicians because most physical systems are inherently nonlinear in nature. Nonlinear equations are difficult to solve and give rise to interesting phenomena such as chaos. The weather is famously nonlinear, and simple changes in one part of the system produce complex effects throughout. Society is another example of this same type of system. It is deterministic, dynamic, and nonlinear.

An attractor is a set to which a dynamical system evolves after a long enough time. That is, points that get close enough to the attractor remain close even if slightly disturbed. Geometrically, an attractor can be a point, a curve, a manifold, or even a complicated set with a fractal structure known as a *strange attractor*. Describing the attractors of chaotic dynamical systems has been one of the achievements of chaos theory. A trajectory of the dynamical system in the attractor does not have to satisfy any special constraints except for remaining on the attractor. The trajectory may be periodic or chaotic or of any other type.

Attractors are parts of the phase space of the dynamical system. A phase space, introduced by Willard Gibbs in 1901, is a space in which all possible states of a system are represented, with each possible state of the system corresponding to one unique point in the phase space. Dynamical systems in the physical world tend to be dissipative: if it were not for some driving force, the motion would cease. The dissipation and the driving force tend to combine to kill out initial transients and settle the system into its typical behavior. This one part of the phase space of the dynamical system corresponding to the typical behavior is the attracting section or *attractee*.

Some dynamical systems are chaotic everywhere, but in many cases chaotic behavior is found only in a subset of phase space. The cases of most interest arise when the chaotic behavior takes place on an attractor, since then a large set of initial conditions will lead to orbits that converge to this chaotic region.

An easy way to visualize a chaotic attractor is to start with a point in the basin of attraction of the attractor, and then simply plot the attractor's subsequent orbit. Because of the topological transitivity condition, this is likely to produce a picture of the entire final attractor, such as the general shape of the Lorenz attractor.

This attractor results from a simple three-dimensional model of the Lorenz weather system. The Lorenz attractor is perhaps one of the best-known chaotic system diagrams, probably because it is not only one of the first, but it is also one of the most complex shapes and as such gives rise to a very interesting pattern that looks like the wings of a butterfly.

Unlike fixed-point attractors and limit cycles, the attractors that arise from chaotic systems, known as *strange attractors*, have great detail and complexity. Strange attractors occur in both continuous dynamical systems (such as the Lorenz system) and in some discrete systems (such as the Hénon map). Other discrete dynamical systems have a repelling structure, called a Julia set that forms at the boundary between basins of attraction of fixed points. Julia sets can be thought of as strange *repellers*. Both strange attractors and Julia sets typically have a fractal structure, and a fractal dimension can be calculated for them.

In the human system we call society, individuals are the strange attractors. Actually, to be more specific, it's their ideas that are the strange attractors. Since ideas originate in the mind of a single individual, it seems more accurate to classify people as the strange attractor in the society system. As America is the subject of this book, it's American society with which we are concerned.

Whenever a person first has an idea, and that idea is transmitted or communicated to others, if it takes root and begins to grow, that is others adopt the idea as something they believe, then a specific trajectory of that attractor or idea starts to emerge. As more people adopt the idea or ideas as part of their belief systems, it becomes the basis of action.[41] Action toward creating that idea results in a pattern that emerges from the action of multiple individuals. Over time, a specific pattern is constructed; it becomes an object such as a philosophical, social, economic or political system. As these are formed, the object that emerges from that pattern is American society.

These objects, while invisible, are no less real that any tangible object such as a car or a boat. They occupy the three dimensions of space—length, depth, and width—and the one dimension of time. In order for these objects to solidify, the mathematical formulation on the Cartesian plane must be either additive or multiplicative to create it. For it to be destroyed, the opposite must be true. It must be divided or subtracted. Such patterns are possible through the multiplicative and additive functions of the sheer number of people involved in the activity or activities that are necessary for the action, and by extension the sustainability of the object. From an individual perspective in the day-to-day living, the formed object is the result of our work. When objects of American society no longer meet the needs of the people, such as an economic or a political system, these objects begin to break down and decay. America must build new structures, and this falls on the backs of its citizens. It is the individual work efforts of all American citizens that make this possible.

All work must contribute to this object called American society, whether it's the work of the doctor, lawyer, teacher, truck driver, restaurant owner, or manager. Remember, power is the rate of application of energy to the accomplishment of work in a system. Right now, America is inert because the power to build and maintain the system doesn't exist. It won't exist until we drastically change. That change must come from the American people.

THE CAUSE AND EFFECT OF CHANGE

People who create new things have the power to change in that they can move from something that didn't exist to something that now does exist. In essence, they have changed the world around them. This power to create is an absolute power given to each human being on the face of the planet. If allowed to use our power to make changes driven only by our passions and whims, this power is not channeled toward productive uses. If left unchecked, the potential to do harm is immeasurable. However, when this power is directed toward building and creating something constructive, it can have positive results and a positive influence on our society.

Joseph Schumpeter described this process as *creative destructionism*.[42] In his book, *Capitalism, Socialism, and Democracy*, Dr. Schumpeter popularized this term to describe the process of transformation that accompanies radical innovation. In his view of capitalism, innovation by entrepreneurs was the force that sustained long-term economic growth, even as it destroyed the value of established companies that enjoyed some degree of monopoly power. He states that "the essential point to grasp is that in dealing with capitalism we are dealing with an evolutionary process. It may seem strange that anyone can fail to see so obvious a fact which moreover was long ago emphasized by Karl Marx."[43] Capitalism as an economic system of production "incessantly revolutionizes the economic structures from within, incessantly destroying the old one, incessantly creating a new one [*such as in American society*]. This process of Creative Destruction is the essential fact about capitalism."[44]

While the power to create would seem to be a positive desired thing, especially within a capitalistic society such as America, it is not something that everyone wants to see happen. Such structures, the economic structures for example,

34

have millions of people with vested interests in those very same structures. As is true with all human beings, the tendency is to protect one's own interest. Companies have the same tendency when threatened with competition. Such a threat doesn't come from the entrepreneurial endeavor until it results in the destruction part where individual and corporate interests are threatened with their survival at issue. It is in this scenario that those in power to do so will use that same power to resist making the changes they should make. As Machiavelli observed in 1515, "there is nothing more difficult to execute, nor more dubious of success, nor more dangerous to administer than to introduce a new system of things, for he who introduces it has all those who profit from the old system as his enemies."[45]

Choices as a basis of action, when these are based on false beliefs, can be disastrous. When these choices are based on knowledge, it means that it is based on truth. If a person knows something, then that knowledge must also be true. Actions based on belief, when false, can lead to dire, unintended consequences. This is the reason that the creative power of the human spirit cannot be left unchecked. This creative power is based on an idea and/or an ideal. Ideals are simply a means for organizing people to perform work toward a common goal. When such ideals are used to inform belief systems, and these ideals are based on false assumptions, the result is disastrous. In this respect, America is held captive by its set of ideals that are used as drivers for the construction and ongoing production of our society.

Ideals are illusions. They are used as magician's tricks to control masses of people. In the hand of leaders who abuse and misuse their position, this power is dangerous and leads us down a road toward self-destruction. So often, our leaders fail to understand the dire consequence of such misuse and abuse. Power is limited and controlled by dividing people through our social, economic, political and philosophical systems. However, the power should actually reside with each individual person; it is the people who have the power to make changes to existing structures through choices. It is not government, not religious leaders, not business leaders, or captains of industry who are forces of change.

For America and Americans to return to prosperity, our power must be restored to its rightful owners. The human spirit has the power to create. In order for this to happen, an individual must have knowledge; that same person must have wisdom to direct the power of that knowledge; he or she must be under authority—the power to create cannot be unchecked. At the same time, no individual must be unlimited in their freedom of choice.[46]

CHAPTER 3: AMERICA IN TRANSITION

The only thing we have to fear is fear itself.

Franklin Delano Roosevelt

AMERICAN INDUSTRIALIZATION: A BRIEF HISTORY

The process of industrialization describes the change from an agricultural society to one based on industry and a shift from home to factory production. Although no specific date can be given as to its beginnings, the industrial society started to rise sometime in the latter part of the eighteenth century in Britain. It was there that new production methods invaded several key industries, and the result was a dramatic shift in industry operations. These new methods included different machines, fresh sources of power and energy, and novel forms of organizing business and labor. For the first time technical and scientific knowledge was applied to business practices on a large scale. Humankind had begun to develop mass production. The result was an increase in material goods that could be used for consumption by the mass population.

The Industrial Revolution began in Great Britain because social, political, and legal conditions encouraged changes in several key industries. A government policy of hands off industry facilitated Britain's industrialization in areas such as iron and steel, steam engine production, and textiles. Fresh methods and ideas created a new machine-building sector that quickly spread mechanization to throughout the economy. Skilled laborers often were replaced with new machines.

One of the most obvious changes to people's lives was that more people moved into the urban areas where factories were located. Migration provided a ready work force for new industries in urbanized centers. The movement into industrial cities created stresses for many people in the labor force. In the factories, long hours, harsh conditions, and often few rewards were the norm. The Industrial Revolution divided the production process into basic, individual tasks rather than a single worker doing the entire job.[47] Such division of labor greatly improved productivity, but reduced factory life to repetitive, boring work. Factory work hours were long, often more than twelve hours a day, six days a week. Strict rules and close supervision by managers and overseers were common; the clock ruled a worker's life in the industrial society.

Although it began in Great Britain, by the nineteenth-century America was fully engaged in the industrialization process. The United States enjoyed many advantages that made it fertile ground for an Industrial Revolution. A rich, sparsely inhabited continent lay open to exploitation and development. It proved relatively easy for the United States government to buy or seize vast lands across North America from Native Americans, from European nations, and from Mexico. In addition, the American population was highly literate and most felt that economic growth was desirable. With settlement stretched across the continent from the Atlantic Ocean to the Pacific Ocean, the United States enjoyed a huge internal market. Within its distant borders there was remarkably free movement of goods, people, capital, and ideas.

The young nation also inherited many advantages from Great Britain. One initial American advantage was the fact that the United States shared the language and much of the culture of Great Britain, the pioneering industrial nation. This helped Americans transfer technology to the United States. As descriptions of new machines and processes appeared in print, Americans read about them eagerly and tried their own versions of the inventions sweeping Britain. Machines and knowledgeable people were essential for furthering industrialization in the United States. It quickly adopted many of the technologies, forms of organization, and attitudes shaping the new industrial world, and then proceeded to generate its own advances.

Soon the United States was pioneering its own innovations. Because local circumstances and conditions in the United States were somewhat different than those in Britain, industrialization developed somewhat differently. America had many plentiful natural resources. For example the abundance of wood led Americans to use that material much more than Europeans did. They burned wood widely as fuel and also made use of it in machinery and in construction. Taking advantage of the vast forest resources in their country, Americans built the world's best woodworking machines.

Industrialization brought deep and often distressing shifts to American society. The influence of rural life declined, and the relative economic importance of agriculture dwindled. Although the amount of land under cultivation and the number of people earning a living from agriculture expanded, the growth of commerce, manufacturing, and the service industries steadily eclipsed farming's significance. The proportion of the work force dependent on agriculture shrank constantly from the time of the first federal census in 1790. From that time until the end of the nineteenth century, farm workers dropped from about 75 percent of the work force to about 40 percent.[48]

New technology was introduced in agriculture. The scarcity of labor and the growth of markets for agricultural products encouraged the introduction of machinery to the farms. Machinery increased productivity so that fewer hands could produce more food per acre. New plows, seed drills, cultivators, mowers, and threshers, as well as the reaper, all appeared by 1860. After that, better harvesters and binding machines came into use, as did the harvester-threshers known as combines. Farmers also used limited steam power in the late nineteenth century, and by about 1905, they began using gasoline-powered tractors. At about the same time, Americans began to apply science systematically to agriculture, such as by using genetics as a basis for plant breeding. These techniques, plus fertilizers and pesticides, helped to increase farm productivity.

Transportation and communication were special challenges in a nation that stretched from the Atlantic to the Pacific Oceans. Economic growth depended on tying together the resources, markets, and people of this large area. Despite the general conviction that private enterprise was best, the government played an active role in uniting the country, particularly by building roads. From 1815 to 1860, state and local governments also provided almost three-quarters of the financing for canal construction and related improvements to waterways. By 1860 more than half the railroad tracks in the world were in the United States.

The most critical nineteenth-century improvement in communication was the telegraph invented by Samuel Morse. The telegraph allowed messages to be sent long distances almost instantly by using a code of electronic pulses passing over a wire. The railroad and the telegraph spread across North America and helped create a national market that in turn encouraged additional improvements in transportation and communication.

Another challenge in the United States was a relative shortage of labor. Much more than in continental Europe or in Britain, labor was in chronically short supply in the United States. This led industrialists to develop machinery to replace human labor.

Along this line, continuous-process manufacturing was invented in America. This process involved making large quantities of the same product in a nonstop operation. In a closely related development, American manufacturers shaped a set of techniques later known as the American system of production. This system involved using special-purpose machines to produce large quantities of similar, sometimes interchangeable, parts that would then be assembled into a finished product. The American system extended the idea of division of labor from workers to specialized machines. Instead of a worker making a small part of a finished product, a machine made the part, speeding the process and allowing manufacturers to produce goods more quickly. This method also yielded goods of much more uniform quality than those made by hand labor.

As American manufacturing technology spread to new industries, it ushered in technical and organizational advances that carried industrial society to new levels. Factories and their production output became much larger than they had been in the earlier years of the Industrial Revolution. Some industries concentrated production in fewer but bigger and more productive facilities. In addition, some industries boosted production in existing (not necessarily larger) factories. This growth was enabled by a variety of factors, including technological and scientific progress; improved management; and expanding markets due to larger populations, rising incomes, and better transportation and communications.

American industrialist Andrew Carnegie built a giant iron and steel empire using huge new plants. John D. Rockefeller, another American industrialist, did the same in petroleum refining. Soon there were enormous advances in science-based industries—for example, chemicals, electrical power, and electrical machinery. Just as in the first revolution, these changes prompted further innovations that led to further economic growth.

It was in the automobile industry that continuous-process methods and the American system combined to greatest effect. In 1903 American industrialist Henry Ford founded the Ford Motor Company. His production innovation was the moving assembly line, which brought together many mass-produced parts to create automobiles. Ford's moving assembly line gave the world the fullest expression yet of industrialization, and his production triumphs in the second decade of the twentieth century signaled the crest of the industrial society wave.

Just as important as advances in manufacturing technology were a wave of changes in how business was structured and work was organized. Beginning with the large railroad companies, business leaders learned how to operate and coordinate many different economic activities across broad geographic areas. During the first phase of the Industrial Revolution, many factories had grown into large organizations, but even by 1875, few firms coordinated production and marketing across many business units. Leaders such as Carnegie and Rockefeller changed this, and firms grew much larger in numerous industries, giving birth to the modern corporation.

Within the business unit, Americans pioneered novel ways of organizing work. Engineers studied and modified production in search of the most efficient ways to lay out a factory, move materials, route jobs, and control work through precise scheduling. Industrial engineer Frederick W. Taylor and his followers sought both efficiency and contented workers. They believed that they could achieve those results through precise measurement and analysis of each aspect of a job. Taylor's *The Principles of Scientific Management* (1911) became the most influential book of the Industrial Revolution. By the early twentieth century, Ford's mass production techniques and Taylor's scientific management principles had come to symbolize America's place as the leading industrial nation.

Industrialization in the United States led to major social changes. With its negative aspects and its benefits, the Industrial Revolution has been one of the most influential movements in America. Urban population grew, rural population declined, and the nature of labor changed dramatically. The nature of work became worse for some people, as industrialization placed great pressures on traditional family structures with work outside the home. But industrialization also brought economic improvement for many Americans in terms of increased material well-being. The industrial way of life provided a constant flow of new goods and services that gave consumers more choices. A rising middle class, increased prosperity, improved health, better education, and a general better standard of living of all are just a few of the many significant social changes of the industrial society.

POSTINDUSTRIALISM: A TIME OF CHANGE

As is true of previous epochs of human history, it's impossible to assign a specific date to mark when different phases of a society begin and end. For example, when did America move from an agricultural society to an industrial society? No specific dates can be given, but major components of industrialization began in the early to middle nineteen hundreds. This is true also with the transition to the postindustrial society. At best, we can only surmise that the beginning of the postindustrial society was sometime shortly after World War II, and it continues to some degree even today, in the early part of the twenty-first century.

When things start to change around us, we, as human beings, begin to take notice. Eager for some explanation of those changes, it's common to see commentators express interest and begin to pontificate an explanation of those changes. Where did these changes come from and what do they mean? The last fifty years of the twentieth century were no different. As new social changes emerged such as those experienced in the latter part of the twentieth century, Daniel Bell's *Post-Industrial Society* in 1973 was the first to identify the postindustrial society.

Although Daniel Bell coined the term postindustrialism in the late 1950s,[49] he himself began substituting *information* and *knowledge* for the prefix postindustrial around 1980, when a tidal wave of enthusiasm for futurology was swelled by interest in developments in computer and communication technologies. The term *information society* became the frequent language of postindustrial society writers. At first, the differentiator between the postindustrial and information society seems to be the fact that postindustrial society is traditionally a sociological term and information society is a lay term used by writers and futurists. However, these lines of distinction began to blur over the course of time, as the two terms began to be used interchangeably throughout the literature. Although considerable overlap, the postindustrial society and the information society are two different phases of societal development within the United States of America.

The World Bank released *Beyond Economic Growth: Meeting the Challenges of Global Development* in 2000 in which postindustrialization was defined as deindustrialization. They suggest that leading developed countries such as the United States are deindustrializing. In short, it's the decline of industrialization in America. The postindustrial society signified not only the decline of industrial society but also the rise of the information society. Essentially, two macro-level processes overlapped at a given point in human history to define a transitional moment in two distinct phases of American society.

Postindustrialism is the notion that the process of social change took America beyond the industrial society order. It is based on the production of information, rather than on the production of material goods. According to those who favor this concept, contemporary society is currently experiencing a series of social changes as profound as those that initiated the industrial era some two hundred years ago. We are entering a new system, a postindustrial society that, while it has several distinguishing features, is characterized throughout by a heightened presence and significance of information. Information and knowledge are crucial for *Post-Industrial Society* both quantitatively and qualitatively.

Within the postindustrial society, we saw the emergence of a new social framework heavily dependent upon telecommunications. New infrastructures that utilize information technologies contribute decisively to the way economic and social exchanges are conducted, the way knowledge is created and retrieved, and the nature of work and occupations in which people must now be engaged. The computer and the Internet play a key role in this new information revolution.

While new information technology plays a central role in the postindustrial society paradigm, it's not just about technological change. The social changes witnessed during this same time period have been just as deep. It is impossible to argue that new information technology did not play a role, and I wouldn't attempt to do so. However, such assumptions around the role of information technology that is described as technological determinism insists that technology acts as an independent force in our life. If this is true, then people are the servants of technology instead of its master. I reject the claim of technological determinism, as technology operates in a context not always of its making. It is so often shaped by social structures such as economics, politics, and culture.

New technology is one major instrument that serves to bring about social change. This newer information technology has served as the basis of the postindustrial society paradigm. While few would deny that technological advances in computing and telecommunications collectively known as information technology, the idea that this convergence is the start of the age of information technology and that everyone would welcome such a marked beginning is highly doubtful. However, the assumption that deserves exploration is the one that places the relation between society and technology solely as technology's influence on society.

Information technology in contemporary society seems qualitatively different from new technology of past societies. Perhaps, this can be explained in three ways. First, current technology is more powerful than any before it. For example, with the shovel man could dig a hole in the ground, but with a single cell phone we can talk to people today on the other side of the world tomorrow. Second, the explicit awareness of technology as a critical determinant of social life and social institutions was instigated by the quality of modern technology. Third, the result is that contemporary society is going to great lengths to understand and control technology for good social purpose, and therefore much effort is expended to measure the influence of technology and its effects beyond simply the economy.

An examination of the technical texts that give an historical account of the marriage of computing and telecommunications reveals a tale that maintains that convergence is based purely on technologic events.[50] Certainly such events are vital, and they make their contribution to changes around us that place us squarely in the age of information technology and the information revolution. However, such accounts give the impression that new technology is somehow outside society, impinging upon it, that the marriage is an entirely spontaneous technical affair that gives birth to a new, contemporary society.

While it is already clear that the social influence of information technology is profound, though not necessarily for the reasons given by the more visionary technologists, to focus only on the influence is to take the new technologies and their convergence as given. This neglects the equally important question of the origins of the technologies, and the nontechnical reasons why they have converged. There are at least three reasons for this. First, the social influence is poorly understood unless the origins of new technologies are taken into account. To take the most extreme position, information technology reduces the likelihood of a global nuclear disaster. It is difficult to square this with the palpable fact that military and defense-oriented requirements and funding provide the biggest single thrust behind information technology. Besides military involvement, one must also consider the involvement of commercial interests in information technology—companies and businesses wish to sell new technologies. Furthermore, governments whose activities are bound up with military and commercial interests, also promote information technology in specific ways. Technological impacts are seen more clearly when such social origins are examined.

Alongside these macro-level interests are many familiar micro-level movements, organizations, and processes that mediate the economic and political interests to the population at large, acting as social carriers of new technologies. They drive to put computers in schools or in other instances, mediate government and commercial interests. On the domestic front, crazes like computer games, the advertisers' promise of greater choice in entertainment, and the magazine racks laden with computer-related magazines are obvious instruments of commercial interest.

Secondly, and on a more theoretical point, the perspective that concentrates on social consequences of given technology neglects the role of human action within the technological process. To give it its proper name, technological determinism assumes that technology has a kind of life of its own that then shapes social existence. It's true enough that no one living in the nineteenth century could have guessed that the motorcar would have contributed so deeply to everyday life in the twentieth-century. Too often cities built with car transport in mind discourage pedestrians and cyclists, pollute the atmosphere, and oblige people to make many transactions—shopping, sporting, and eating, and so on—at some distance from their homes. Moreover the car has been augmented internally by modifications for luxury, safety, and speed and externally by generating new forms of support and service. It seems to have grown almost autonomously.

Here is the major point—none of this could have occurred without people being involved in its development. Technology—whether one is talking about machines or systems or both—possesses no life of its own. It is a human product, a social construction. Very powerful social forces, especially military, economic, and political ones, achieve their social shaping. But in these cases it is also clear that active human agents are involved; people are constantly monitoring, evaluating, and justifying their activities.

Thirdly, if the interplay between the social shaping of technology and the technological shaping of society is examined, then the door is opened for reshaping, redirecting, or simply resisting certain technological developments. The worst forms of hype present contemporary society as unavoidable; a result of the social diffusion of information technology, but there is nothing that is inevitable about it at all.

Along this line of thinking, it is quite plausible that technological change only appears to induce social change in that it creates new opportunities for human beings and for societies, and it produces both positive and negative consequences that result in new problems. There is a close relationship between technological and social change. This relationship itself helps to identify the reason any technological development such as those experienced within contemporary society induce massive social changes. Technological advance creates a new opportunity to achieve some desired goal. This opportunity requires alterations in social organization if advantage is to be had. This is turn means that existing social structures will be interfered with, and the end result is that older structures that were adequate to meet goals are now inadequate.

To summarize, social change occurs when great advances in technology are experienced within a society. However, it is not the technology itself that causes the social change to occur. From the postindustrial society perspective, technology is the centerpiece that acts as an impetus for social change. Information technology is a social object that needs to be studied and better understood. However, technology is but a tool; it is a prerequisite and an enabler for information that defines the new opportunities within society, and thus the catalyst for the social change experienced within contemporary society.

MORE THAN TECHNOLOGICAL ADVANCEMENT

There is no doubt that the transitional period referred to postindustrial society is heavily reliant on an advanced information technology infrastructure, and information and knowledge are central to this phase of development in society. However, the conceptualization goes much deeper and must also include an examination of the forces of production. In doing so, one aspect of postindustrial society that must be considered is that of social class.

In the industrial society, one central focus was on inequality among certain groups such as women, elderly, and minorities. If the information society has in fact replaced the old industrial society way of life, then what does this mean for these same groups? There are three possible views of class in the information society. One, information society is characterized by classlessness achieved by technical not social revolution. Two, information technology strengthens the hand of the already powerful capitalists simply reinforcing class lines. Three, the introduction of new technology tilts the balance of power in different ways, realigning classes and releasing new social movements, and this redefines social class altogether.

The cornerstone of the popular information society thesis is that a new *information sector* comprising *information workers* has become a dominant economic factor in advanced societies. However, the evidence points, not to an information sector but to the increase of a diverse range of information activities whose social significance depends on a complex series of variables. Many kinds of work are likely to become information intensive, but this does not add up to a new sector. This does not add up to a new social class.

Similarly mistaken is the notion that the new classes may be accompanying the spread of information technology. Education and skill levels are becoming a more important criterion for determining social position, but this does not affect the basic social divisions based on property ownership.[51] Some technocrats may have more power but do not rule. On the other hand, the simple Marxian view of class polarization is also open to serious question. First, a smooth transition to an information society is highly unlikely. Second, the idea that class struggle is the only axis along which conflicts occur in modern societies is not reasonable. To restate, new technology mediates other kinds of social relationships as well as class.

For example, information technology, the centerpiece of postindustrial society, often designed, developed, sold, and used by some to channel power. Yet women are not meekly accepting such subordination. The slowly increasing strength of female participation in technology may open up new areas of contested terrain over fundamental issues. While women are challenging male predominance in high-technology jobs, their involvement also leads to a refusal to make the sharp separation between work, family, and personal life that is dictated by the male work world.

Traditionally, women have had slightly higher levels of formal education than men. Postindustrial occupations in areas such as health, education, and research that are based on education are now open to women. Today, women make up about 49 percent of the managerial class, about 30 percent of the natural scientists, about 40 percent of the college teachers, 30 percent of the lawyers, and more than 50 percent of the teachers, librarians, designers, and psychologists.

Minorities do not appear to enjoy the same level of positive social change that seems to have accompanied women's roles within the postindustrial society. The distinguishing factor for minorities within the postindustrial society is in the new interactions that are enabled through the use of technology such as the Internet to form new social networks. One of the consequences of these networks is an increase in the importance of social capital and social influence. Social capital is the awareness of new opportunities and possibilities for advancement through new information, by acquiring social relationships.

In agricultural societies, the elderly exercised considerable power and were given a very high status. However, in the industrial society, they exercised relatively little power and were given a low position of status. American society has a well-developed and sophisticated educational system that is designed specifically to train and prepare young people for entry into their chosen professions. However, the institution is ill equipped to retrain older workers when new technologies require additional schooling. In a rapidly changing society younger people are nearly always better educated and posses more knowledge of recent technology than their elders; thus, the latter lose their utility and the basis of their authority.

The use of and access to information technology throughout all levels of society is tied to economics. Technology is a necessary prerequisite to the creation and distribution of information throughout the postindustrial society. The U.S. Department of Commerce identified the *digital divide* as the prohibitive cost of technology and suggested that this factor acts as a deterrent for some groups to access the Internet.[52] Therefore, not all people will have access to the Internet at the same time. This argument around the digital divide presumes that access to the Internet is the same as Internet usage. However, giving the poor access to technology does not guarantee equality. That is to say, that just because all people have Internet access, there is no a priori reason to assume equality will be evident in Internet usage.

Therefore, one model of the postindustrial society must encompass a micro-level view of social changes embodied by the lifestyle of people within society. Such a lifestyle reflects the technical, informational, economic, social, and cultural dimensions that are manifested in the way people live, work, and play in society. Central to lifestyle is a determination of how life chances mitigate life choices around Internet usage that results in an *informatizationalized* lifestyle within the information society. A lifestyle is a collective pattern of related behavior based on choices from options available to people, and an informatizationalized lifestyle is a collective pattern of behavior based on choices from Internet usage options available to people according to life chances. A person's life chances are socially determined by his or her socioeconomic status, age, gender, race, ethnicity, and other factors that influence informatizationalized lifestyle choices.

Lifestyle is what distinguishes one status group from another, such as Internet users and non-Internet users, or to use another term the information rich and the information poor. The famous sociologist Max Weber in 1922, put forth the notion that life chances refers to the probability of acquiring a particular lifestyle such as the informatizationalized lifestyle described here. In order to have a chance to gain that lifestyle, a person must have the financial resources, status, rights, and social relationships to support that lifestyle.

Internet access is a prerequisite before one can make the choices about the activities and behaviors that result in an informatizationalized lifestyle. However, Internet access does not automatically dictate Internet usage around those choices. As stated previously, the informatizationalized lifestyle must encompass not only the technical (i.e., computer ownership and Internet access are technical in nature) and economic (i.e., Internet access requires computer ownership and access via an Internet service provider both of which cost money), but also informational, social, and cultural dimensions that are manifested in the way people live, work, and play in the information society. Specifically, the informatizationalized lifestyle of contemporary society is recognizable as activities and behaviors surrounding Internet usage resulting from the choices they make. The choices available around Internet usage include such activities as sending and receiving e-mail; taking educational courses online; doing research for school; checking news, weather, or sports; making phone calls; searching for information; searching for jobs; doing job-related tasks; shopping; paying bills or other commercial activities; and playing games. Moreover, a person's life chances in the information society are socially determined by their socioeconomic status, age, gender, race, ethnicity, and other factors that influence those choices, thereby resulting in the informatizationalized lifestyle.

Unfortunately, lifestyle studies have not focused on lifestyle in the postindustrial society. The informatizationalized lifestyle as defined by Internet usage choices by examining differences in a person's life chances as determined by the individual's socioeconomic status, age, gender, race, ethnicity, and other factors that influence lifestyle choices. Informatizationalized lifestyle choices are defined as Internet usage based on the options that are available for those who have Internet access at home. By examining only those who have access at home, the technical and economic barriers defined by the digital divide are less important.

TRANSITION TO THE INFORMATION SOCIETY

If postindustrial society simply defines a transitional period for America from the middle of the twentieth century until today, what then is an information society? Such a conceptualization is readily apparent throughout the literature in the use of terms such as *information workers* and *information revolution*. During this time period, new information technologies that quickly permeated offices, industrial processes, schools, and homes seemed to be everywhere. With the arrival of such technologies, came many sudden changes and a desire to better understand these changes and their impact. The changes in contemporary society are certainly obvious in terms of technological innovations, but they also have significance in terms of social change.

Just as there was a transition from an agricultural society to an industrial society, so, too there was a transition from the industrial society to the information society. The information revolution of the last fifty or so years saw a shift from production of material goods through physical labor in industries to intellectual work and an increase in consumption of services. In 1993, Dordick and Wang used *informatization* to describe the process of social change that resulted in an information society. A new and challenging explanation of a changing social structure resulted in a definition of the information society as one whose *infrastructure* is closely defined by *information technology* and characterized by the development of a large *service sector* that is heavily dependent upon *professional and technical occupations* denoted by the increasing *intellectualized nature of work* that can only be performed through *ongoing educational endeavors* where the *knowledge theory of value* gets translated into *information* and treated as *commodity*.

Using this definition as the starting point, a simplistic view of the information society can be constructed. Specifically, the information society involves four key areas that serve as pillars to both anchor and support the basic social structure of the information society within twenty-first- century America. These four pillars are information, technology, human capital, and a political economy. To illustrate the importance of each and the role it plays in the information society, there are five conceptions of the information society that include technological, economic, occupational, spatial, and cultural.

The technological conceptualization is probably the most common definition of the information society. Technology provides the infrastructure of the information society. It emphasizes technological innovation and the idea that breakthroughs in information processing, storage, and transmission through IT (information technology) have applications in every sphere of life. The design, production, and use of technology are human activities that produce tools. The development of technology, therefore, is significantly dependent on human capability and will to create and generate new solutions and unique products and systems.

The economic view is based on the idea that information industries such as media, education, and information technology, and research-based industries such as pharmaceuticals are making an ever-greater contribution to the economy. Globalization, which characterizes contemporary society, has accelerated over the past thirty years and is more visible now than ever. Positive economic growth, combined with constantly growing foreign investments and higher international trade, are the main characteristics of the global economy. This produces a growing inequality and widening of the wage gap in developed societies, while in developing countries, there is a dramatic drop in the number of people living in poverty. Globalization influences the rise of human aspirations on a personal level; it also increases immigration and heterogeneity within a society, while people develop a multiple identity.

The occupational definition focuses on the change in organizations and the nature of work. There is a significant job increase in the field of automatic management of information, while other jobs have a psychological element that brings about new and, until now, unknown work-related satisfactions. White-collar employment in manufacturing industries will be drastically reduced, although the number of white-collar jobs in service industries will not necessarily increase sufficiently to absorb job losses in the manufacturing sector; thus, advances in information technology will likely bring more unemployment, hold down the growth of unskilled workers' wages, and widen income and regional disparities.

This is similar to the claim that automated technologies are not only diminishing the proportion of manufactured work available but rapidly shrinking the need for human labor in the white-collar sector as well. With manufacture and service work daily displacing workers with new technologies, and with the shift from mass employment to elite employment, joblessness will become widespread. But just as there are notions of jobs becoming scarce, people seem to be working harder than ever as demonstrated by the fact that in the United States work time has actually increased since 1948 and Americans now work 320 more hours than their west European counterparts.

The spatial conceptualization of the information society stresses space and place. The changes that occur when information networks connect locations dramatically change the organization of activity in time and space. Urbanization is a dynamic social and economic process that transforms societies from primarily rural to primarily urban ways of life. There is a spatial reorganization of population and economic activities in postindustrial societies where a large majority of people, jobs, and organizations are concentrated in or dominated by urban agglomerations.

Lastly, the cultural dimension of the information society is probably the most easily acknowledged but also the most difficult to define or measure. This perspective has emerged particularly with the convergence of communications and information technology, which is now turning computer networks into mass-media networks and communication systems such as satellite TV, the World Wide Web, and mobile phone networks. Media and communication provide people with more than information. The messages received in the form of sounds, images, texts, and stories can reinforce or challenge a person's identity, values, ideas, understanding, and ways of relating to the world and to one another.

Workers engaged in intellectual work (whether called information or knowledge) now are the owner of the means of production. This change represents a significant shift in the production processes of the information society. In the early 1960s, economists and social scientists began to think about a fourth occupational sector of the work force, one in which workers were engaged in knowledge- or information- intensive occupations.

This led to a heated debate on the social and economic consequences of American society and its growing information industries. About this time, an increasing share of government expenditures was in activities that produced no material output, and increasing amounts of resources were being spent by industry on similar nonmaterial outputs. Such expenditures are necessary for the production of knowledge and are centrally important to the nation's economy.

Knowledge is anything that is known by somebody, and knowledge production is any activity by which someone learns of something that was previously unknown. Following these definitions, five groups of knowledge-producing activities—education, research, and development, media and communication, information machines, and information services—constituted the knowledge industry. Knowledge-producing occupations such as professional and technical workers, managers, officials and proprietors, clerical and sales workers, and craftsmen and foremen in printing trades were responsible for a growing percentage of knowledge work in the United States, which would account for 29 percent of the gross national product and slightly less than 31 percent of the work force would be engaged in knowledge-producing industries in 1959.

Another way of thinking about knowledge industries is that they include only research, higher education, and the production of knowledge as intellectual property. Instead of trying to pinpoint knowledge workers across multiple occupations, it is much simpler to include only two groups of professionals—scientists and engineers. This estimate of information workers yields a much smaller contribution to a nation's gross national product. In examining changes in the information or knowledge work force over time through longitudinal data for the contribution of knowledge industries and workers to the nation's gross national product, the importance of knowledge and/or information in the American economy and the information society is better defined and understood.

Ancillary workers and firms who support the production and distribution of information and who generate income by information activities are not limited to the selling price of a product. It is a better basis of measurement because it more accurately reflects the wealth generated by the information economy. Activities may not be directly involved in the production of information, but they contribute to the value of the product or service produced and should therefore be included. For example, the use of information obtained by remote sensing satellites is used in the fishing industry to locate schools and increase the catch. While not produced in an information industry, the information gathering by satellite is attributed to information consumed internally by the fishing industry.

Other research of importance has been conducted by the U.S. Department of Commerce to examine the differences in computer ownership and access to the Internet. As previously covered, the digital divide is the unequal level of Internet access by specific groups. By the end of 1998, over 40 percent of Americans had computers in their homes and about 25 percent accessed the Internet. By the end of the third quarter of 2001, that number had increased with over 66 percent of the population owning a computer and 54 percent were using the Internet regularly.

Second, Internet usage is increasing for all groups regardless of location, marital status, income, education level, age, race, ethnicity, or gender. However, there are disparities within these groups. High-income urban households are more likely to have a computer and access the Internet than low-income rural households. Single mothers with children have the highest growth rate in Internet usage but still lag behind other groups. Those with higher incomes are more likely to access and use the Internet as compared to those with lower incomes. The better educated use the Internet more than the less educated. People over the age of fifty are the least likely to use the Internet, while children and teenagers use computers and access the Internet more than any other age group. Whites and Asian Americans are the most likely to use the Internet. Blacks and Hispanics are the least likely to use the Internet. Males are more likely to use the Internet than women.

Third, not all people have access to the Internet at home. Public access to the Internet through locations such as schools and libraries plays an important role for those groups who have the least access such as lower-income, less-educated, and minority groups. However, those with access to the Internet at home have a clear economic advantage. Fourth, Americans are expanding the range of activities and behaviors in making choices about the use of the Internet. By 2001, about 45 percent of the population used e-mail, 33 percent searched the Internet for product and service information, and about 39 percent make purchases online.

LIFESTYLE IN THE INFORMATION SOCIETY

Observable macro-level changes in a society also influence micro-level changes in the lives of the people who are a part of that society. In America in the latter part of the twentieth century and the beginning of the twenty-first century, these social changes are apparent in the day-to-day lives of people, including work and leisure activities. To more fully understand these changes, a different body of literature must be examined that covers the postmodern society ideas. In the postmodern tradition, there's a different focal point in terms of explaining the social changes within contemporary American society. In this body of literature, theorizing and study is more focused on culture and is deeply engrained in Weberian theory of lifestyles.[53] Among the classical theorists, Max Weber provides the deepest insight into the lifestyle concept. Lifestyle is linked to status by highlighting prestige as the distinguishing characteristic of status, which is normally expressed by the fact that a specific style of life is expected from all those who belong to that status. Status, not class plays the larger role in Weber's perspective. Status groups originate through a sharing of similar lifestyles or as a means to preserve a particular style of life.

Lifestyles were based not so much on what people produced but on what they consumed. One might thus say that classes are stratified according to their relations to the production and acquisition of goods, whereas status groups are stratified according to the principles of their consumption of goods as represented by special styles of life. In other words, lifestyle differences between status groups are based on their relationship to the means of consumption not the means of production, although this does not mean that consumption is independent of production. The economic mode of production sets the basic parameters within which consumption occurs, but it does not determine or even necessarily affect specific forms of consumption because the consumption of goods and services conveys a social meaning that displays the status and social identity of the consumer. Consumption can then be regarded as a set of social and cultural practices that establish differences between social groups, not merely as a means of expressing differences that are already in place because of economic factors. The use of particular goods and services through distinct lifestyles ultimately distinguishes status groups from one another.

In the information society, a lifestyle represents definable patterns of behavior that reflect the current conditions now prevalent in American society. Lifestyles in postmodern society are mixed, interwoven, and flexible, and thereby preclude clear maintenance of hierarchical distinctions and a standardization of lifestyles. Such lifestyles grounded in consumerism, such as choices of clothes, leisure activities, consumer goods, and bodily dispositions are not fixed to specific status groups. This situation is not evidence of a dramatic change in groups, but this development is a new improvement within the existing class hierarchy consisting of an expansion and legitimization of upper- and middle-class lifestyles.

Lifestyles are utilitarian social practices and ways of living adopted by individuals that reflect personal, group, and socioeconomic identities. They consist of self-selected forms of consumerism, involving particular choices in food, dress and appearance, housing, automobiles, work habits, forms of leisure, and other types of status-oriented behavior. The social changes currently experienced in the late twentieth and early twenty-first century involve massive social, economic, technological, and political changes that dramatically influence lifestyles. Lifestyles comprise patterns of related behaviors, values, and attitudes adapted by groups of individuals in response to their social, cultural, and economic environments. As Weber argues, lifestyles are realized primarily by choice within the social context provided by chance. Lifestyles typically consist of choices and practices influenced by an individual's life chances or probabilities for realizing them.

Just as early modernization dissolved the structure of feudal society and created the industrial age, modernization today is changing industrial society and modernity is being established. One way is the effect of modernity on the individual, especially in relation to the metropolis and the mature money economy. Yet the dialectical opposite of the submersion of individuality under the weight of modern living is the greater intensity, stimulation, and diversity of urban life that enhance the opportunity for individualization. Although the metropolis, science, and especially the money economy foster the dominance of abstract, analytical, calculative, and rational modes of thought that promote impersonal forms of interpersonal relations, they also promote a sense of individuality. Lifestyles are one way in which individuals seek to define their identity in relation to mass population. A goal of individuals is to determine their self-identity as a fixed and unambiguous point of reference. It is up to individuals to produce their own identity, and lifestyles are a strategy for accomplishing this.

Weber's insight concerning the interplay of choice and chance remains the central feature of the lifestyle concept. However, in the rapidly changing late or postmodern situations, lifestyles not only provide self-identity, but they also promote a sense of stability and belonging for an individual by providing an anchor in a particular social constellation of style and activity. He believed that choice is the major factor in the *operationalization* of a lifestyle, but the actualization of choices is influenced by life chances. Life chances are not a matter of pure chance. Instead, they are the chances people have in life because of their social situation. Chance is socially determined, and social structure is an arrangement of chances. Lifestyles are, therefore, not random behaviors unrelated to structure but are typically deliberate choices influenced by life chances. Choices and constraints work off each other to determine a distinctive lifestyle for each individual or group. People have needs, goals, identities, and desires that they match against their chances and probabilities of acquiring. They then select a lifestyle based on their assessments and the reality of their circumstances. Unrealistic choices are not likely to be achieved or maintained, whereas realistic choices are based on what is structurally possible and are more likely to be operationalized, made routine, and can be changed when circumstances permit.

Individuals have a range of freedom but not complete freedom in choosing a lifestyle. That is to say, people are not entirely free to determine their lifestyle, but they have the freedom to choose within the social constraints that apply to their situation in life. Lifestyle constraints, in a Weberian context, are primarily socioeconomic in origin; therefore, they can account for the interplay of individual choice and structural constraints in operationalizing a lifestyle. Those who have the desire and the means may choose, while those lacking in some way cannot choose so easily and may find their lifestyle determined more by external circumstances.

Weber's overall contribution to the understanding of contemporary lifestyles is that lifestyles are associated with status groups and are principally a collective, rather than an individual phenomenon; represent patterns of consumption not production; and are formed by the dialectical interplay between life choices and life chances, with choice playing the greater role.

The mode of social life resulting from the industrial revolution influences contemporary lifestyles. Modernity differs from all previous forms of social order because of its dynamism, global influence, and the degree to which it undercuts traditional customs and habits. The more tradition loses its hold, the more individuals are forced to negotiate lifestyle choices among a variety of local and increasingly global options. Modernity promotes a diversity of lifestyles, and even people in the lowest social classes have some choice. No culture eliminates choice altogether in day-to-day affairs, and even the poor have distinctive cultural styles and activities that require choices. People are likely to be pushed by social situations into choosing a particular lifestyle; in other words, it is necessary to adopt the appropriate lifestyle of a specific group or strata if one wishes to belong and move within it. A lifestyle involves a cluster of habits and orientations, and hence has a certain unity that connects options to a more or less ordered pattern. As such, an individual's particular lifestyle choices tend to fit a pattern that makes alternative choices out of character.

Lifestyles not only fulfill utilitarian needs but also provide material form to one's self-identity. Self-identity is not something that is just assigned to the individual by significant others or by the society. It is something that has to be routinely created and maintained through the activities of the individual. Everyone, to some extent, is forced to adopt a representative and reflexively constructed lifestyle. New conditions that transform time and space combined with certain disembodying systems, such as increasingly sophisticated and abstract money systems and the dissemination of technical knowledge throughout society, promote social change. As social life becomes more open, the contexts for action more plural, and authority more diverse, lifestyle choices are increasingly more important in the construction of self-identity and daily activities.

While postmodern conditions promote uncertainty and diversity in lifestyle choices, they also push people toward greater individual responsibility. Postmodern conditions are characterized by a fragmentation of traditional centers of authority and accelerated individualization. Although these processes would suggest that choice plays a greater role than chance in lifestyle selection, this is not necessarily the case. Choices are shaped by the individual's life chances, which are grounded in a particular reality such as socioeconomic, gender, age, or racial. Life chances, therefore, remain an especially powerful component of lifestyle options, even though traditional social structures are undergoing a major transition. Not only do life chances constrain choices, but the revolving character of the postmodern society also complicates matters.

Lifestyles may provide relief in a rapidly changing world by reducing complexity, that is, lifestyle choices can promote a sense of stability and belonging for an individual by providing an anchor for the person in a particular social constellation of style and activity. Lifestyles, like institutions, can be seen as opportunity structures. People take what they need from them, while adopting them as the preferred way to live. Chance mitigates choice. Life chances, as depicted by Weber, are predominantly socioeconomic. When it comes to lifestyles, it would appear that most people engage in certain behaviors regardless of their socioeconomic position, but different social classes are likely to pursue different avenues in terms of quality, distinctiveness, and probabilities for success. On the other hand, there is little empirical evidence to suggest that the contemporary patterns of social behavior that are referred to as lifestyles are merely deliberate products of independent individuals.

Chance is then an especially strong component of a lifestyle.[54] Individuals have life chances in society that can either make or break them; therefore, any concept of lifestyles needs to pay particular attention to chance. Life chances influence lifestyles through socioeconomic resources and perceptional boundaries derived from socialization and experience in a particular social milieu.

Most theories and concepts regarding lifestyle in the twentieth century are centered on the social stratification. The relationship between lifestyle and other forms of status, such as gender, age, race, ethnicity, religion, and sexual preference have not been fully explored, and neither have other variables such as peer relations and the influence of advertising and mass media campaigns. However, variables such as age and gender may in fact induce age-specific or gender-specific lifestyles that transcend class boundaries; thus, socioeconomic status cannot be considered the sole determinant of a lifestyle.

The term lifestyle implies complexity and structure but nonetheless infers a unity, pattern, or integrated set of behaviors. The appropriate strategy is to identify these integrated sets of behaviors in relation to the groups that practice and reproduce them. This process is not a case of pure rational choice because the choices made are not completely autonomous. People may have control over their choices but not over the principles and conditions underlying those choices. [55]

This consistency and routinization most likely prevails even in postmodern conditions where people are detached from the certainties and modes of living of the industrial age and subjected to evolving social circumstances with greater behavioral options. Moreover, lifestyles are opportunity structures in that people adopt them for the gains they feel they can acquire, which include both a material form to their self-identity and an anchor in a particular social constellation of style and activity. On the other hand, individuals do make choices that fit nonetheless to a structural scheme grounded within group behavior.

Many structural approaches emphasizing the effects of life chances on individuals tend to underestimate the creativity of social agents. In the same manner, many microsociological approaches concentrate on the perspective of the social agent and tend to underestimate the interdependence of patterns of social behavior and life chances that produce the structure of lifestyles. It is necessary to focus on a number of variables that must be analyzed if the typical structure of a pattern of behavior is to be reproduced. Lifestyles are grounded in life chances that include age, gender, race, and ethnicity, as well as the options those chances provide. The choice–chance relationship must be conceptualized as a complex form of interaction involving the interplay of the two.

A lifestyle is not simply a collection of behaviors nor is it merely a variable; today's lifestyles are a recent postmodern phenomenon most clearly visible in the culturally and economically empowered middle classes. In fact, the very idea of what constitutes a contemporary lifestyle has been triggered by changes in middle-class ways of living. Lifestyles have significant implications for understanding class and gender relations, cultural orientations, self-control, and the role of lifestyle generally in an information society.

PROBLEMS WITHIN THE INFORMATION SOCIETY

Fortunately, the explosive technological changes characterizing the latter part of the twentieth century seemed to fit quite well with the post-industrial society concept. Daniel Bell's 1973 book *The Coming of Post-Industrial Society* provided a ready-made model, and it was quickly recognized as the standard for many commentators on this subject. It is obvious that technology plays a critical role in the emerging social system described by Daniel Bell as the *postindustrial society*. However, the explosion of information technology such as computers and the Internet that began in the late seventies and continued through the eighties and nineties was not yet realized.

CHAPTER 3: AMERICA IN TRANSITION

Recent developments in information technology must be considered to understand the current information society paradigm in which America now finds itself. The convergence of telecommunication technology with computers is a not a new trend, but the latest developments in this area as represented by the Internet are a recent phenomenon. Technological advancements such as those presented by the Internet do not serve to bring about social changes because social changes can only occur when people are involved. For example, social-networking sites may allow people to get together over the Internet through the use of the technology, but they do not guide the social relations that result from the sites. So it is a given that the technological capabilities afforded by information technology must be available before certain social changes can occur. Who could have foreseen the technological changes that would occur in information technology that currently exists in contemporary society? Now there are desktop computers with capabilities that could not even be achieved by mainframes in the eighties and early nineties. In 1973, *PC* was not even a term. Furthermore, the Internet was in its infancy in 1973, and it certainly bore little resemblance to the Internet we have today.

Weber makes the pertinent observation that lifestyles are based on what one consumes and not on what one produces. For example, purchasing a product or service on the Internet is nothing more than an information-producing activity that results in the consumption of that product and/or service. The company providing the service and/or product must produce the information about the product (i.e., description, cost, etc.), and the buyer or individual must produce information in order to acquire the product (i.e., credit card information, delivery address, etc.). Internet usage presents individuals with opportunities to realize certain choices such as the ability to shop, to pay bills, to search for information, to use the phone, to play games with others from around the world, to communicate via e-mail, and to take educational courses online; these choices are in fact definable patterns of behavior that constitute a style of living in the information society. Furthermore, these choices are mitigated by life chances as defined by an individual's social situation such as socioeconomic status, gender, ethnicity, age, race, marital status, and residential location.

Social class has not disappeared within the information society. It simply needs to be reframed to reflect the changing social structure that currently exists within the information society. Social class is a combination of education, occupation, and income within the information society as defined by Weber as socioeconomic status. Examination of the interaction of socioeconomic status with other social groups in terms an informatizationalized lifestyle reveals a stratification system that reflects differences in lifestyle choices within the information society. Given the current trends, two classes are likely to emerge—the service class and the information and knowledge class.

Not all groups within the information society are the same with regard one's informatizationalized lifestyle. Differences in power and inequality exist among groups such as women, minorities, and the elderly within the information society, albeit for different reasons. Some argue that there is evidence that women may be achieving a higher status position within the information society. Almost no work has been done on the role of ethnicity in the information society. Minorities often lack *social capital* and that hinders social mobility within the information society. The elderly may enjoy less status within the information society than they did within previous phases of society. Now everything one needs to know is at his/her fingertips and with the rapid rate of change in the labor market, job skills become outdated quickly.

Does an informatizationalized lifestyle within the information society remain the same regardless of residential location—say rural versus urban? Geography does not play the same role within the information society, and it is no longer the controller of costs. Distance becomes a function not of space but of time, and the costs of time and the rapidity of communication become the decisive variables. Worksites are less meaningful. While this is primarily due to technological change, it also is related to the increasing role of information as a part of work. For example, a trader with a company in New York can now live and work in the Colorado mountains. This is clearly one aspect of geography in relation to an informatizationalized lifestyle within the information society.

But there is another perspective on the role of residential location. Those with the least access to computer and online services are people with low incomes who live in rural areas, those living in poorer central-city areas, blacks, single-parent households (particularly those headed by women), and those with limited schooling. With the technological advancement and the increased role of information in the information society, these differences may actually exacerbate the existing inequalities. Yet it is not just access to the technology that is perpetuating the inequality, it also has much to do with the skills and resources necessary to achieve access. To restate, one can now become a member of the information-poor class regardless of residential location.

The informatizationalized lifestyle of the information society is not conducive to traditional family relationships. Very little has been written, if anything, to give an account of social relations within the information society. However, the Internet serves as a medium to establish new interactions that are, in fact, social networks. Such is the case for online chat rooms and online data services. Now, more than ever before single people can meet others from around the United States, and, for that matter, from around the world. It seems plausible that traditional social relations in connection to the informatizationalized lifestyle of the information society will continue to change.

INFORMATION SOCIETY IN TWENTY-FIRST CENTURY AMERICA

This chapter is significant for three reasons. First, it serves as a foundation for blending theories of lifestyles with certain aspects of Bell's theories on postindustrial society into a more appropriate model of the information society that can be used to better understand the social changes that are reflected in the informatizationalized lifestyle currently found within American society in the twenty-first century.

Second, here we examine how choices are related to one's life chances and how this is intertwined with social class and socioeconomic status. Given the current evidence supporting the information rich and the information poor thesis, inequalities clearly exist even in the information society. If Internet access is all that is required for equality in the information society, can it be assumed that some will not be better off than others? Given the history of capitalism in the United States, this hardly seems like a plausible hypothesis. Moreover, when one excludes the economic barriers that keep certain groups from owning and accessing the prerequisite information technology, is it a safe assumption that groups such as blacks, women, and the elderly will make the same choices as their counterparts?

Finally, the trends in the information society have certain policy implications. For example, current policies from the federal government are established to address the digital divide by bringing access to all by making Internet access affordable to every home. Part of this policy initiative is based on the belief that inequality stems from the unequal access to the Internet. A very different picture may emerge where it is not a lack access that dictates inequality but a lack of Internet usage. These implications would necessarily mean different policy initiatives to address not only infrastructure and access but also services and usage via the Internet (i.e., skill development).

The purpose of this chapter was to define the informatizationalized lifestyle that is emerging within the information society. As defined earlier, the informatizationalized lifestyle consists of many different observable activities and behaviors around Internet usage. Such choices are constrained by life chances that are structurally determined by gender, race, ethnicity, age, marital status, residential location, and socioeconomic status.

Daniel Bell and his work on postindustrial society are heavily driven by social changes within the techno-economic structure of society where property relations are determined by the relationship between the forces of production and the social relations of production. More specifically, Bell's contribution to this study is found in his theory of postindustrial society that identifies technology as a lever for social change that is deeply tied to the economics of a highly skilled, highly professional, intellectualized, and services-based society. The Internet best represents the current technology that forms the basic technical infrastructure to support the informatizationalized lifestyle within the information society.

As previously stated, Weber observed that lifestyles were based not so much on what people produced but on what they consumed. The consumption of goods and/or services indicates specific styles of living that are represented by the specific choices a person makes. Choices are constrained by a person's ability to realize those choices based on that person's life chances. In other words, lifestyle differences are based on an individual's relationship to the means of consumption not the means of production. However, consumption is not independent of production. Consumption can then be regarded as a set of social and cultural practices that establish differences between social groups and not merely as a means of expressing differences that are already in place because of economic factors. Of particular interest are the differences between sociodemographic groups of Internet users in terms of their choices around Internet usage that in turn leads to or constitutes an informatizationalized lifestyle.

Informatization is the process of social change that results in an information society. Informatization contains technical, informational, economic, social, and cultural dimensions that are manifested in the way people live, work, and play in the information society that make up a style of living. However, the term *informatizationalized* was used as a way of establishing a term that implies changes that have taken place instead of changes that are in the process of taking place.

The importance of this nuance lies within the ability to measure the lifestyle that is represented by the choices one makes around Internet usage.

As noted earlier, the use of and access to information technology throughout all levels of the information society is directly tied to economics. Access to the Internet has associated costs, hence the digital divide. Some assume that providing all people with access to the Internet can close the digital divide. However, simply giving the poor access to technology does not guarantee equality. Moreover, there is no reason to assume economic disparities will no longer exist in Internet usage once universal access is achieved.

Internet usage and the way that it is used (or not) by various socioeconomic groups are important for theories on lifestyle in the information society. That is, not all sociodemographic characteristics of Internet users are useful for classifying and understanding the informatizationalized lifestyle as suggested by the current theories. Lifestyles are not random behaviors unrelated to structure but are typically deliberate choices influenced by life chances. Remember Weber's pertinent observation that lifestyles are based on what one *consumes* and not on what one produces.

Internet access presents individuals with opportunities to realize certain choices. Products and services that are available for consumption via the Internet provide individuals who have Internet access with a wide array of choices and a particular lifestyle based on those choices. However, consumption of these products and services is not independent of production. Socioeconomic status sets the basic parameters by which consumption can occur. The ability to make choices that result in consumption of the products and services that are available on the Internet is constrained by social structures that define an individual's social situation such as socioeconomic status, gender, ethnicity, age, race, marital status, and residential location.

Members of the same status group share a similar lifestyle, for example, middle class in America. One main distinguishing factor between groups is lifestyle. That is to say, that one's lifestyle is a reflection of the types and amounts of goods and services one consumes. The types and amounts of goods and services one consumes in the information society reflect their informatizationalized lifestyle. But consumption is not independent of production and cannot occur without income. The income arises from performance of intellectual work that is based on the new owners of the means of production—the information worker of the twenty-first century information society. When the work product, i.e., the information commodity, is exchanged in the marketplace, the exchange must result in capital that can pay for the basic necessities of life and also other commodities that represent a specific information society lifestyle.

These social changes hold a number of important questions that will be explored in the chapters throughout the remainder of this book. More specifically, if individual workers now own the means of production, how do members of a society contribute to the production process in the information society? That is, how are human beings to become more productive if the main mode of production relies on intellectual capital? Moreover, how is money made? Is this a new form of entrepreneurship? It's easy to see that such intellectual production processes rely on human capital and the development of brainpower.

The development of human capital—the human mind—is a lengthy process that requires ongoing educational endeavor beginning almost at birth and continuing throughout an entire career. What then is the role of education in this new information society system? It would seem that there's now even more of a need to provide a continuous flow from elementary to secondary and post-secondary educational endeavors while connecting the education process to the demands of the intellectual work production processes within the information society. How does this affect education in the information society? Do current education institutions provide this continuity?

What is the role of government in policy development to drive this new betterment of its citizens within the information society? Given the bureaucratization of the current government, it would seem at odds with the streamlined informatization lifestyle of the information society. Do government institutions need to be reformed to become representative of a democratic information society? Given the government's role as representatives of the people within the information society, for the economic well-being of the populace as a whole, we can't decouple politics from economics. How then does the intersection of business and government, and their relationship change within the information society to meet the demands of the new political economy of the information society?

Given the impact of globalization and a global economy on jobs and capital within the United States, how does the information commodity influence this situation? That is, if what America now has to export is intellectual capital, how do we exchange this value for money in the world marketplace? Do models of globalization need to change to reflect the different phases of development of a particular society? That is, societies would be classified as information producers, industrial producers, and agricultural producers.

The big final question is What if? What if America does not change? What if institutions do not reform? What if government doesn't change its current practices? There are specific indicators that are examined based on that scenario in chapter 8. This is then followed by a synthesis and presentation of the major challenges facing America in the twenty-first century. How well we meet those challenges will determine our future in America.

CHAPTER 4:
FROM THEOLOGY TO THEORY TO TRUTH

The thoughts a society thinks have profound repercussions on what it does.

Author Unknown

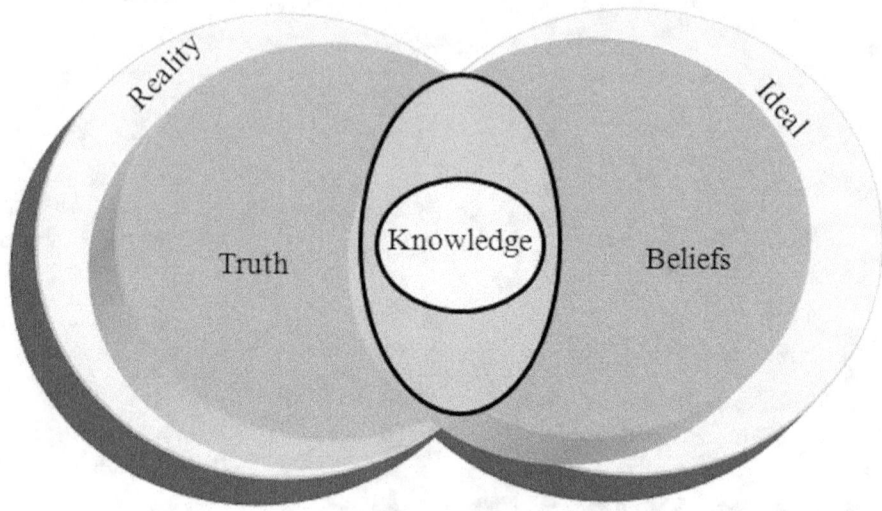

Figure 1: A Belief System

Ideas are like seeds; when planted in the fertile soil of a human mind, they grow. The extent to which they grow, persist, or survive is dependent on how well they take root and the soil in which they've been planted.[56] Some ideas never take root; some take root and grow or persist for a little while; still others fall on fertile ground and multiply. When these ideas are based on false beliefs, the results can be disastrous. When an idea is strong and is on fertile ground, it can persist across many people, their lives, and even across many nations. Such ideas are strong, and they have strong roots systems, but they also have an expiration date. However, ideas that are so strong as to have persisted for a long time die a quite painful death. The main reason for this is that people just can't seem to let them go. Even in the face of insurmountable evidence that it's time for the ideas to die, human beings often have trouble with letting go. The death of an idea can be quite a painful experience; especially to the person or persons who are faced with the death.

Ideas originate in the mind of a human being, and as these ideas are transmitted from one person to another, from one generation to another, from one society to another, they collectively form the basis of a belief system. It is important to understand the connection between ideas and belief systems because belief systems form the basis of human action. The very social structures that support and enable civilization arise from actions based on collectively held belief systems. In sum, to make changes to the social, political, economic, and philosophical systems, we must first inform our belief system with new knowledge thereby destroying old ideas that are false and no longer apply to our everyday reality.[57] When we start to make changes to these structures, we disrupt reality. It would seem that once it's proven that these ideas should be changed and those changes reflected in the social structures of America, it should be a simple matter to make the changes. It's not. We must realize that these structures have vested interests of millions of people.

Some of these ideas are hundreds and even thousands of years old. Some go as far back as the beginning of human civilization when God first created Adam and Eve.[58] Some go back 2,400 years ago when Greek philosophers such as Aristotle sat around and pontificated about the meaning of everything.[59]

Realize that Aristotle never read the Bible; for that matter, none of the famous Greek philosophers had ever even heard of the Bible.[60] However, many of the ideas that were used to create America were heavily influenced by Aristotle, if not directly then indirectly through others who were Aristotelian thinkers. Many of these early thinkers read both Aristotle and the Bible. How then did they reconcile the thoughts and ideas of Aristotle to the teachings of the Bible? St. Thomas Aquinas was one of the first to attempt this resolution of the two bodies of the Judeo-Christian belief system with that of the Greek philosophy of Aristotle.[61] He was not the only one. Other thinkers such as John Locke, Rene Descartes, Thomas Hobbes, Jean-Jacques Rousseau were influenced by both Greek philosophy of Aristotle and Judeo-Christian theology. In fact, many of these thinkers used ideas that dated back to Aristotle to formulate the Declaration of Independence and the U.S. Constitution.

To modern ears, Aristotle's view of universe may seem mythical. However, if we follow his reasoning, which lead him to affirm that there must be an immaterial, perfect being he would've called God, we can see how his reasoning provided a model for later thinkers to prove the existence of a God. This was not the same as Aristotle's God, but the God of Genesis; the God who created the world out of nothing.[62] But there remains one fundamental question, even to this day. Is there a God? Did this same God create all that there is or ever will be? Did he create human beings?

PHILOSOPHY AND GOD

Philosophy is the study of general and fundamental problems concerning subjects such as existence, knowledge, values, reason, mind, and language. There are at least two senses in which the term philosophy is used. In the more formal sense, philosophy is an academic discipline focusing on the fields of metaphysics, logic, ethics, epistemology, and aesthetics. In the more informal sense, a philosophy is an attitude to life or way or principle of living whose focus is on resolving the most basic existential questions about the human condition.[63] Philosophy is distinguished from other ways of addressing fundamental questions (such as mysticism or mythology) by its critical, generally systematic approach and its reliance on reasoned argument. Philosophy comes from the Greek term *philosophia*, which translates to *love of wisdom*.

Aristotle, a student of Plato, was an early influential philosopher who argued that ethical knowledge is not *certain* knowledge (like metaphysics and epistemology) but is *general knowledge*. Because it is not a theoretical discipline, a person had to study and practice in order to become *good*; thus if the person were to become virtuous, he could not simply study what virtue *is*, he had to be virtuous by undertaking virtuous activities

Rationalism is any view emphasizing the role or importance of human reason. Extreme rationalism tries to base all knowledge on reason alone. In epistemology and in its modern sense, rationalism is any view appealing to reason as a source of knowledge or justification. In more technical terms it is a method or a theory in which the criterion of the truth is not sensory but intellectual and deductive. Rationalism typically starts from premises that cannot coherently be denied, then attempts by logical steps to deduce every possible object of knowledge. This type of knowledge gained is said to be a priori because it is knowledge gained independent of experience.

Modern rationalism begins with Rene Descartes.[64] Reflection on the nature of perceptual experience, as well as scientific discoveries in physiology and optics, led Descartes to the view that we are directly aware of ideas rather than objects. This view gave rise to three questions:

1. Is an idea a true copy of the real thing that it represents? Sensation is not a direct interaction between bodily objects and our sense but is a physiological process involving representation.
2. How can physical objects such as chairs and tables or even physiological processes in the brain give rise to mental items such as ideas? This is part of what became known as the mind-body problem.[65]
3. If all the contents of awareness are ideas, how can we know that anything exists apart from ideas?

Descartes tried to address the last problem by reason. He began, echoing Parmenides, with a principle that he thought could not coherently be denied: I *think*, therefore I *am* (often given in his original Latin: *Cogito ergo sum*).[66] From this principle, Descartes went on to construct a complete system of knowledge (which involves proving the existence of God, using, among other means, a version of the ontological argument). His view that reason alone could yield substantial truths about reality strongly influenced those philosophers usually considered modern rationalists (such as Baruch Spinoza, Gottfried Leibniz, and Christian Wolff), while provoking criticism from other philosophers who have retrospectively come to be grouped together as empiricists.

IS THERE A GOD?

In Western philosophy, the basic philosophical positions on the problem of free will can be divided in accordance with the answers they provide to two questions:

1. Is determinism true?
2. Does free will exist?

Determinism is roughly defined as the view that all current and future events are causally necessitated by past events combined with the laws of nature. Neither determinism nor its opposite, indeterminism, are positions in the debate about free will.

The standard argument *against* the existence of free will is very simple. Either determinism is true or indeterminism is true. These exhaust the logical possibilities. If determinism is true, we are not free. If indeterminism is true, our actions are random and our will lacks the control to be morally responsible.

Theological determinism is the thesis that there is a God who determines all that humans will do, either by knowing their actions in advance through some form of omniscience or by decreeing their actions in advance. The problem of free will, in this context, is the problem of how our actions can be free, if there is a being who has determined them for us ahead of time.[67]

Jewish philosophy stresses that free will is a product of the intrinsic human soul, using the word *neshama* [breath], but the ability to make a free choice is through *Yechida* [singular], the part of the soul that is united with God, the only being that is not hindered by or dependent on cause and effect. Thus, freedom of choice does not belong to the realm of the physical reality, and the inability of natural philosophy to account for it is expected.

In the American context, historians use the term Judeo–Christian to refer to the influence of the Hebrew Bible and New Testament on Protestant thought and values, most especially the Puritan, Presbyterian, and Evangelical heritage.[68] The founding generations of Americans saw themselves as heirs to the Hebrew Bible, and its teachings on liberty, responsibility, hard work, ethics, justice, and equality. They took from the Bible a sense of being chosen and an ethical mission to the world, which became key components of the American character—the American Creed. These ideas from the Hebrew Bible, brought into American history by Protestants, are seen as underpinning the American Revolution, Declaration of Independence, and the U.S. Constitution. Other authors are interested in tracing the religious beliefs of America's founding fathers, emphasizing both Jewish and Christian influence in their personal beliefs and how this was translated into the creation of American institutions and character.[69]

To these historians, the interest in the concept Judeo–Christian lies not in theology but in actual culture and history as it evolved in America. These authors discern a melding of Jewish thought into Protestant teachings that, in combination with the heritage of English history and common law, as well as Enlightenment thinking, resulted in the birth of American democracy.

Nineteenth-century historians wrote extensively on the United States of America having a distinctively Protestant character in its outlook and founding political philosophy. It is only since the 1950s that the term Judeo–Christian has been applied to this philosophy, reflecting the growing use of that term in American political life. Some use the term casually as an inclusive synonym for the religious. Others argue the term is appropriate in its own right, capturing a distinctively Old Testament dimension (though not necessarily that of Judaism) in the Puritan character of early American Protestantism especially the work ethic.[70]

The notion of a distinctive religious basis for American democracy and culture was first described and popularized by Alexis de Tocqueville in the 1840s, in his influential book, *Democracy in America*. In chapter 2, De Tocqueville describes America's unique religious heritage from the Puritans. His analysis showed the Puritans as providing the foundational values of America, based on their strong Hebrew Bible view of the world, which included fighting for earthly political justice, an emphasis on laws and education, and a belief in the Jews as a chosen people that the Puritans identified with, giving them a sense of moral mission in founding America. As de Tocqueville observed, the puritan's biblical outlook gave America a moral dimension that the Old World lacked. De Tocqueville believed these biblical values led to America's unique institutions of religious tolerance, public education, egalitarianism, and democracy.

How are we like God? It is our ability to create. Human beings are the only living thing on the planet with the ability to come up with an idea and then transform that idea through the use of natural resources into something real, a tangible finished product. People use their labor to make ideas a part of the physical world that surrounds us.

God had an idea. He created man from that idea. In this way we are not only like the Creator, but we are creators ourselves.

Our ability to use our mind to create is innate in human beings.[71] It is as much a part of who we are as the necessity to breathe air and eat food. All of creation is but the transfer of energy through the application of power to work. Focused power upon labor gives a physical shape to our ideas. It transforms our thoughts into a shape others can see, feel, and experience. The American dream is such an idea. Ideas are but theories that have yet to be tested. The scientific method says that theories have to be tested in order to accumulate knowledge. The way that works is to use those ideas/theories to formulate social policies.

Freedom of choice is an absolute necessity to create. This freedom only comes from liberty. When liberty is denied, our freedom of choice is curtailed, and thus our power to create is limited, if not downright denied. The ability to transform ideas into a concrete form requires the focused effort of more than one person when it is a complex object. That is why we have a division of labor.[72] Each person has a role to play and a certain piece of the work to get accomplished. The more complex and abstract the object, the more important it is to clearly communicate to others the needed direction to get the work accomplished. Tools can help to facilitate this process of work, but all technology is a tool. No matter how sophisticated a tool is, it still requires someone who knows how to use it. No single person possesses all the knowledge or the tools to build a complex object like a skyscraper.

The ability to create is a force that must be controlled. It is a power, and power unchecked can be used for both good and evil. That means we must have restrictions in the form of the rule of law, due process, responsibility, and accountability. These must be absolute—no favors for the rich and powerful. But freedom in the form of complete liberty carries with it responsibility for choices that result in actions, especially when those actions harm others.

THE CONNECTION BETWEEN NUMBERS AND GOD

Man is three in one—body, soul, and spirit. God is three in one—Father, Son, and Holy Spirit. The union of the two is equivalent to the number six. The multiplicative of the two (three times three) is nine. Thus God is represented as three-zero-six-nine with two numerical properties. First, the whole can't be more than the sum of its parts. Second, the maximum value of any number is it's multiplicative.

Mathematics, or more specifically numbers, are also important to politics, but not for the same reasons that pollsters think. It takes an agreement of at least two to arrive at a consensus to move forward. This is also necessary for America to move forward. However, our political parties can't agree on anything except the fact they don't want a new political party to steal any of their power. As long as America only has two major political parties, we will never move forward as a nation. The reason for this is that the net sum gain of two equal but opposing forces is zero. That's right; our political parties essentially cancel each other out. So, two divided is one. One party pushing against the other party to control the direction of America results in zero.

One is the loneliest number because one is powerless. Our society as a system is powerless to move forward because we lack the agreement of at least two that is needed to achieve a maximum of force that will drive our society forward. As I stated elsewhere the laws of physics apply to American society because it is also a system that is used to accomplish the work of our nation. Right now, the structures, including our political structure, don't facilitate the motion required to move our nation forward in accomplishing the work of our society. In short, we are powerless. We lack the power to move forward.

Let's do some math to illustrate the principles I've just described. From this exercise, we can see how the power of numbers when applied to the American society system has resulted in a net sum gain of zero. More importantly, we can see how this contributes to the *Inert America* condition.

Let's assume the coordinates of three-zero-six-nine equals GOD. The whole is the sum of its parts, and it can never be more than that. Is God a number?

Absolutely not; God is the Creator of the universe; he is not a number. I am simply stating that within our system, the number three-zero-six-nine represents God. To that end, God also created a numerical system to control it. Within that numbering system, he is represented by a numerical value.

Evidence of this system is all around us. If God exists, then we must conclude this system is deterministic and the events we see are not random but chaotic. It can be difficult to tell from data whether a physical or other observed process is random or chaotic because in practice no time series consists of pure *signal*. There will always be some form of corrupting noise, even if it is present as rounding off or truncation error. Thus any real time series, even if mostly deterministic, will contain some randomness.

All methods for distinguishing deterministic and stochastic processes rely on the fact that a deterministic system always evolves in the same way from a given starting point. Thus, given a time series to test for determinism, one can:

1. pick a test state;
2. search the time series for a similar or nearby state; and
3. compare their respective time evolutions.

Define the error as the difference between the time evolution of the test state and the time evolution of the nearby state. A deterministic system will have an error that either remains small (stable, regular solution) or increases exponentially with time (chaos). A stochastic system will have a randomly distributed error.

Essentially all measures of determinism taken from time series rely on finding the closest states to a given test state. To define the state of a system, one typically relies on phase space embedding methods. Typically one chooses an embedding dimension and investigates the propagation of the error between two nearby states. If the error looks random, one increases the dimension. If you can increase the dimension to obtain a deterministic-looking error, then you are done. Though it may sound simple, it is really not. One complication is that as the dimension increases the search for a nearby state requires a lot more computation time and a lot of data (the amount of data required increases exponentially with embedding dimension) to find a suitably close candidate. If the embedding dimension (number of measures per state) chosen is too small (less than the true value) deterministic data can appear to be random, but in theory, there is no problem choosing the dimension too large.

When a nonlinear deterministic system is attended by external fluctuations, its trajectories present serious and permanent distortions. Furthermore, the noise is amplified due to the inherent lack of linearity and reveals totally new dynamical properties. Statistical tests attempting to separate noise from the deterministic skeleton or inversely isolate the deterministic part risk failure. Things become worse when the deterministic component is a nonlinear feedback system. In presence of interactions between nonlinear deterministic components and noise, the resulting nonlinear series can display dynamics that traditional tests for nonlinearity are sometimes not able to capture.

God created life, and life on planet Earth could not be sustained except by the combination of three things—the Earth, the Sun, and the Moon. There are nine planets in our solar system.

The maximum of any number is achieved by its multiplicative except for 0, 1, and 2. Relating this mathematics to our political parties in the United States, we can see why we have the *Inert America* condition. The parties are divided $2 \div 2 = 1$. The maximum that can be achieved by the number of 1 is 1 or ($1 \times 1 = 1$). The net sum gain of two equal but opposing forces is zero. You do the math ($1 - 1 = 0$). In order to move forward, we must have at least the power of two because that number represents agreement ($2 \times 2 = 4$). Mathematically, our problems in America could be solved by the addition of a third political party. With a third political party, we could then achieve enough power to move forward. This third party could represent the middle class of America.[73]

WHAT IS KNOWLEDGE?

There are five different type of knowledge, but the one Aristotle attached to the world is when human beings understand truths that are self-evident. Realize that John Locke was an Aristotelian thinker, so when Thomas Jefferson wrote "we hold these truths to be self-evident," it was not an accident. Aristotle recognized four other types of knowledge. 1.) The well-founded opinion (belief) of mathematical thought. 2.) The well-established generalization of scientific research (the scientific method). 3.) The philosophical opinions that are based on common experiences. 4.) The opinions about particular facts that historians support through historical research.[74] These four types of knowledge are less weighty because they represent opinions or beliefs that can be true or false. That is, they are not absolutes. Unfortunately, these other four types of knowledge have become the common standards for knowledge creation. I say unfortunately because it seems that people, including renowned scientists, are content with standards of knowledge that are not based on self-evident truth.

In philosophy, empiricism is a theory of knowledge that asserts that knowledge arises from experience. Empiricism is part of the epistemology or *theory of knowledge*. Empiricism emphasizes the role of experience and evidence, especially sensory perception, in the formation of ideas, while discounting the notion of innate ideas (except in so far as these might be inferred from empirical reasoning, as in the case of genetic predisposition).

In philosophy of science, empiricism emphasizes those aspects of scientific knowledge that are closely related to the evidence, especially as discovered in experiments. It is a fundamental part of the scientific method that states that all theories must be tested by constructing hypothesis against observations of the natural or physical world.

The term *empiricism* has a dual etymology. It comes from the Greek word ἐμπειρία, which translates to the Latin *experientia*, from which we derive the word *experience*. It also derives from a more specific classical Greek and Roman usage of *empiric*, referring to a physician whose skill derives from practical experience as opposed to instruction in theory.

The term *empirical* was originally used to refer to certain ancient Greek practitioners of medicine (empiric school) who rejected adherence to the dogmatic doctrines of the day (dogmatic school), preferring instead to rely on the observation of *phenomena* as perceived in experience. The notion of *tabula rasa* [clean slate or blank tablet] dates back to Aristotle and was developed into an elaborate theory by Avicenna and demonstrated as a thought experiment by Ibn Tufail. The *doctrine* of empiricism was later explicitly formulated by John Locke in the seventeenth century. He argued that the mind is a *tabula rasa* (Locke used the words *white paper*) on which experiences leave their marks. Such empiricism denies that humans have innate ideas or that anything is knowable without reference to experience.

According to the empiricist view, for any knowledge to be properly inferred or deduced, it is to be gained ultimately from one's sense-based experience. As a historical matter, philosophical empiricism is commonly contrasted with the philosophical school of thought known as *rationalism,* which, in very broad terms, asserts that much knowledge is attributable to reason independently of the senses. However, this contrast is today considered to be an extreme oversimplification of the issues involved because the main continental rationalists were also advocates of the empirical scientific method of their day. Furthermore, John Locke held that some knowledge (e.g., knowledge of God's existence) could be arrived at through intuition and reasoning alone.

Logical positivism is a school of philosophy that combines empiricism, the idea that observational evidence is indispensable for knowledge of the world, with a version of rationalism. Rationalism is any view appealing to reason as a source of knowledge or justification. It is a method or theory in which the creation of the truth is not sensory, but it is intellectual and deductive.

One of the reasons rational choice theory is inept at explaining human behavior is because its proponents assume that people make choices based on knowledge. For any choice or choices to be rational, it must be based on knowledge of the truth. Unfortunately, people so often make choices based on what they believe and not on what they know. Beliefs can be both false and true. However, if choices were based on knowledge of the truth, they would always be rational and predictable. Truth is truth; it is absolute, and any choice made as a basis of action that is based on knowledge would logically be the same. However, because beliefs differ, choices made based on beliefs seem irrational because they are not based on truth. They are false. False beliefs lead to irrational behavior. Because choices are not necessarily based on rationalized knowledge where truth is the standard of measurement, there is a certain uncertainty that can only be understood through the use of mathematics by the use of probability theories to explain behavior. Probability theory can only give you the most likely outcome most of the time. It is not an absolute measure because choices are not absolute. If truth were to be used as the standard of measurement, probability theory would no longer be necessary, as choices would be rational all the time. There are not multiple truths, as some would have you believe. There is but one truth. It is absolute and unalterable. To know something is to make it true, which again makes it absolute. There is no mystery here and no need for probability to predict the most likely outcome.

All mathematics exemplifies rationalized knowledge. For example, $2 + 2 = 4$ is a simple mathematical problem. We know that $2 + 2 = 4$, therefore it must be true. However, we can't know it based on our experience. We can't know that $2 + 2 = 4$ through the use of sight, sound, taste, touch, or smell. It's something that we can only know, therefore it must be true. Even though we can't know that this simple equation is true through experience, we can know it is true through reason and rational thought. Interestingly, all things created by the human beings from ideas such as buildings, and which we define as real, are only possible through the use of mathematics in one form or another. Oddly, rationalized knowledge or mathematics makes possible the reality of our everyday experience by transforming ideas into physical entities that we can define as real because we can see, taste, touch, hear, or smell it.

If these assertions are true concerning everything in existence today that we define as real, then it must also be true that we can know that God is real and that he created all that there is on planet Earth through the use of science called mathematics. We can know this by the reality of all things that exist on planet Earth that are natural, and therefore not manmade. If we can know that math is real, then we can know that God is real and that the truth of his existence lies in the fact that he used mathematics to create everything on the planet. If not, then we can say that the Empire State Building came into being through a sheer act of random events.

It's absolutely necessary for us to arrive at the knowledge of the truth of God through the use of a rationalized process if we hope to move forward as a nation. We must create an information society and a knowledge-based economy, and align our social, political, economic, and philosophical systems to the three macro-level trends identified in chapter 1 if we wish to return to a state of prosperity that is drive by growth and innovation. How can we do this if we can't even arrive at the truth of God as the Creator of the universe? An information society with a knowledge-based economy is a rational society. It exists out there in an abstract form; it's not something we can experience through touch, taste, sight, hearing, or smell.

CHAPTER 5: THE U.S. CONSTITUTION AS A SOCIAL CONTRACT

Man is born free; and everywhere he is in chains.

Jean-Jacques Rousseau

THE HISTORY OF THE SOCIAL CONTRACT

When men gathered in Philadelphia, Pennsylvania, on June 7, 1776 and declared their independence from the tyranny of England because of the unjust taxation levied on the people of the colonies, it was a significant event in human history. At no other time in the history of the planet and among any civilization had a group of men undertaken such bold actions. When we examine the men involved in these actions that were viewed as treasonous by England, we have to also consider the language used in drafting the Declaration of Independence, as well as the ideas the document represents and where these ideas originated. It is especially significant to remember that Thomas Jefferson was the original drafter of the Declaration of Independence. The language used may have been his exclusively but the ideas used were not his alone. They were based on ideas of other men, some of whom can be traced all the way back to Aristotle and the early Greek philosophers. Some of those influential ideas came from thinkers such as Thomas Hobbes, Jean-Jacques Rousseau, and especially John Locke. You see, unlike the politicians of today, our Founding Fathers were veracious readers.[75] They didn't have TVs, the Internet, and an army of staffers to do the reading and thinking for them. They relied on the written word as the transmitter of ideas. A close examination of the first two paragraphs of the Declaration of Independence as drafted by Thomas Jefferson illustrates this point. Many of these ideas come directly from John Locke.

When in the Course of human events it becomes necessary for one people to dissolve the political bands which have connected them with another and to assume among the powers of the earth, the separate and equal station to which the Laws of Nature and of Nature's God entitle them, a decent respect to the opinions of mankind requires that they should declare the causes which impel them to the separation.

We hold these truths to be self-evident, that all men are created equal, that they are endowed by their Creator with certain unalienable Rights, that among these are Life, Liberty and the pursuit of Happiness.—That to secure these rights, Governments are instituted among Men, deriving their just powers from the consent of the governed,—That whenever any Form of Government becomes destructive of these ends, it is the Right of the People to alter or to abolish it, and to institute new Government, laying its foundation on such principles and organizing its powers in such form, as to them shall seem most likely to effect their Safety and Happiness.[76]

After the signing of the Declaration of Independence, Thomas Jefferson wrote to Richard H. Lee some three years later "that it had not been his task at the time to find new principles and arguments, but to place before mankind the common sense of the subject."[77] Just as there are always disagreements among men as to the proper course of things, the wording that charts such a course and its actual execution of the course never finds agreement among more than one person without compromise. The same was true for the Declaration of Independence. For example, the wording crafted by Thomas Jefferson of inalienable rights of Life, Liberty, and the pursuit of Happiness was influenced by John Locke's writings on political theory in which he said that all men are born in a natural state where all people are equal. In this natural state, each individual has the natural right to defend his life, health, liberty, or possessions.[78] Although it lacks common agreement as to the change in wording, some believe that it was changed in order to downplay the ownership of property as a role of government. It is further conjectured that this idea was put into place to appease the many landowners among the signers of the Declaration.

Such ideas were consistent with ideas we might call political philosophy or political theory, and such ideas were mediated by not only individual philosophical beliefs and views but also by their economic interest. Such early ideological formulations of political and economic structures as a basis of modern day United States of America were consistent with the particular time period in which they were born, planted, took root, and grew. We must realize, however, that the Declaration of Independence and the ideas represented by the declaration did not form a sovereign nation state. The declaration itself simply set free the residents of the thirteen colonies from the monarchial power of England. Once free, according to Locke's social contract theory, they reverted to their original State of Nature.[79]

Once the Revolutionary War was fought and the independence of the colonists was firmly established, there remained the task of forming sovereignty—a civil society that would operate based on the principles set forth in the Declaration of Independence, one of which was the consent of the governed. But what form would this new government take that would embody those principles? Clearly, John Locke's political philosophy articulated a social contract theory that favored the idea of classical liberalism that was popular during that time period. We would not know the form that the new government would take until eleven years later, when on September 17, 1787, the Constitution of the United States of America was adopted by the Constitutional Convention in Philadelphia, Pennsylvania. What emerged was not a true form of classical liberalism but a form of republicanism.[80]

THE U.S. CONSTITUTION AS A SOCIAL CONTRACT

The ideas that were used to form America based on the Declaration of Independence and the U.S. Constitution were heavily influenced by classical liberalism. Classical liberalism is a set of ideas that arose in the seventeenth and eighteenth centuries out of conflicts between a growing, wealthy, propertied class and the established aristocratic and religious orders that dominated Europe. Liberalism cast humans as beings with inalienable natural rights (including the right to retain the wealth generated by one's own work), and sought out means to balance rights across society. Broadly speaking, it considers individual liberty to be the most important goal because only through ensured liberty are the other inherent rights protected.

There are many forms and derivations of liberalism, but the central conceptions trace back to three main ideas. Early thinkers such as John Locke, Jean-Jacques Rousseau, and Adam Smith saw humankind beginning in the state of nature, then finding meaning for existence through labor and property, and using social contracts to create an environment that supports those efforts.

The U. S. Constitution is such a social contract. The formation of the United States of America was not possible without the Constitution. As a social contract is serves a number of functions. First, it serves as a foundation of American civil society that enables the formation of the major social structures of America—philosophical, social, political, and economic. Second, it establishes an agreement between the governing and the governed. Because this arrangement is based on the consent of the governed, governance is based on the general will or public opinion of the citizens.[81] Like all contracts, it's an agreement between two parties. The party of the first part is the government, and the party of the second part is the governed. When the party of the first part violates the provisions of the contract, the contract is rendered null and void. In strict legal terms, such language is easy to understand and interpret. As a contract, it is a binding agreement formed as a basis of a civil society in which all members agree to do certain things. When one party to this contract fails to abide by it and perform his part of the agreement, then the other party has become aggrieved. Such grievances are grounds for a renegotiation of the contract.

Certain political forces in the country would be happy to separate and destroy the country. They spend their time criticizing and sidestepping the U.S. Constitution by arguing that it is only a document and that it has no meaning for twenty-first century America. This type of thinking puts America on a very dangerous, slippery slope. I submit that if there is no such thing as the U.S. Constitution, then there is no such thing as the United States of America. We're just a geographical location with a mass of people at around 300 million who reside in North America. We are no longer a sovereign nation state. Why is this important to understand?

No power in heaven or on planet Earth can undermine the sovereign will of God.[82] All of his creation, including human beings, must comply with the universal laws he has established. Remember, when human beings are not bound by a social contract, they revert to their natural state and live under the laws of nature established by God. All power that is under each individual's domain of control must conform to the laws of nature and the sovereign will of God. In this condition, an individual's actions are bound only by his or her personal power and constrained by God. When a social contract is formed, the power that resides with each individual is delegated or transferred to the governing body that is formed on the basis of the social contract. The U.S. Constitution, from this perspective, is an operating agreement on how government is supposed to conduct itself; it's a covenant with the Creator of the universe that establishes how a body of people will conduct themselves as a nation. It also serves as an agreement between two parties—the government and the governed.

A social contract only establishes a body of government; it doesn't specify the particular form the government takes such as a constitutional monarchy, a democracy, or a republic. In the United States, the Constitution created a republic. Republicanism is the ideology of governing a nation as a republic, where the head of state is appointed by means other than heredity, often by election. Remember, the point of the Revolutionary War was to throw off the chains that placed extreme tax burdens on the colonists by the king of England. To replace one monarch with another was not an option.

Although conceptually separate from democracy, republicanism included the key principles of rule by the consent of the governed and sovereignty of the people. In effect republicanism meant that the kings and aristocracies were not the real rulers but rather the people as a whole were. Exactly how the people were to rule was an issue of democracy since republicanism itself did not specify how. In the United States, the solution was the creation of political parties that were popularly based on the votes of the people and which controlled the governments of republicanism. Founding Fathers such as Benjamin Franklin and Thomas Jefferson were strong promoters of representative democracy. However, other supporters of republicanism, such as John Adams and Alexander Hamilton, were more distrustful of majority rule and sought a government with more power for elites.

Almost as soon America was formed as a nation, political parties were also formed that represented both philosophical ideals and economic interests.[83] In late-nineteenth-century terms, this would be described as a political economy.[84] In the latter part of the twentieth century and the early twenty-first century, this would be articulated as conservatism. Such an intellectual interpretation, however, is merely a reformulation "of classical liberalism in an entirely unclassical age of the twentieth [and twenty-first] century; it is the image of a society in which authority is at a minimum because it is guided by the autonomous forces of the magic market. The 'providence' of classic conservatism becomes liberalism's generalization of the 'unseen hand' of the market, for, in secular guise, Providence refers to a faith that the unintended consequences of many wills form a pattern, and that this pattern ought to be allowed to work itself out. Accordingly, it can be said that there is no elite, that there is no ruling class, that there are no powerful centers which need defense."[85]

Oddly, what passes for liberalism in today's terms is diametrically opposed to the classical liberal tradition. Articulated it would be called collectivism in which government uses social policies to establish positive rights whereby the many are made to pay for the few. It is government interference in the natural operations of economics in which control is sought through centralized planning to establish a fair and equitable distribution of wealth even when such wealth isn't earned through the application of the Protestant work ethic. In the late-nineteenth and early-twentieth centuries, it would have been called socialism or communism.

As both parties—Democrats and Republicans—set about to articulate their political philosophies, they are intent on garnering votes during elections, while protecting the special interests that represent their power bases. This divides the nation and prevents agreement when it comes time to formulate and pass social policies that serve the interests of the people. As Machiavelli wrote in the early sixteenth century, when there is no agreement, in order to exercise power, the prince who holds the reins of power must resort to force in order to ensure that his will is done.[86] In *The Prince*, Machiavelli examines the acquisition, perpetuation, and use of political power in the Western world. Machiavelli wrote *The Prince* to prove his proficiency in the art of the state, offering advice on how a prince might gain and keep power. He justified rule by force rather than by law. Accordingly, his work seems to justify a number of actions intended solely to perpetuate power. In twenty-first-century America, the furthering of power results in one party controlling the presidency, the House, and the Senate, which translates into a loss of the checks and balances originally established to protect citizens from government abuses of power.

CHAPTER 5: THE U.S. CONSTITUTION AS A SOCIAL CONTRACT

When checks and balances in government cease to exist, corruption abounds and the interests of the people are forgotten and their voices are unheard. Persuasion versus coercion: this is the difference between dictatorships and other sole-control government systems in comparison to democratically elected republics. This force of will translates into a government exercise of power on the people. In this scenario, government becomes the master, and the citizens of the state become slaves. In such a situation, the people are no longer able to enjoy liberty, and, therefore, their freedom of choice is restricted. Such an exercise of power violates the inalienable rights established by the Declaration of Independence, the Bill of Rights, and the U.S. Constitution.

When liberty and freedom are taken away, or even greatly restricted, it's hard to say that you're free. One of the oddities of the twenty-first century is that liberalism, liberty, and liberation all have the root Latin word of *liber* [free], but when the term *liberalism* is used, many people run in the opposite direction. It is a fundamental rejection of their freedom.

Perhaps a more accurate analogy of this condition in America is the term *serf*.[87] What is a serf? Serfdom is the socioeconomic status of unfree peasants under feudalism. It was a condition of bondage or modified slavery that developed primarily during the High Middle Ages in Europe. Serfdom was the enforced labor of serfs on the fields of landowners for protection and the right to work their leased fields. We have been reduced to serfs in America.

Do you think we are not serfs in America? Try not paying your taxes. Try not making your house payment. Try not paying your tax bill on your house even though you've paid for the property and own it outright with no mortgage. Watch how fast the government shows up at your door and confiscates your "property."

Political pundits who are busy espousing political philosophies often do nothing but harm by spewing poison onto the American population. These folks seem to have no shame, and the fact is that they are only dividing the population, often for their own gain, and essentially usurping the power of the people. In twenty-first-century America, the last thing we need is division among the population. There is nothing wrong with diversity. When we celebrate our diversity and pull together as one nation under God, the American spirit is unstoppable. If there has ever been a time where we need to work together, it is now. We have to stand together united on the document that created the nation of America—the U.S. Constitution. It's the tie that binds, and without it, there is no United States of America.

What are we to do when our leaders no longer listen to the voice of the people? It's sad to say it, but it's obvious that politicians no longer listen to the citizens of this country. If they did, they would hear a very angry middle class that is tired of working to support the 5 percent of the upper class and the 15 percent of the lower class that do not work. They rely on government programs and social policies to meet their every need. They rely on government programs and social policies to give them their every advantage. Neither group pays any taxes, albeit for different reasons. If politicians began to listen to America's middle class, they would hear that they're tired of working just to make ends meet, raise their children while being taxed to death just to support the lower and upper classes. The poor don't pay taxes. The rich don't pay taxes. The burdens are pushed onto the backs of the hard-working middle class families. It's enough already.

If our government were truly listening, they would quickly realize that Americans are angry. They're tired of it. They say they're helping by printing up a trillion here and a trillion there, but no one ever comes to the door to pass out all the money that magically appears and then just as magically disappears. It's just debt that future generations have to pay. Perhaps such thinking doesn't penetrate the thinking of Washington, but it's on the mind of every American.

The other side of the coin is that these actions literally put our children and grandchildren into debt. It's not freedom or economic prosperity—it's debt that must be paid at some time in the future. Perhaps that statement is not politically correct, but it's completely accurate. With trillions in debt and trillions more likely to be added as baby boomers retire over the next decade, it is a mathematical impossibility that the next generation will ever be able to work enough, produce enough to pay even the interest on that debt. How can prosperity flow from that situation? It can't. We need a new social contract; one for an information society and a knowledge-based economy that can represent the interests of the people in the twenty-first century.

A SOCIAL CONTRACT FOR A KNOWLEDGE-BASED SOCIETY

The purpose of this book is not to place blame on the backs of those whose ideas have become our prison. The purpose is to challenge existing beliefs and, by extension, alter those beliefs. This will provide a way to escape the bondage that robs us of American liberty and is maintained though the use of established interests that serve to enforce and reinforce the very structure of American society. To accomplish this task is to throw off the chains of imprisonment and regain freedom through the reinstatement of inalienable rights of life, liberty, and the pursuit of happiness. This is the true American ideal created by our Founding Fathers because it guarantees the rights of all American citizens while clearly defining the powers of government. To once again free citizens of America and restore them to that constitutional status of free human beings is true liberty, and it is liberating.

The social contract establishes the state, which derives its power from individuals. This is accomplished in the United States through the Constitution. As our Founding Fathers knew, this was necessary to maintain a civil society that could progress forward for the well-being of all citizens. This has changed dramatically in the twenty-first century. It almost appears that no one in our government even recognizes the limitations of power established to control government.

The twenty-first century calls for a new social contract by which liberty is no longer taken away from American citizens, but its citizens are granted liberty to the fullest extent so that they might pursue happiness in whatever form that may take. Such actions on the part of the U.S. government will establish social policies that support the economic engine of the twenty-first century in a knowledge-based economy. What does that mean? In a nutshell, control over resources must be put into the hands of the people to direct and use those resources as they see fit. This idea of a paternalistic government who knows what is best and should therefore control your resources, especially financial resources through taxation, is a holdover from a bygone era. American citizens are not children who need guidance of government parents. As discussed in chapters 6 and 7, this will require a new political system and a new economic system.

If knowledge is power, then we must establish the means by which that power can be harnessed to accomplish the work that is ahead for America as we sit at this crossroads in our history as a nation. To accomplish this task, we must recognize three important macro-level trends. First, production processes are now decentralized. Second, we no longer need to control time and space of people resources. Production must now be managed by performance outcomes. Third, individuals are now the new owners of the means of production because knowledge itself resides with individuals. In order for America to bring back prosperity, we must align social policy to reflect these trends. This can only happen by establishing a social contract that is based on the U.S. Constitution and clearly defines the government's role and powers that don't interfere with individual rights and personal liberty. Such an effort will require a major overhaul of the current political and economic systems.

CHAPTER 6: POLITICS AND GOVERNMENT

It would not be for the public good to have [a majority in Congress of one party] greater [than] two to one.

Thomas Jefferson

THE HISTORY OF POLITICAL PARTIES

Although the classical liberalism of the eighteenth and nineteenth centuries best describes the ideas that went into the Declaration of Independence and the U.S. Constitution, the opinions of the Founding Fathers in forging a new nation were not unanimous. The U.S. Constitution was signed in 1787, but almost as soon as the ink was dry, various factions that held competing interests as to how this new government should go about the job of governing were formed. The U.S. Constitution is silent on the subject of political organizations, mainly because most of the Founding Fathers disliked them. Yet, groups soon arose and resulted in the formation of political parties.

The first party system of the United States featured the Federalist Party and the Democratic-Republican Party. The Federalist Party grew from Washington's secretary of the treasury, Alexander Hamilton, who favored a strong central government. The Democratic-Republican Party was founded by James Madison and by Washington's secretary of state, Thomas Jefferson, who strongly opposed Hamilton's agenda. The era of good feelings (1816-1824), marked the end of the first party system. Political consequences of Federalist opposition to the War of 1812, as well as other factors, first reduced the Federalist Party to merely local significance and ultimately to complete disappearance. The era of good feelings thus marked a brief period in which only one party, the Democratic-Republican party, was significant at the federal level.

In 1824 and 1828, The second party system saw a split of the Democratic-Republican Party into the Jacksonian Democrats, who grew into the modern Democratic Party, led by Andrew Jackson, and the Whig Party, led by Henry Clay. The Democrats supported the primacy of the presidency over the other branches of government and opposed the Bank of the United States, as well as modernizing programs that they felt would build up industry at the expense of the taxpayer. The Whigs, on the other hand, advocated the primacy of Congress over the executive branch as well as policies of modernization and economic protectionism. Central political battles of this era were the bank war and the spoils system of federal patronage. The 1850s saw the collapse of the Whig party, largely as a result of deaths in its leadership and a major intraparty split over slavery as a result of the compromise of 1850. In addition, the fading of old economic issues removed many of the unifying forces holding the party together.

The third party system stretched from 1854 to the mid-1890s and was characterized by the emergence of the antislavery Republican Party, which adopted many of the economic policies of the Whigs, such as national banks, railroads, high tariffs, homesteads, and aid to land-grant colleges. The fourth party system, 1896 to 1932, retained the same primary parties as the third party system but saw major shifts in the central issues of debate. This period also corresponded with the Progressive Era and was dominated by the Republican Party. The fifth party system emerged with the New Deal coalition beginning in 1933. There is debate over whether it ended in the 1960s along with the New Deal coalition, in the mid 1990s, or continues until today.

The modern political party system in the United States is a two-party system dominated by the Democratic Party and the Republican Party. Candidates from either of these two parties have won every United States presidential election since 1852; since at least 1856, either party has controlled the United States Congress. Several other third parties have achieved relatively minor representation at the national and state levels from time to time.

MODERN POLITICS

Today's political parties are reminiscent of two boys playing with matches who accidentally start a forest fire. Thousands of acres of trees and many homes are burned. The end result is thousands of dollars of damage. Of course, the two boys are scarred and pretend they had nothing to do with the fire. Upon investigation, it's found that they started the fire. Once identified, they deny any involvement. After conclusive evidence shows they started the fire, and they can't deny their involvement, they point their fingers at each other and say, "He made me do it." Sadly, this is how our political parties seem to operate in America.

Modern politics is not that much different than politics of old. The politicians have become more sophisticated, more adept at hiding their self-interest in terms of public interest, but it's still the same old story. Every four years, we are presented with a choice to vote Republican or Democrat. This is not really a choice since both parties are guilty of the same practices and the same tactics. They both seek to control government for self-gain; they use government to control the population and push their ideas and ideologies on everyone else in the nation. They never seem to acknowledge that even with a majority of the votes, it generally represents about 20 percent of the population at most. It so often is presented to the public that the general will of the people has been expressed, and that the rest of the nation should allow 20 percent of the populace to tell 80 percent what to do. This was not the intent of our Founding Fathers as they forged a new nation.

General will, much like individual will, forms the basis of action within a republic. As such, it represents the direction a society must take. This general will is commonly called public opinion.[88] Smart politicians understand that in order to maneuver into a position where they can utilize their power of government, they must inform public opinion and use this to establish an agenda, that is, a course of action for a nation. This works well, except in cases where this mechanism is used to push specific political and personal agendas that are based solely on the self-interest of one or only a few. In this instance, it can hardly be said that the action taken represents the will of the majority, since the will of the majority is based on manipulation by a few to gain access to power.

Public opinion, from this perspective, functions as a theory of civil society that can be traced to philosophically based ideas underpinned by theory. It is created. When the creation isn't understood and controlled by its creator, it can be a creature with very destructive uncontrollable powers. Modern political parties create such creatures though social policies reflective of their political philosophies.

Public opinion, when informed by media who distribute information that supports such specialized interests, can hardly be said to provide an unbiased opinion. Unfortunately, you can't believe everything you hear and everything you read, regardless of source—TV, radio, or a blog. These also represent interests that often aren't aligned to the best interest of the public good. Both parties in the United States use this mechanism to sway public opinion in their favor.

The Democratic Party is one of two major political parties in the United States. It is the oldest political party in the United States and among the oldest in the world. The Democratic Party, since the division of the Republican Party in the election of 1912, has consistently positioned itself to the left of the Republican Party in economic and social matters. The economically left-leaning philosophy of Franklin D. Roosevelt, which has strongly influenced American liberalism, shaped much of the party's economic agenda since 1932. Roosevelt's New Deal coalition usually controlled the national government until the 1970s. The civil rights movement of the 1960s has continued to inspire the party's liberal principles, despite having lost the more conservative South in the process. In 2004, it was the largest political party, with 72 million voters (42.6 percent of 169 million registered) claiming affiliation. The president of the United States, Barack Obama, is a Democrat, and since the 2006 midterm elections, the Democratic Party is the majority party for the 110th Congress. The party holds an outright majority in the House of Representatives and the United States Senate. Democrats also hold a majority of state governorships and control a plurality of state legislatures.

Modern progressivism insists that we need to change. Unfortunately, the progressive form of change generally is a push toward more government control, more government programs, and more socialism. They believe that more centralized power in the hands of government is a good thing. They suggest this is necessary to support centralized planning that is fundamental to a planned economy. What they fail to understand is how this only creates more bureaucracy that makes it harder to get things done. They maintain that this form of government is necessary for the twenty-first century. It's fundamental to those things we hold dear such as liberty. This is the Democrat Party.

The Republican Party is one of the two major contemporary political parties in the United States of America. It is often referred to as the Grand Old Party or the GOP. Founded in 1854 by antislavery expansion activists and modernizers, the Republican Party rose to prominence with the election of Abraham Lincoln, the first Republican president. The party presided over the American Civil War and Reconstruction and was harried by internal factions and scandals toward the end of the nineteenth century. Today, the Republican Party supports a conservative platform (as far as American politics are concerned), with further foundations in economic liberalism, fiscal conservatism, and social conservatism. George W. Bush was the nineteenth Republican to hold the office of president. Republicans currently fill a minority of seats in both the United States Senate and the House of Representatives, hold a minority of state governorships, and control a minority of state legislatures. The party's nominee for president of the United States in the 2008 presidential election was Senator John McCain of Arizona. It is currently the second largest party with 55 million registered members, encompassing roughly one-third of the electorate.

The twenty-first-century Republican Party doesn't provide a better solution. Their ideas and ideology are bankrupt. The current trend within this party is one of moralism. They also want to tell you how to live your life, but they want to take a higher moral ground as the basis of arguments against change. They also use government as a means of control over the rest of the population to push the agenda and their ideals.

Rob Atkinson in his book *The Past and Future of America's Economy* describes the stance of both parties extremely well. He maintains that both current liberal

Democrats and conservative Republicans are statists who wish to maintain the status quo by returning to bygone eras—"conservative Republicans to the social order of the 1950s and the economic order of the 1920s and liberal Democrats to the social order of the 1960s and the economic order of the 1940s."[89] Both are wrong and their ideas and ideology is simply out of date and out of touch with the needs of the American population of the twenty-first century.

Liberty is not freedom; liberty *guarantees* freedom. More government control can never result in more freedom, especially freedom of choice. Choice as a basis of action must also have responsibility attached. As explained by Frederick A. Hayek, central planning doesn't allow for liberty, as it restricts an individual's ability to make choices—it's not what you want, it's what the government thinks is best.[90] This form of government destroys a complex society's ability to get work done, such as is the case of America in the twenty-first century. Central planning is cumbersome and restrictive in an agricultural society. It is very costly in an industrial society where the economy relies on the control of time and space of each worker involved in the production process. In an information society with a knowledge-based economy, it is impossible.[91]

In the twenty-first century, we must approach government from a different philosophy with a different set of ideas—one that encourages growth. This philosophy must embrace the macro-level trends, especially the one where individual human beings are the owners of the means of production, by embracing and encouraging entrepreneurship. This philosophy must go further by understanding and implementing an open market process, lowering taxes to support entrepreneurship, innovation, and by extension economic growth, while at the same time respecting the civil rights guaranteed by the U.S. Constitution. This type of government cannot include a welfare state, nor can it tolerate any form of imperialism.[92]

Although people who support these ideals go by different names—libertarian, classical liberal, conservative, and liberal—none of these seem to fit the bill. The Jeffersonian philosophy of limited government, liberty, the free market, and the rule of law that protects the unalienable rights of life, liberty, and the pursuit of happiness must be reinstated to its original form. *Liberal* is the most appropriate term, but in contemporary America, when many hear the term *liberal*, they run in the other direction. Interestingly, the root word for *liberal*, *liberalism*, *liberty*, and *liberation* is the Latin term *liber*, which means free, not slave. When you reject liberalism, you are rejecting your freedom. One reason for this is because the term was adopted by FDR and the New Deal era, and it became associated with government programs and the welfare state. Now, people in America interpret liberalism to mean a form of socialism, and/or a lack of morality and a moral center. None of these are true.

GOVERNMENT AS MASTER – PEOPLE AS SLAVES

As Thomas Jefferson wrote, "in a free society, differences of political sentiment result in different political parties. These sentiments resolve themselves naturally into two basic parties: the authoritarian (or monarchist, tory, etc.) that favors government that controls the people, and the democratic (or republican, liberal, etc.) that favors government controlled by the people. The body of the nation chooses a path that is mapped by one or the other of these parties." It is a nice thought to think that the politicians we elect to represent our interests actually represent our interests. Nothing could be further from the truth. It's a sad statement of the role of government in the United States, but it's the way it is.

What most people fail to recognize is what happens when we go to the booth to cast our vote every four years. It is through this action that we transfer our power to the politicians we elect. This power is used to vote yea and nay in Washington to establish social policy—our laws of the land. There's nothing wrong with this form of government when it works the way it's supposed to work. Unfortunately, it just doesn't work anymore. When the power of the vote is directed by self-interest and special interest, it no longer represents the people of this nation and their interests.

The current system of government lacks integrity because it lacks accountability. When there is no accountability for actions, corruption rules. In this way, government is completely corrupt and corrupting. It is rotten to the core. When things rot, they then decay eventually disappearing into nothingness. How much longer do we have before the American government dissipates into nothing and ceases to exist?

A corrupt government can never serve the needs of the people because it is self-serving. White House for sale—how does that yard sign strike you? Impossible? Not hardly. In the 2008 presidential election, around one billion dollars was spent just to get a job that paid only $400,000. How does this make sense? What is the return on investment? If the cost of becoming president is one billion dollars, then how many people can afford that job? The truth is that it has nothing to do with the monetary compensation. It is about serving self-interests. The choice for America in the twenty-first century is not one ruled by either Republican or by Democrat. As we sit at this crossroads, the choice is not one of right or left. The choice is one of government and more government or liberty. To this choice, I offer the same thoughts shouted by Patrick Henry in 1775, "Give me liberty or give me death."

THE CURRENT STATE OF GOVERNMENT

For the baby boom generation, the war to end all wars was not World War II. That war was their father's war. Their war was the Vietnam War, and it defined their generation. The war abroad in the fight against Communism, and the social unrest here at home in America had a profound effect on that generation—a profound effect that is still being felt today.

Unfortunately the rest of America is also caught in the downward spiral that defined that time period. The Vietnam War was a war of ideals and ideology, and it is still playing its tunes today in the hearts and minds of those affected by it. The struggles of that time period are still haunting our nation's halls of power throughout all levels of our society. It's the same issue, the same tired arguments, the same ideological principles; it's just a different time and now the baby boomers are all grown up and facing their own mortality. America is caught in the middle. The pathway to prosperity has never been war. That path can only be peace. Let's declare peace before it's too late.

When we consider the debt accumulated by the baby boom generation, it's easy to say I'm unimpressed at the accomplishments of my father's generation. So much debt has been foisted on future generations just to support their ideological positions, and that debt will continue to climb over the next decade. In fact, it will never be paid off. With the anticipated national debt expected to land somewhere between 35 and 50 trillion by 2020,[93] it is a mathematical impossibility to work enough and to produce enough goods and services that will result in enough value to even service the debt, let alone pay down the principle. Our children have literally been sold into debt slavery. And to my sadness, the total cost of the debt of the baby boomers is unknown—it's impossible to predict with accuracy. When we consider the aging population of the baby boomers, their issues of old age, and the influence of their retirement on productivity in that decade, I can predict nothing less than total economic devastation for the

U.S. economy. But let us not despair; for we have hope, and, most importantly, we have time. Time is running out, however, so we must act now. We must put aside ideological differences that only serve to divide us, and celebrate the diversity that defines this nation in order to achieve the greatness that can be America once again. This can only be accomplished through massive social changes in all major social structures. We simply can't put new wine in old barrels. We need new barrels.

The Republican Party saw its ideology, which can be traced directly to economic policies of the 1920s, totally demolished. The Democrat Party is in danger of the same thing happening in the next decade. Economic liberalism, laizze-faire capitalism, and free market economics didn't contain nor restrain corporate greed—$700 billion to bailout banks with taxpayers footing the bill.[94]

There's a certain irony that the party responsible for the creation of the welfare state should also be in power when the welfare state crashes the system.[95] Social welfare, social security, Medicaid, socialism, free will, and individualism didn't work either. Although the total price tag is not known, we've started with a one trillion dollar stimulus plan to begin a new administration's democratic policies in 2009. Again, taxpayers foot this bill as well. The sad reality is that it's not the people who created the mess who will be paying the bills. They will be dead when it finally comes due. To my knowledge, no debt has ever been paid from the grave.

America is in a pickle. Hard-working American citizens are hurting. The middle class is disappearing at an alarming rate, and no one has any answers. Our politicians play politics while our lives are in shambles. Why?

Thomas Jefferson once said that to control a nation's economy is more dangerous than a standing army. How true! America will never be defeated militarily but economically? That's another story altogether. The Roman Empire was never defeated, yet it doesn't exist today. If that great empire that persisted for thousands of years fell, might America meet with the same fate?

Consider this fictitious conversation between a man and his god.

Here's the scene: a man is born. As he grows, he realizes that he must have a means to meet his need for food, shelter, and clothing. So, he kneels to pray to his god.

"Oh, money god, I am in need," says the man.

"Yes, my son? How may I help? Tell me of your needs," says the money god.

The man prays, "I need food, clothing, and shelter. Please provide for me money god and send these things to me."

"Here is some money for you, my son. Go forth and spend it to meet your needs. All I require from you is to do work to return this to me," the money god commands.

The money god saw that it was good.

As time passed and the money ran out, the man knelt to pray again. "Oh, money god, I have a few other things on my list that I want. Can you also supply me with those wants?" said the man.

The money god responded enthusiastically, "Yes! I'm going to give you the money you require in the form of credit. This credit is debt, but you have no need to worry about that. Just ask, and you shall receive."

The man responded, "Oh, money god, I don't have the money today to pay for those things."

"No problem," said the money god. "You can pay it off in the future as you work. However, I must charge you interest on that money."

"Why, money god? I thought it was free," inquired the man.

"You have to pay homage to me. I am the lord your money god," the money god responded with anger.

A few months passed, and the man lost his job.

"Oh, money god, I lost my job today, and I can't find work," said the man.

"My child, this is bad. No more money for you. I have spoken," said the money god.

In a panicked tone, the man said, "But wait money god, haven't I worked hard? How will I feed my children? Why can't you just provide me with another job? Don't you control this too?"

"That's another department," was all that the money god said.

With a pleading tone, the man said, "Oh money god, are you still up there? Are you still listening? Oh, money god, my children are hungry. I am without shelter, as my house has been foreclosed. Oh, money god, don't you care? Where are you, money god?"

Sadly, this scene on some level is playing out throughout America. Money is the solution to all our problems – right? Not hardly.

The problem with this scene is that the man lost his job. As long as he is capable of finding a job and paying on the debt, the money train keeps moving. Here's where people get into trouble—debt is a form of slavery. While Americans consider themselves free, it's hard to have freedom when all that you have and own is debt. It reduces the average American to nothing more than a serf, and freedom in a country that his forefathers set free is denied. Such a future was predicted by Thomas Jefferson.[96]

Why is it that when we get into the situation that we are in today, the government is capable of printing up trillions of dollars, but that money never actually gets out to the working public? After it's printed, the money is sent out to banks who loan it out to people with interest. However, they won't loan you money if you don't have a job. There seems to be a pattern here. The money god forgot to coordinate with the serf department, and the lender of last resort who thought there was no connection between money and work failed to print a large enough money supply so that the money god could meet all the needs of the people. As work ceased due to structural changes caused by bad social policies, the Prince Repub and the Prince Dem both moved to intercede on behalf of the people to encourage the money god to print up more money. Prince Repub pushed conservative values in the form of moralism and said that liberalism is socialism, and that the free market is the only way. Prince Dem said that change was necessary, and that he was now Progressive because he had heard the voice of the people. All the while, both princes promoted bankrupt ideas that are illustrated by a bankrupt nation and bankrupt people who are caught in a continuous time loop that never changes.

As time passed, and we prayed to the money god for relief, he became unresponsive, so the prince unleashed the leviathan.[97] As the leviathan grew, he required more money in the form of taxes. The more he grew the more money he needed; until all that was left was people working to pay taxes to support the leviathan. The princes who were supposed to be protecting the people sold us out. Here we are in America the land of serfs.

How is it that the American dream has now turned into a nightmare, and how do we wake up from this nightmare?

A NEW POLITICAL PARTY AND A NEW GOVERNMENT

The emergence of a new society in America is at hand. It will require considerable work to put the new structures into place that will support the current and all future generations. How it will look will greatly depend on its creator. We, like God, have been given the special ability to create things in our own image. If left unchecked, forces will push our new society to ideas and beliefs of specific groups within our society. If current political parties have their way, it will look a lot like Prince Dem or Prince Repub, depending on who can gain control, wield the power, direct public opinion, and in the end, have the final say. Our political leadership will be presenting its version to the U.S. population as though it represents a single choice—the only choice. They present the choice as though it is a difference between the two when, in reality, they are one and the same. That sameness is found in the fact that both parties wish to use government to push their own ideologies and their ideological brands.

I suggest that the choice for our new society to be made by the American public is not one of government that consists of Prince Repub or Prince Dem. The choice before our populace is one of government and more government or liberty and freedom. That is why we are at this crossroads here in America. We have to make a choice. As we sit at this crossroads, we could take a left or a right (Democrat or Republican philosophy), but that choice would only keep the country traveling in circles. After all, if Prince Repub is the right, and Prince Dem is the left, then when we look at it these directions in terms of a geographical map representation, right would represent east and left would represent west. If you travel east far enough then you eventually end up west. Conversely, if you travel west far enough, then you also end up east. Although you will never get our two political parties to agree on this, they essentially represent the same thing. It is the same coin, just different sides.

America must move forward—not east, not west, not left, not right—forward. Neither the Republican Party nor the Democrat Party offers the solution to this problem. If fact, many of the problems we are experiencing right now are the result of their leadership, their social policies, their ideologies, in other words, their bad leadership. However, neither party is willing to accept blame for the consequences from these bad policy decisions, but they are both quick to take all the glory for the good outcomes resulting from their decisions. Interestingly, if you really knew what they were doing, you would conclude logically that they would only make *good decisions*. Who intends to make bad decisions? Also, it stands to reason that if either party knew and understood what is going on, that they would move to control the current crises enveloping America – even stop it. The truth is that they haven't such abilities, as their knowledge and understanding isn't any greater than that of the average American citizen. Our politicians are just better at pretending that they have an answer.

To mediate the differences between two extremes found in each political party, I suggest a different term. I think the term *constitutional liberal* should be used. Although these have traditionally been thought of as opposites that represent either the far right or the far left, I contend that these two terms are used by interests in both extremes to mask identity, intent, and purpose. This term could be used to identify people who value the U.S. Constitution and what it stands for, namely small government with limited powers and individual rights and liberties; it could be used as a platform to create a new power base to form a new political power base.

Neither the Republican nor the Democrat parties welcome such ideas. In fact, the only thing that each party can agree on is that they don't want a third party to capture seats in the House or Senate or win the presidency. It is, however, the entrenched interests represented by these parties that prevent American from moving forward. They do so by dividing the voting population down the center, thereby usurping our power as a nation to move forward.

Imagine stepping on the gas to make the car move forward; well, society also has an accelerator. It's the power of force that comes from the individual creative energy created by the combustible engine of innovation as knowledge gasoline is ignited and translated into productivity through our work. This is the same power we need to move America forward, neither to the right nor to the left, but straight ahead. This is the power that will bring about the structural changes we need for American society to move forward in the twenty-first century.

As explained in the previous chapter on the social contract, that power is not derived from the government. Government is not the power source; the power comes from the people. What is this power and what is its source? What are its limits? These seem like simple questions, but for the average American, they are not simple.

At birth, every human being is born with power. That power has limits of course, but it is available to all. This power is the power to create, or, put another way, it's the ability to produce. This is simply another way of saying that we have the power to work by transforming our ideas into finished products. A spark of creativity in the form of an idea that is brought to fruition through directed action could change your world and the lives of others. Sadly, many never come to this understanding. They never arrive at the knowledge of the truth of their power. They never realize that they have the power to create. The power to create can be used for both good and evil. This power can be either constructive or destructive.

In short, the power to move forward, to make the changes we need to make as a nation, resides with the people. The people of this nation are its only true asset. The nation's strength and greatness can only be maintained if liberty in terms of power is returned to the people. This doesn't mean that there's no rule of law. In fact, the opposite is true. The greater the liberty, the greater the need for an absolute rule of law where all are equal before the law with the eyes of justice blindly applied in all circumstances. This system of government not only allows people to retain their power, it makes them responsible for the choices they make and the actions they take in using this power.

The American society is a system. Within this system, power is the rate at which work is performed. Energy is the ability to do work or cause change. Change is the key to moving our society forward into a prosperous century. We must escape the powerlessness or entropy currently enveloping the nation. The gas in a knowledge-based society is knowledge itself. Knowledge is power. Knowledge, like all power, must be applied with wisdom. Here is wisdom.

Power is the ability to do work, and work creates the productivity we need for the twenty-first century. This productivity is the only real value. This value is what props up our currency. If we wish to have prosperity, we must have hyper-productivity that is only possible through major systemic structural changes that support a twenty-first information society with a knowledge-based economy. This can only happen when government establishes social policies that represent the interests of the people and not self-interest and special interests. This must translate into a new political economy—one where individuals have the power, people are the masters, and government is the slave. In its current form with the current political parties, it's unlikely that such changes can or will happen. We must return to a government by the people, of the people, and for the people in order to protect the prosperity of this nation for all future generations.

CHAPTER 7: THE NEW POLITICAL ECONOMY

I have two great enemies, the Southern Army in front of me and the bankers in the rear. Of the two, the one at the rear is my greatest foe.

Abraham Lincoln

THE HISTORY OF ECONOMIC THOUGHT

Economics and economic thought is still in its infancy. The men who have pursued this area of science, like all men of science, are constrained to write and speak ideas that they may refer to as theories like all other people engaged in any scientific endeavor. Like other theories, they must prove these out; they must be tested against the real world of daily affairs. What so often goes unnoticed by those who aren't privy to the thoughts of these men is just how influenced their thinking is by others, within and without the discipline of economics. Just like the ideas that can be traced back to the beginnings of America's political philosophies, we also have the early beginnings that can be traced back to thinkers of bygone eras and their economic philosophies.

"The ideas of economists and political philosophers," wrote Lord Keynes, a great economist, "both when they are right and when they are wrong, are more powerful than is commonly understood. Indeed the world is ruled by little else. Practical men who believe themselves to be quite exempt from any intellectual influences are usually the slaves of some defunct economist. Madmen in authority, who hear voices in the air, are distilling the frenzy from some academic scribbler of a few years back. I am sure that the power of vested interests is vastly exaggerated compared with the gradual encroachment of ideas."[98] Such ideas are embodied throughout the history of economics, and these very same ideas can be traced back to Adam Smith, David Ricardo, Karl Marx, John Maynard Keynes, and Joseph Schumpeter to name a few of those titans of economic thought.

The idea that some human beings are free, and that their plight in life is not determined by their birth, is a relatively new idea. For example, around 2,400 years ago Aristotle wrote that some men at birth are marked for subjection and slavery, while others are born to rule.[99] It wasn't until 1776 that the idea that men are born free and endowed with certain inalienable rights took root here in America. With this idea of freedom, there also came the need for betterment and improvement. Such needs required action or work—human labor. It was during this same year that Adam Smith published *Inquiry into the Nature and Causes of the Wealth of Nations*.[100] With this work, men began to understand how freedom and liberty translated into economic well-being, and how the tasks that they performed fit into the whole of their society.

The Wealth of Nations, as it is commonly referred to, is an account of economics at the beginning of the Industrial Revolution that advocated a free market economy as more productive and beneficial to society as a whole. Key to the themes expressed in Adam Smith's work is the "invisible hand" that naturally guides society through self-interest. He felt that where free markets are concerned if capital flows naturally on its own accord that it would, without the assistance of government, flow to the most productive hands, as the individual simply strives to better his own condition. Smith states that "the greatest improvement in the productive powers of labor, and the greater part of the skill, dexterity, and judgment with which it is anywhere directed, or applied, seem to have been the effects of the division of labor." To illustrate this, he describes the extensive division of labor within the "trifling" industry of pin manufacture, along with the astounding resultant productivity and laborers' dexterity; then he levers this as an introductory microcosm of the greater, yet less obvious division of labor in the broader economy. The advantages of this division were likely the driving force behind diversification of the trades and industry, and this diversification was greatest for nations with more industry and improvement. Agriculture is differentiated from industry for its comparative lack of division of labor, and the attendant lack of improved productivity; hence, while poor nations could not compete with rich nations in manufactures, they could compete in agriculture. Smith lists three causes, arising from division, of improved productivity:

- the laborer's dexterity - due to specializing, year-round, in a specific task;

- time not wasted passing from one task to the next - as in agriculture, as well as the more consistent and focused effort when working in just one area; and

- the machines and tools that have evolved in conjunction with increasingly specialized labor.

Of all the ideas expressed in his work, one of the most influential in classical economics is the idea of the labor theory of value. The labor theories of value (LTV) are economic theories of value according to which the values of commodities are related to the labor needed to produce them. Labor theories of value prevailed amongst classical economists, including Adam Smith and David Ricardo, culminating with the socialist theories of Karl Marx. Such ideas were a part of mainstream economic thought until the earlier part of the twentieth century. Classical economist David Ricardo's labor theory of value holds that the value of a good (how much of another good or service it exchanges for in the market) is proportional to how much labor was required to produce it, including the labor required to produce the raw materials and machinery used in the process.[101] David Ricardo stated it as, "The value of a commodity, or the quantity of any other commodity for which it will exchange, depends on the relative quantity of labor which is necessary for its production, and not as the greater or less compensation which is paid for that labor." In this heading, Ricardo seeks to differentiate the quantity of labor necessary to produce a commodity from the wages paid to the laborers for its production. However, Ricardo was troubled with some deviations in prices from proportionality with the labor required to produce them. For example, he said "I cannot get over the difficulty of the wine which is kept in the cellar for three or four years [i.e., while constantly increasing in exchange value], or that of the oak tree, which perhaps originally had not 2 s. expended on it in the way of labor, and yet comes to be worth £100." Of course, a capitalist economy will stabilize this discrepancy until the value added to aged wine is equal to the cost of storage; if anyone can hold onto a bottle for four years and become rich, it will be done so much it will be hard to find freshly corked wine. There is also the theory that adding to the price of a luxury product increases its exchange-value by mere prestige. Ricardo's labor theory of value is not a normative theory, as are some later forms of the labor theory, such as claims that it is *immoral* for an individual to be paid less for his labor than the total revenue that comes from the sales of all the goods he produces.

If the endeavor of all human beings is the economic well-being and self-betterment of each, then why do some have so much more? It didn't take long for the self-awakened eyes of liberty and equality of all men to see a strange inconsistency of economic inequality among men. With this, questions arose as to why. Why are some individuals poor and some rich? The economic distribution of wealth that should've benefited all of society only seemed to benefit a few. With such questions, other economists such as Karl Marx tried to explain this economic inequality.

Marx uses his labor theory of value to derive his theory of exploitation under capitalism. Unlike Ricardo, Marx distinguishes between labor power and labor.[102] *Labor power* is the *potential* or *ability* of workers to work, given their muscles, brains, skills, and capacities. It is the *promise* of creating value possessed by human labor that has not yet been expended. *Labor* is the actual *activity* of producing value. The profit or surplus-value arises when workers do more labor than is necessary to pay the cost of hiring their labor-power. To explain the normality of exploitation, Marx describes capitalism as having an institutional framework in which a small minority (the capitalists) monopolizes the means of production. The workers cannot survive except by working for capitalists, and the state preserves this inequality of power. In a normal role, force is a structural part of the usual workings of the system. The reserve army of unemployed workers continually threatens employed workers, pushing them to work hard to produce for the capitalists.

Marx's historical analysis of capitalism as a system of production was scathing. From this perspective, the only people who could better themselves were the capitalists because they controlled all the money. To say that Marx was not a fan of capitalists is putting it mildly, and his strong opinions become obvious in *Capital: A Critique of Political Economy* where he describes them as "Mr. Moneybags." Marx's analysis suggested that all men did not have an equal opportunity to pursue means of self-betterment and improvement. He further maintained that the capitalist's ability to maintain that power position over the workers was enforced and reinforced by the political structures that were controlled by moneyed and propertied interest that maintained power by controlling government. He concluded that capitalism didn't work as an economic system and that a form of government that supported that type economic system was very one sided, and therefore, it didn't work either. His was an outright rejection of both economic liberalism and laissez faire capitalism. "For Marx recognized that the economic difficulties of the system were not insuperable. The Marxist prediction of decay was found on a conception of capitalism in which it was politically impossible for a government to set the system's wrongs aright; ideologically, even emotionally, impossible. The cure for capitalism's failings would require that a government would have to rise above the interests of one class alone."[103] His vision of an economic system that worked for the benefit of everyone in society was socialism.[104]

In economics, laissez-faire means allowing industry to be free of state intervention, especially restrictions in the form of tariffs and government monopolies. Initially, the economic liberalism had to contend with the supporters of feudal privileges for the wealthy, aristocratic traditions and the rights of kings to run national economies in their own personal interests. Economic liberalism is the economic component of classical liberalism.[105] It is an economic philosophy that supports and promotes laissez-faire capitalism by opposing government intervention in the free market, and supporting the maximum of free trade and competition. By the end of the nineteenth century and the beginning of the twentieth, these were largely defeated.

"Certainly the signs of prosperity were visible at every hand. America in the late 1920s had found jobs for 45 million of its citizens to whom it paid some

$77 billion in wages, rents, profits, and interest—a flood of income comparable to nothing the world had ever seen." When Herbert Hoover said with earnest simplicity, "We shall soon with the help of God be within sight of the day when poverty will be banished from the nation."[106] It, poverty, was not. It, poverty, still is not.

This idea of noninterference in the market place by government persisted into the earlier part of the twentieth century. In 1929 with the stock market crash and the ensuing Great Depression this idea died. Enter John Maynard Keynes.[107] Dr. Keynes was considered the father of macroeconomics;[108] until that time the discipline was concerned with microeconomics.[109] The theories forming the basis of Keynesian economics were first presented in *The General Theory of Employment, Interest and Money,* published in 1936. Keynesian economics advocates a mixed economy—predominantly private sector but with a large role of government and public sector—and served as the economic model during the latter part of the Great Depression, World War II, and the postwar economic expansion (1945–1973). Realize that the era in which Dr. Keynes wrote his magnum opus on employment was during the heart of the Great Depression in which millions of people were out of work and a great deal of suffering was occurring across the nation. With so much suffering and people out of work, how could we eliminate poverty from planet Earth?

Franklin Delano Roosevelt and his social policies were heavily influenced by these same economic theories. It was a push to put people back to work and the nation on the road to prosperity once again. However, the interference of government into the lives of people and commerce represented a marked departure in the political philosophy of the role of government based on classical liberalism ideology. The interference of government during this time resulted in the adoption of many different social programs through social policies put into place by legislating it into law by the U.S. government of the time. Philosophically, this move by government resembled a move toward socialism and communism.[110] President Roosevelt didn't want to be accused of being a socialist, so he adopted the term *liberalism.* Confusion has ensued over the terms liberalism and socialism ever since.

Just like political debates, economic debates have ensued over the causes of the Great Depression. These didn't end with Dr. Keynes and the Keynesian economics school of thought. The Austrian school of economics, and specifically Joseph Schumpeter, also had much to say about the causes of the Great

Depression and the role of government in that time period.[111] Austrian economics was ill-thought of by most economists after World War II because it rejected mathematical and statistical methods. However, the Austrian school is credited with predicting the Great Depression. Frederick A. Hayek made his prediction of a coming business crisis in February 1929.[112] He warned that a financial crisis was an unavoidable consequence of reckless monetary expansion.

The Austrian school and Austrian economists have made significant contributions to mainstream economic thought. For example, they were very influential in the development of the neoclassical theory of value, including the subjective theory of value on which it is based, as well as contributions to the economic calculation debate, which concerns the allocation properties of a centrally planned economy versus a decentralized free market economy. The subjective theory of value, which says that value of a good is not determined by how much labor, was put into it but by its usefulness in satisfying a want and its scarcity. None, however, have been more influential that Joseph Schumpeter.

Joseph Alois Schumpeter was born in Austria in 1883, the same year John Maynard Keynes was born. While both men shared many social views, they came to very different views as to the future of capitalism.[113] Dr. Schumpeter was less optimistic about the future of capitalism and its survival. Schumpeter's view of capitalism was one "whose flow of production is perfectly static and changeless, reproducing itself in a "circular flow" that never alters or expands its creation of wealth." The system is stationary and because it lacks momentum, inertia sets in. Most importantly, "in this changeless flow competition will have removed all earnings that exceed the value of anyone's contribution to output." Here, workers and landowners get rents or whatever value their resources contribute to the circular flow. The capitalist get nothing, except his wages as management. "That is because any contribution to the value of output that was derived from capital goods they owned would be entirely absorbed by the value of the labor that went into the making of those goods plus the value of the resources they contained." This thought process led Dr. Schumpeter to the question vexing many other economists before him. Where do profits come from? "Profits, he said, did not arise from the exploitation of labor or from the earnings of capital. They were the result or quite another process. Profits appeared in a static economy when the circular flow failed to follow its routinized course." The disruptions he was referring to is the result of technological or organizational innovations into the circular flow. "As a result of these innovations a flow of income arises that cannot be traced either to the contribution of labor or of resource owners." An innovation implies an innovator. He called these individuals entrepreneurs and maintained that their innovations were the source of profit in the capitalist system. These entrepreneurs are responsible for profit because they combine the factors of production in new ways, resulting in economic growth.[114]

Such ideas have been integral in forming and shaping the modern economic system that is a part of twenty-first century American society. Just like the men who espoused these ideas, this system is not without flaws. Ideas come and ideas go; perhaps, it's time for new ideas.

THE CONNECTION OF POLITICS TO ECONOMICS

Politics and economics are inextricably linked. The economic system in America supports the political system and vice versa. To change this link would require a major readjustment and realignment of existing social structures that are currently girded by entrenched political and economic interests. When the framers of Americas system of government created the Constitution, they put safeguards into place to control the interplay of the two interests. That line of demarcation has steadily been redrawn and/or ignored by both political parties within the United States. It is absolutely absurd to think that any company would contribute thousands, even millions of dollars, to a politician and his/her campaign without the expectation of a return on investment in the form of a political favor, new legislation that establishes social policies in their favor, etc. "When both economic and political institutions were small and scattered—as in the simpler models of classical economics and Jeffersonian democracy—no man had it in his power to bestow or to receive great favors. But when political institutions and economic opportunities are at once concentrated and linked, then public office can be used for private gain."[115] Self-interest takes hold and greed ensues; it's a formula that, put simply, is a part of the age old effort to get rich and then to become richer. When such interests interact, it's easy to see how corruption becomes a normal part of day-to-day operations in both the political and economic worlds of the twenty-first century.

Although the period before the New Deal was notable for the limited extent of the federal government, the Austrian school suggests that there was a considerable degree of government intervention in the economy—particularly after the 1860s. Notable examples of government intervention in the period before the Civil War include the establishment of the First Bank of the United States and Second Bank of the United States as well as various protectionist measures (e.g., the tariff of 1828). Several of these proposals met with serious opposition and required a great deal of horse trading to be enacted into law. For instance, the First National Bank would not have reached the desk of President George Washington in the absence of an agreement that was reached between Alexander Hamilton and several southern members of Congress to locate the capital in the District of Columbia. In contrast to Hamilton and the Federalists, was the opposing political party the Democratic-Republicans.

Most of the early opponents of laissez-faire capitalism in the United States subscribed to the American school (economics). This school of thought was inspired by the ideas of Alexander Hamilton, who proposed the creation of a government sponsored bank and increased tariffs to favor northern industrial interests. Following Hamilton's death, the more abiding protectionist influence in the antebellum period came from Henry Clay and his *American System*.

In the mid-nineteenth century, the United States followed the Whig tradition of economic liberalism, which included increased state control, regulation, and macroeconomic development of infrastructure. Public works such as the provision and regulation transportation such as railroads took effect. The Pacific Railway Acts provided the development of the first transcontinental railroad. In order to help pay for its war effort in the American Civil War, the United States government imposed its first personal income tax, on August 5, 1861, as part of the Revenue Act of 1861 (3 percent of all incomes over US $800; rescinded in 1872).

Following the Civil War, the movement toward a mixed economy accelerated with even more protectionism and government regulation. In the 1880s and 1890s, significant tariff increases were enacted.[116] Moreover, with the enactment of the Interstate Commerce Act of 1887, the Sherman Antitrust Act, the federal government began to assume an increasing role in regulating and directing the country's economy. The Progressive Era saw the enactment of even more controls on the economy, as evidenced by the Wilson Administration's new freedom program. Following World War I and the Great Depression, Keynesian policies turned the state into a mixed economy.

Government interference in the economy and the economic lives of individuals with the United States has been a constant. It's not a recent phenomenon. Unfortunately, such interference in today's fast-paced world has served to tie the hands of the people who need to move with deliberate actions—the American middle class. We cannot, however, underestimate the role of special interests in this process. So long as these interests do not interfere with or constrain the rest of America, it's generally ignored. I would even suggest that most Americans do not even recognize that such actions by lawmakers even occur. It's when these interests no longer represent the middle class that such shenanigans become painfully clear to the rest of America. These times and years of the first decade of the twenty-first century serve as a prime example of how Washington and elected officials have effectively tied the hands of the nation by such actions.

As alluded to previously, middle class America is the backbone of the country; it's where all the work is done. This class of people includes the truck driver, the medical doctor, the restaurant owner, the college professor, and the countless others who work every day to make this country run. These are the workers who build America on a daily basis through the sweat and toil of labor. Without their work, nothing is produced. It is through these means that productivity of the population leads to prosperity for our nation. Liberty is the pathway that leads us toward that prosperity, because it serves as a guarantee to the freedom of choice that is the basis of action. Nowhere is this better stated than by Thomas Jefferson in the Declaration of Independence in the inalienable rights of life, liberty and the pursuit of happiness.

When social policies constrain freedom of choice by limiting liberty and rights guaranteed by the Constitution in order to protect moneyed interests and special interests, then the entire system breaks down; it is effectively rotten to the core and in a state of decay. Structurally speaking, these policies don't promote productivity and growth, which are vital to a thriving economy and prosperity; they, in fact, constrain them by promoting special interests that are not in the best interests of the masses of the population.

When such events occur through the actions of government, it has the same effect of violating the social contract—the U.S. Constitution. It, in essence, renders the contract null and void. This contract—the U.S. Constitution—is the means by which the two pillars of American society, our political and economic systems, are established and function to meet the needs of the population. Without these, society then begins to break down, lawlessness occurs, economic activity stagnates, and the government moves to maintain social control. We are currently operating without a social contract in the twenty-first century.

By realigning social policy with the current macro-level trends, freedom of choice is reestablished, and liberty is guaranteed. Of course, liberty without the rule of law and due process is anarchy, and this certainly doesn't reflect the intent of the framers of the Constitution. Freedom of choice guarantees liberty, and this freedom puts the power back into the hands of the people. The "invisible hand" characterized by Adam Smith in the *Wealth of Nations* (originally published in 1776) cannot move forward in promoting the common good, if individuals are denied the freedom of action, i.e., choice. Liberty must be the cornerstone of our nation, and it cannot happen without freedom of choice. Liberty, then, takes on a whole new role in promoting economic prosperity, and the common good.

Liberty puts responsibility for action back into the hands of the people. Government is no longer the force that moves people; people are the force that moves our society forward. This, of course, will require a major shift in our social, political, economic, and even philosophical beliefs. As such, this move will certainly change the status quo, and thereby expel entrenched interests. The battle to regain liberty in this country will be difficult. There are too many folks who have a free ride, and far too many who do not value the Protestant work ethic.[117]

Social policy must promote the common good and not just the interest of a few, even when those few (the minority) are in control of all three houses of government. The rule of the majority of the nation by a minority is not democracy, as so often portrayed when one political party claims victory at election time. This is nothing more than mob rule. It is only their interests that get addressed, even if those interests do a great harm to the rest of the country. Economic prosperity must be promoted through social policies that benefit all, not just special interests.

PRODUCTION AND CONSUMPTION

The key to a prosperous America where the American dream is still possible is drastic changes to our economic system. These changes won't happen easily or quickly. In September of 2009 in a scathing article in the *New York Times*, Paul Krugman posits the question, "How Did Economists Get It So Wrong?" as he explores the shortcomings and missteps by economists of all flavors—both micro and macro—that lead to the economic disaster of 2009.[118] It's clear that economists got it wrong as evidenced by the outcome, but getting them to admit it is something entirely different. Moreover, the politics, especially political parties, would also have to take responsibility for the social policies put into place that *let* economists get it wrong. As stated previously, you really can't separate the two. Originally, political economy meant the study of the conditions under which production or consumption, within limited parameters, was organized in the nation-states such as the United States. Here we explore production and consumption again within those parameters.

In examining economics and economic theories, you must consider two different concepts—value versus price. In an economic system, production and consumption create the necessity of exchange. In an economic system, supply and demand acts as a driver of price of a given commodity that is used in that exchange. They are related, but the two are distinctly different concepts. The determining factor of price is the law of supply and demand[119], the cost of creating a product or delivering a service as drivers of profitability, and the utility of the commodity. These must remain constant whether considered at the micro level of each individual transaction or at the macro level as in the whole of society. Production and consumption, however, drive something vastly different called value. As mentioned in chapter 3, consumption is not independent of production.

The fact that these are often confused by economists is obvious when you trace through the history of economic thought. A few economists like David Ricardo, Karl Marx, and John Maynard Keynes have tried to address the issue, but in the end, did they get it right? The short answer is yes and no. The system of production is different than the economics of production in that the system of production creates value while the economics of production drives price. They misunderstood this point. For example, Marx thought of labor as the key factor of production, and from this he constructed his labor theory of value, which really was a labor theory of price.

Value is created when people work. Work is a function of the production process. How the work is performed is irrelevant to the creation of value in a system of production—work can be mental or physical, but work is work. The output from that work results in a commodity. The price of this commodity may be determined by the cost of labor, the utility of the product, etc. They are inputs into the production process that are collectively called the factors of production.[120] Price, however, is not the same thing as value. People create value in an economic system when they apply their creative abilities to the construction of a commodity or output. As I stated in chapters 2 and 4, American society is both a deterministic and a dynamic system. Later in this chapter, I will illustrate both principles in the context of an American economic system that is driven by a system of production.

In the capitalist system of production, capital or money is one of the drivers around price because price determines the amount of profit. Profits and profitability cannot be ignored in the system of production because to do so generally results in losses, and losses mean you're out of business. From this perspective, the profit motive is a powerful motivator.[121] However, we can't ignore that manipulation of government does occur in which social policies and laws are engineered in a fashion to maximize profit. Free market capitalism proponents are benefited by government deregulation of financial industries because it allows those in economic positions of power to manipulate the economic system and drive profits (money) into their hands. For example, deregulation is thought to be the primary culprit behind the banking collapse. It was driven by the lack of oversight by the Federal Reserve because Alan Greenspan, the chairman of the Federal Reserve from 1987 to 2006, thought that that there was no such thing as a housing bubble.[122] He is a free-market economist. Additionally, through deregulation, large investment firms were allowed to buy up and store large quantities of oil reserves. By doing so, it appears that demand has greatly exceeded supply. When prices go up, huge profits are made such as witnessed in 2008. The oil is then dumped back into the marketplace, which makes it appear that demand has dropped and that supply has exceeded demand. Most importantly, this type of manipulation by economic forces does not accurately represent a healthy, thriving economic system. Politicians who allow such manipulation through voting on social policies that give businesses the legal means to do so are just as guilty as the ones who actually do the manipulating.[123]

The real problem with an economic system that allows such manipulation is that it is corrupt. Because it is corrupt, it doesn't meet the needs of a society as a whole. In America, the capitalist system of production is corrupt. While many criticisms could be heaped at the system as it exists today, I prefer to point out that the biggest problem is that it isn't putting people to work. When an economic system doesn't provide a society with the type of structure that allows people to have a job, perform work, and earn money, it collapses and ceases to function. People have to have jobs to earn money to meet their needs. On the most basic level, survival demands an individual be able to obtain food, shelter, and clothing. It short, it is consumption.

From a different perspective, consumption is based on choices, and those choices result in a style of living. This style of living as evidenced by the food you eat, the house you live in, the car your drive, etc. It is possible only through the standard of living afforded to the citizens of the United States because of jobs they hold that result in incomes that allow them to make buying decisions based on that income. People have to work in order to consume. The medium of exchange, in this case the American dollar, allows them to pay for that house, buy that food, pay the mortgage, and pay for college for their children. It provides them with the means to meet the necessities of life—a standard of living.

If a few people have all the money, the primary driver behind the means of production, the rest of America suffers greatly. Prices may be driven by the law of supply and demand, but the basic reality is that if you don't have a job to make money to use to buy stuff, then the price of any commodity is absolutely irrelevant. On the other hand, if the financial system has been flooded, thereby devaluing the currency and reducing the buying power to almost zero, then you can work as long and as much as you want and still not make enough to pay for the basic necessities of life. From this perspective, the capitalist system of production as an economic system leaves a little to be desired.

The major problem we seem to be faced with is unemployment. Unemployment is a symptom or side effect of the current economic structure, and it is systemic. With high unemployment levels, the system does not meet the needs of society, and it becomes painfully obvious, especially to those who are unemployed. In this scenario, value is not being created. When the system doesn't create value, the production and consumption of a society forces it into a depression. There is no growth because there is not opportunity to grow. People and companies become reactionary and start to constrict their activities. Recession sets in, and then, without stimulus and a plan to move forward, depression is inevitable.

What so many economists and politicians fail to recognize in their theorizing and implementation of social policies is just how technology plays a role in the system of production and how this influences societal stages of development. As I discussed in chapter 3, American society has transitioned from an agricultural society to an industrialized society that was based on mass production and mass consumption during the 1920s, 1930s, and 1940s. This transition didn't occur overnight. For one, the technology and infrastructure that facilitated this transition didn't exist. When new technology is applied to old systems of production, productivity explodes and the output from the old system is drastically increased. With these increases in productivity of the work process, prosperity is experienced across the whole of society as I have shown in figure 2.

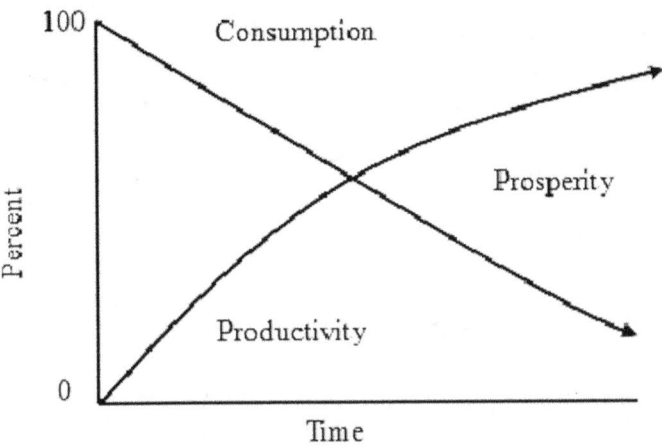

Figure 2: Economic Model Resulting in Prosperity

One by-product of applying new technology to old systems of production is that people become expendable because less people are required to achieve the same level of output. This results in fewer jobs, and unemployment begins to rise. As fewer people work, the value of the system of production begins to drop. Remember, *people* create value. New technology applied to the old system of production didn't increase value; it just built efficiencies into the production process. You can now make more commodities more quickly with fewer people. However, when unemployment rises, that translates into lower levels of productivity in terms of people who are members of that particular society. As shown in figure 3, when fewer numbers of people are working in the system of production, productivity drops even though consumption continues to rise. The distinction I'm making here is between productivity and production. Productivity is based on value created by people involved in the system of production in a society. Production is simply the output that is the result of the work process. From this perspective, the universal law that humans must work in order to consume is violated.

As I have illustrated in figure 4, the aim of a healthy economic system is to provide people the opportunity to work. By driving and keeping a person productive, and then on the aggregate society level, a nation productive, we can manage the economic system by maximizing the input of people in the production process and controlling the consumption of those outputs. That is to say, we can then manage the economic system.

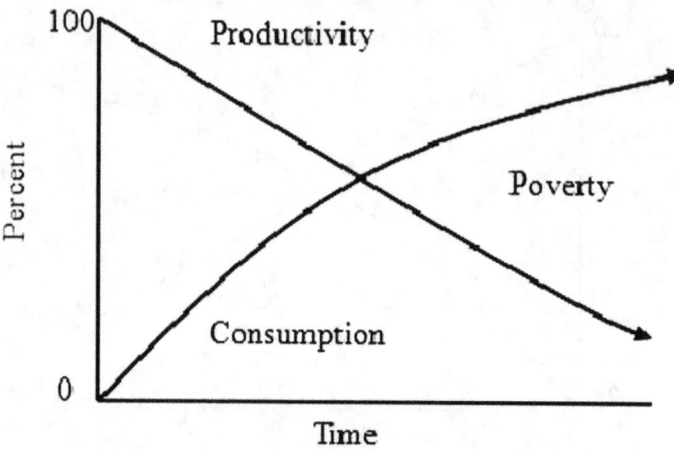

Figure 3: Economic Model Resulting in Poverty

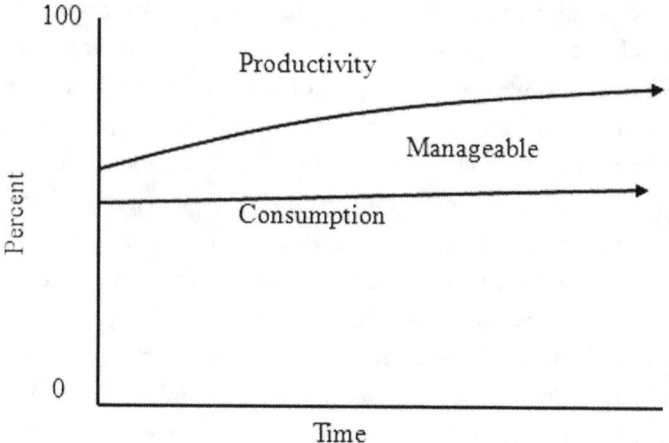

Figure 4: Manageable Economic Model

NECESSITY, THE MOTHER OF ALL INVENTION

Where we are as a nation is just not very clear to most people, including our politicians. We are going through a transition period; it's a major shift in the social fabric of society that is driven by the three macro-level trends identified in chapter 1. The critical area that this will affect is work—how we work, when we work, and who will work. The short-term implication is an adjustment in the number of jobs. What many politicians, Americans in general, fail to recognize is that the current job losses in our economy in 2009 are necessary. Moreover, these job losses are easily explained by the transitional period we are faced with in the twenty-first century. Let me elaborate. The number of baby boomers retiring within the next decade is somewhere around 80 million. Current job losses are around 7 million in 2008 and 2009 When all the baby boomers retire, who will fill those positions? There would be no one to do all the work. Our focus now must be on policies that facilitate the transition of a workforce of 80 million baby boomers to one with fewer workers to fill those positions.

This can only be accomplished through structural changes within American society. The problems in our economy now are related to structural issues that are causing unemployment. This necessitates major changes in our social, political, economic, and philosophical structure of our society. We will have fewer people to do the work. This is the reason we must prepare this generation and the next generation for the hyperproductivity that must follow suit. What does that mean? How is that related to the macro-level trends identified in chapter 1 and alluded to earlier? What must our politicians do to set policies that can address this issue and other related issues for the twenty-first century while we make this transition from an industrial society to an information society—from a capital-based economy to a knowledge-based economy? These are important questions we will answer in this chapter.

There's absolutely no way that Franklin Delano Roosevelt (FDR) and the people of the New Deal era could've foreseen that their investments in the infrastructure of their day would pave the way to mass production, mass consumption, and mass transit; all prerequisites to meet the needs of the future baby boom generation that was yet to come into existence during the time period of 1946 through 1964.

Although we could contribute such activities to sheer foresight, there is no evidence to support the proposition that government had any preconceived notion that such an infrastructure would be necessary to support the baby boomers of America and usher in prosperity experienced since the 1940s. Foresight is always zero; therefore, to pretend that planning was the instrument that made it all happen is to ignore the obvious flaws that are inherent in government—mainly that government by the people, of the people, and for the people is also run by people. These flaws are inherent in the entire human race, and there's no evidence that contradicts this fact. They, the people of the New Deal and depression era, simply thought that it was necessary to put people back to work in order to get the country out of the depression of the 1930s.

The government did not *know* the future. To know the future needs of the baby boomer generation would've required a priori knowledge that didn't exist in their thinking. Their ideas about the depression and what was causing it were only beliefs. These beliefs were not the same as knowledge, and therefore couldn't be considered to be the truth.

It's only through an historical interpretation of the events that we can know the truth. Planning that leads to perfect results that are a means to an end can only come from knowledge of future events. For it to be successful, it must be based on truth, because truth can provide a foundation of reality upon which to build. If it is only based on beliefs and belief systems, it is a house of cards that easily crumbles when the storms of life come. The foundation is the same as sand, and with the wind and rain, it washes away, and the foundation ceases to exist. Our society too is crumbling, in large part because the basic economic structure of our society no longer provides a foundation that can support future generations.

ECONOMICS FOR TWENTY-FIRST CENTURY AMERICA

As noted earlier, the key to a prosperous America where the American dream is still possible is drastic changes to our current economic system. This chapter emphasizes what those changes look like, and, more importantly, how they relate to the macro level changes identified in chapter 1. This chapter is not meant to be a textbook on economics and economic theory, but these are essential areas that need to be explained in order for the reader to understand the forces that have brought us to where we are today in America.

Many economists will disagree with the approach I've taken in this chapter. So be it. After many hours of study and reading countless books on these theories, I can honestly say that most of the economic theories that are used today to drive economic and monetary policy in the United States are absolutely wrong. Perhaps they made important contributions at one time, but like sour milk, these theories have passed their sell-by date. It's time to discard them and start anew. New economic theories and a new economic system will revitalize the American economy and return us to our place of prosperity, if used correctly.

CHAPTER 7: THE NEW POLITICAL ECONOMY

While we are busy making changes, we should make major changes to our economic theory and in our economy. These changes are not mere suggestions for improvement, but they are absolutely necessary for future generations of Americans to have any hope to enjoy the prosperity of their parents. If we hope to leave a powerful nation for future generations, economic prosperity must return.

After conducting an exhaustive review for this book, I have come to one unmistakable conclusion—the American dream is an illusion. Most Americans feel that it is their right to enjoy the American dream. What they don't understand or accept is that it's not a guarantee. It's not a right, and it's not a reality that most people ever really achieve. Interestingly, most economic theorists posit theories or simply their ideas about how to achieve this dream. Oddly, very few of them ever achieve it. It seems logical to ask, if they know so much, why don't they have all the money?[124] The truth is that they too are working stiffs trying to make ends meets, build a career, and take care of a family. They are no different than the rest of America. They want a piece of the pie, too.

Unfortunately, what this translates into for the rest of us is a rat maze, where these theories are tested out in trial-and-error experiments. When the results come in and these theories are proven false, it is usually too late for many because their state has become far worse than it was before. You might ask, don't people in the government and our elected officials know this? The short answer is NO! Politicians rely on economists to put forth theories that drive these policies, but few of them even understand the theories, much less the implications of the policies. It would seem rational that only those policies that are based on knowledge would be used to create the policies that affect the lives of the rest of us, but they rarely do. In the end, it's just someone's ideas. Some of those ideas had merit at a particular epoch in human history, but that time has now passed. Unfortunately, when that time came and went, the people forgot to change the theories. If those theories were ever remotely successful creating and supporting a growing economy, then the inclination of the economists who supported them was to push for more of the same. The fact that those ideas no longer applied to the world around us and are defunct and devoid of anything meaningful seems to go unchallenged; perhaps it's professional courtesy, promotion of self-interest, or something else entirely. For most, it is simply a lack of understanding. For some, it is a matter of refusing to give up on that he/she holds dear. Change is difficult. This fact applies to economists as well. For example, look at John Maynard Keynes and the revival of interest in Keynesian economics as a response to the current financial crisis.[125]

America is in transition, and the people are screaming for reform or change. What most do not recognize is why change is necessary, and what changes we need to make. The social changes we need today in twenty-first century America are reflected in the changes needed in America during the thirties or the era of the Great Depression. It was during the thirties that America need to transition from an agrarian society to one based on mass production and mass consumption. These changes required considerable structural changes within the country to make them possible.[126] This transition was extremely difficult for the people of that time. To move from one way of life or style of living to another can be difficult. The interaction of the people with the overarching macro-level societal needs and resultant changes have implications beyond going from something old to something new. It should be noted that the Great Depression wasn't just an economic condition; it also was a psychological condition. Psychologists don't understand economics; economists don't understand people or the psychology of economics. And politicians don't understand either. There you have it.

The social changes of today are no different. This is a different time period, but the conditions are the same. That is to say, we are now in another major transition period. This time we are moving from an industrial society to an information society with a knowledge-based economy. These social changes require significant structural changes.

Knowledge is power. Knowledge resides within the individual—in his/ her brain. Within a system, power is the rate of transfer of energy to accomplish work. Work is the labor that is related to as system of production—it's the productivity of the individual. The productivity of the production process resides within the capabilities of the means of production. In the twenty-first century, the macro-level shift that has occurred is that individuals are now the owners of the means of production. Not only do we have to shift our social structures to reflect this change, we must also make sure that the people make also make this transition. If the means of production now reside with individuals and consumption is not independent of production, then we must, as a society, get people to move to a state of productivity, so that our society can also move back to a state of productivity. Productivity at the individual level is the difference between eating and not eating—it is consumption. When you haven't the means to meet the basic necessities of life, then that is poverty. At the individual level, it is a psychological condition. At the societal macro-level, it is a depression. At this level it is an economic problem. The two are interrelated. These conditions upset the economic theories of today.

One fine example of this is Keynes theory of Propensity to Consume.[127] The consumption at the individual level, where it involves the basic necessities of life and survival is not a choice. In order to survive, people must consume. A better use of terms and their descriptions would've been Necessity to Consume and Propensity to Produce. Given such a rephrasing, consumption becomes the unavoidable constant and production is optional. However, if one doesn't produce, then one doesn't consume.

Keynes Propensity to Consume makes the assumption that consumption is a choice. Consumption is not a choice; it is a necessity for survival and 100 percent of the people on the planet must consume. A better way to look at his economic formulas is this way.

Necessity to Consume X Productivity/

Number of People Working X Hours Work = Total Productivity

Total Productivity – Total Consumption = Standard of Living

Instead of price related to supply and demand, we need formulas that estimate value based on the levels of productivity and consumption within a society. Some have argued that we need to return to the gold standard.[128] I disagree. Gold is a finite resource that only a few have access to in any significant quantity. It is true that we need to anchor our money on something of value. To stabilize our currency and to drive up its value, we must base it on the productivity of the American population. This would also allow the government to better estimate the money supply. If people work and produce goods and services, then the money supply is increased. If they don't, then the money supply is decreased. This would control the effects of inflation and deflation.

If creativity is unlimited, then the ability to produce enough to get money for unlimited consumption remains a threat, since consumption is tied to finite resources on the planet. These are not unlimited. Therefore, the only system of taxation that makes sense is one that is based on consumption, as this would allow control of unlimited consumption based on wants. Needs are absolute, wants are not.

Our political and economic leaders seem perfectly willing to debate the problems facing America, especially middle-class America by standing firmly on their philosophical and political ideologies, so long as they and their families have food to eat. When the average American has nothing to eat, time seems to matter little. However, if our leaders had nothing to eat, they would find themselves in a position where they are a little more humble and a little more willing to compromise their principles, since principles won't fill a belly.

In the twenty-first century, individuals are the producers. In order to produce, they must also be free, that is, they must have liberty. Not some liberty, but absolute liberty because freedom of choice is what makes liberty possible. Choices are what drive a style of living or lifestyle, and a lifestyle is made possible by a standard of living.

Of course, this type of liberty is not unrestrained and anarchistic as some would portray it. To maintain a civil society, we must adhere to the rule of law and due process otherwise anarchy would rein. This would not result in a productive society. Liberty such as this would also mean the elimination of time and space management instilled by industrial production process and Charles Taylor. This was necessary in the industrial society, but it is a dead idea in the twenty-first-century information society. We can no longer manage based on time and space, for they have no meaning. When you pick up a cell phone today and call someone on the other side of the planet tomorrow, then you know that something has changed. This is the final point: production processes have become decentralized. This is made possible by globalization.

With the decentralization of production processes, the nature of such an arrangement makes it impossible to manage people based on time and space. They must now be managed based on performance or outcomes. This also means that people must be held accountable for the outcome and their actions. Responsibility is the new word for this century. If society truly had an Age of Enlightenment, an Age of Reason, then now is the *Age of Responsibility*. While it seems few want to take responsibility for their actions, it must happen if twenty-first century America is to remain competitive in the world. Making this type of transformation in our style of living also has other advantages. This transformation of work literally makes it possible to produce twenty-four hours a day. This is what I term *hyperproductivity,* and this condition will take America into a new age. Why is his necessary?

Work is how we create value through products and services. This value is how we restore and support the value of the American dollar. This is covered in more detail in this chapter on political economy. Suffice it to say here, decentralization of the production process also requires a decentralization of power. Currently the social, political, economic, and philosophical social structures in the United States do not lend themselves to this type of model. They are designed as means of control. If we don't change these systems, prosperity will never return to the United States.

How long it takes to achieve those outcomes is the critical success factor. The critical success factor is getting the work done by utilizing whatever resources necessary. This requires an entrepreneurial mindset.

Price and value are often confused and used interchangeably. This is a misconception that I hoped to clear up in this chapter. What I explained in this chapter, many economists will not accept. Some may even feel nauseated by it. Nonetheless, this is the correct interpretation, and if America hopes to see its economy recover and our country return to prosperity, then we must implement models that follow a different logic than that espoused by current economists. If the economists have all the answers, then why don't they have all the money?[129]

Many classical economists, even Marxists and others, recognize that there is a relationship between money, commodities, price, value, and work. However, they have misinterpreted the relationship between the variables in their economic models. The key to understanding economics is to correctly connect the people, places, and processes involved in the production process. This is what makes the system churn, as it were.

There are three major theories of value commonly used in economic texts— labor theory of value, subjective theory of value, and marginal utility theory of value. Logical these theories postulate the price of a given commodity in relation to certain variables that create the value of the commodity. What each of these assume is that price of a commodity is a direct result of the value assigned to the commodity based on specific criteria, including cost of labor that went into making the product, its subjective desirability by the buyer, and its marginal utility to the person who acquires the commodity. What I propose is that these theories have nothing to do with value. True value is intrinsic, and it cannot be defined simply by quantitative means of price. Moreover, I suggest that all these theories of value only contribute to the overall price for a specific commodity. The final price of a commodity is mediated by the law of supply and demand if left to natural operations of the law without interference from those who seek to benefit by manipulating the law.

While modern economists have sought to establish price as a basis for an economic system that fails on one or the other side of this law—supply-side or demand-side economics. Both have failed to acknowledge and build into their models a true representation of value. This is especially true of monetarists who see money in terms of supply and demand only, and therefore attempt to use monetary system as a basis of controlling the law of supply and demand. Sadly, much of current fiscal and monetary policies established by the government are driven by these outdate theories of economics.

It all centers on establishing true value. What is it, and how is it derived? Until value is determined and established, our economic system will continue through the business cycles of boom and bust, and American families will continue to pay the ultimate price. Here's why.

Work is value. In the knowledge-based economy, work is mental, intellectual. The most valuable commodity in this type of economic system is the human mind, as this is where knowledge is created and accumulated. It is a creative process. It is virtually unlimited. Current economic models assume that value is derived from commodities and their desirability in marketplace. They base their models on the finite natural resources grounded around assumptions of capital (money) and capitalistic motivations. This can be traced to the economic assumptions of the profit motive as incentive to invest in the production of commodities. Accumulated money is wealth, and wealth is power. The shift of wealth into the hands of a few capitalists means that they have all the power. The real underlying problem with this approach to economics is that the wealthy don't work. They control the money supply, but they produce nothing themselves. That is, they produce nothing of value.

There are certain side effects to using money as a commodity that are subjected to the laws of supply and demand. These side effects are inflation and deflation, and both are tied to money supply. Money is paper, and it actually has no value. What it represents is the time and labor contributed to creating something, a commodity. When money is decoupled from anything of value, and the money supply is decreased and increased by the Federal Reserve, this causes inflation and deflation. Both are bad because both affect the real value of the money—your time and labor. If money had any real value, do you believe that the Federal Reserve would destroy billions of dollars of old money every year. Of course not! If they did that then they would be destroying real value.

Value is created by the work of human beings. The Federal Reserve does not create it. It is represented in goods and services we create for exchange. Money was created as a medium to facilitate that exchange. Somewhere, somehow, a few bankers got together and created a mechanism to control the money supply, and by so doing, they would control all the money, all the wealth, and all the power. What they failed to recognize was that money is just a piece of paper and has no real value. The real value rests with the producers—the people who are doing the work that produce the goods and services. It comes from work, and work in the information society is knowledge based. In this type of society, the magician's trick of swapping paper for work doesn't apply. Digits on a computer can also represent the medium of exchange. Once we understand and move to the digitization of money—a paperless society would have no paper money— then the means of control over the population disappears. The Federal Reserve loses its reason for being. If the people of the United States wake up and realize the trickery perpetrated by the Federal Reserve on the working people of this country, there would be a revolt tomorrow. While there may still be a place for the Federal Reserve System in the twenty-first century, it would not be the Federal Reserve in its current form.

CHAPTER 8: THE POWER OF TEN

Poverty is the parent of revolution and crime.

Aristotle

THE POWER OF TEN

In the twenty-first century, education is as important to the information society as the assembly line was to the industrial society. The first Model Ts off the assembly line weren't that appealing, but they got America moving and ushered in new era of prosperity. Education can do the same thing for America in the twenty-first century. It's not the education of yesterday though. It's the education of the twenty-first century. We need a totally new education model. This model has to fit with the social, political, economic, and philosophical structures of a twenty-first-century American society. It has to support and facilitate a new way of teaching, a new way of learning, a new classroom model, and a new school model. In sum, we have to have a new education model. This type of transition won't be easy, but it's necessary. Prosperity of future generations depends on its successful implementation.[130] As I illustrate in this chapter, we can show how and why education needs to change by simply taking the demographic makeup of ten American citizens and then based on a simple projection of those demographic trends over the next decade, see the clear direction of America if we continue down this path. It is the power of ten.

In order for America to stay competitive in the global economy, public education must do a better job of providing the next generation of Americans with the skills and education required for living and working in an information society and a knowledge-based economy. What has been done is not enough. We have unprecedented rate of dropouts in the United States every year, and while explanations are mixed, it is a clear message that education doesn't meet the needs of the next generation. It is outdated. The signs of this are evident in a shrinking middle class. Wealth and power are increasingly concentrated in hands of a few. More money is going out of America than ever before along with jobs that are increasingly sent to Asian countries such as India and China. Unemployment is rising, and with the baby boomers retiring, this trend can have devastating effects on the American dollar. This is not likely to change anytime soon. In fact, all indicators point to it getting worse over the next decade and beyond. For a look at the future, consider this scenario.

Around 2000-2001, a study was released that reported that 40 percent of America's ten-year-olds cannot pass a basic reading test.[131] Now let's leap forward by twenty years. The year is now 2020, and America is entering the third decade of the twenty-first century. We now have the same statistic, but it reads a little differently—40 percent of America's thirty-year-olds cannot pass a basic reading test. How can we run a technologically advanced society with people who cannot read? How does this support a knowledge-based economy? It's not going to happen. How do these people get jobs? Quite simply, they don't. So, four out of ten people can't get jobs in the information society because they don't have the most basic skills required.[132] We also have an aging population with more people retiring in the next few years.[133] Let's say that three people out of those ten are retired. That leaves three working people. At least one of those people will be a child. That leaves two working people. If they make above average incomes of $50,000 a piece, this will translate into $100,000 dollars to divide up among ten people, assuming no taxes and that those two people are willing to share their money with the other eight. We now have $100,000 divided by ten, and that is $10,000 per person. The poverty level is currently around $15,000.[134] So we now have ten people all living in poverty. However, if we could just get those other four people prepared for the future with skills that would allow them to compete globally in the information society with skills appropriate for a knowledge-based economy, this could translate into six people earning $50,000 a year. With $300,000 divided by ten, there is now $30,000 per person. That translates into much better numbers. That's the difference between poverty in America in 2020 and prosperity. Over the next decade, prosperity in America is in jeopardy. We must have a clear direction with a clear vision for the future of America—one that leads us to prosperity, not poverty.

Education is the key to changing the course and direction of America's future. As an institution, it is the reflection of American society. It is the window of opportunity that leads from one generation to the next. This window is rapidly closing. To lose a generation is unacceptable, but dropout rates indicate that is happening. While the above scenario may never happen, all indicators point in this direction. Education is how we keep America great and strong, and get our next generation prepared for life in the information society and global economy. Public education must recognize the importance of its role in the information society and make the changes that are necessary in order to get the next generation where it needs to be. The gap in economic disparity continues to widen, and if public education does not change then it will only get wider. Woe unto

America. However, the blame and responsibility doesn't rest on the shoulders of education alone. The whole of society, including our political leaders, must put social policies into place that facilitates this transition.

THE LACK OF EDUCATION AND THE UNEMPLOYABLE

The rise of the high school movement in the beginning of the twentieth century was unique in the United States, in that high schools were implemented with property-tax funded tuition, openness, no exclusivity, and were decentralized. The academic curriculum was designed to provide the students with a terminal degree. The students obtained general knowledge (such as mathematics, chemistry, composition, etc.) best applicable to the high geographic and social mobility in the United States. The provision of the high schools accelerated with the rise of second industrial revolution industry. The increase in office white collar and skilled blue-collar work in manufacturing reflected in the high demand for high schools.

In the twenty-first century, the educational attainment of the U.S. population was similar to that of many other industrialized countries, with the vast majority of the population having completed secondary education and a rising number of college graduates that outnumber high school dropouts. As a whole, the population of the United States is becoming increasingly more educated. Postsecondary education is valued very highly by American society and is one of the main determinants of class and status. As with income, however, there are significant discrepancies in terms of race, age, household configuration, and geography. Overall the households and demographics featuring the highest educational attainment in the United States are also among those with the highest household income and wealth. Thus, while the population of the United States is becoming increasingly educated on all levels, a direct link between income and educational attainment remains.

In 2007, Americans stood second only to Canada in the percentage of thirty-five- to sixty-four-year-olds holding at least two-year degrees. Among twenty-five- to thirty-four-year-olds, the country stands tenth. The nation stands fifteen out of twenty-nine rated nations for college completion rates, slightly above Mexico and Turkey. The U.S. Department of Education's 2003 statistics suggest that 14 percent of the population (or thirty-two million adults) have very low literacy skills. However, this is but one picture of education in America.

We cannot separate primary from secondary education. We cannot separate secondary from postsecondary. We cannot separate the education experiences in high school or college from the skills needed in workforce. While there may be many reasons to get an education, one of the realities of education is that it teaches skills and transfers knowledge from the current generation to the next in order to prepare them to enter into adult life as a productive member of American society. From this view, education is not a self-betterment proposition; it's an economic proposition. When we lose those individuals before they've completed their high school graduation, it is a serious blow to the future of America.

"High dropout rates are a silent epidemic afflicting our nation's high schools. The dropout epidemic in the United States disproportionately affects young people who are low-income, minority, urban, single-parent children attending large, public high schools in the inner city. But the problem is not unique to young people in such circumstances. Nationally, research puts the graduation rate between 68 and 71 percent which means that almost one-third of all public high school students in America fail to graduate."[135] In this same report, of those they interviewed, the top reason given for leaving schools was that classes were not interesting.[136] Additionally, another reported statistic was that 81 percent of those dropouts interviewed said that what would've improved the chances of staying in school were opportunities for real-world learning to make classes more relevant. This report is telling because it illustrates that what is going on in the classroom is far removed from what is going on around students. That is, the classroom experience doesn't reflect the real-world experience.

"Over a million of the students who enter ninth grade each fall fail to graduate with their peers four years later. In fact, about seven thousand students drop out every school day. Perhaps this statistic was acceptable fifty years ago, but the era in which a high school dropout could earn a living wage has ended in the United States. Dropouts significantly diminish their chances to secure a good job and a promising future. Moreover, not only do the individuals themselves suffer, but each class of dropouts is responsible for substantial financial and social costs to the communities, states, and country in which they live."[137] The cost of dropouts to our nation is extremely high—a cost that we cannot afford over the next decade. How high? "Dropouts from the Class of 2008 alone will cost the nation more than $319 billion in lost wages over the course of their lifetimes."[138]

On top of the growing epidemic of losing the next generation of Americans by virtue of the fact of that they are dropping out of school, America is now in a deep recession with millions of jobs lost through 2008 and 2009. Unemployment rates have also reached epidemic proportions. At the end of 2009, the unemployment rate hit 10 percent. This is a level not seen in a long time, and described as the worst recession since the Great Depression.

If assessed at a high level, the whole story is not apparent. A little history is necessary to put unemployment into its proper context. This helps to demonstrate the connection between politics, economics, and education in America. It helps to explain why we are where we are today.

Unemployment occurs when a person is available and willing to work but currently without work. The prevalence of unemployment is usually measured using the unemployment rate, which is defined as the percentage of those in the labor force who are unemployed. The unemployment rate is also used in economic studies and economic indices such as the United States' Conference Board's Index of Leading Indicators as a measure of the state of macroeconomics. Mainstream economics believes in the main that unemployment is inevitable and a necessary evil to prevent inflation; this is disputed by some schools of heterodox economics. The causes of unemployment are disputed. Keynesian economics emphasizes unemployment resulting from insufficient effective demand for goods and services in the economy (cyclical unemployment). Others point to structural problems and inefficiencies inherent in labor markets; structural unemployment involves mismatches between demand and supply of laborers with the necessary skill set, sometimes induced by disruptive technologies or globalization. Classical or neoclassical economics tends to reject these explanations and focuses more on rigidities imposed on the labor market from the outside such as unionization, minimum wage laws, taxes, and other regulations that may discourage the hiring of workers (classical unemployment). Yet others see unemployment as largely due to voluntary choices by the unemployed and the time it takes to find a new job (frictional unemployment). Behavioral economics highlights phenomena such as sticky wages and efficiency wages that may lead to unemployment.

There is also disagreement on how exactly to measure unemployment. In *The General Theory of Employment, Interests, and Money*, Keynes argued that neoclassical economic theory did not apply during recessions because of private investor timidity. In consequence, people could be thrown out of work involuntarily and not be able to find acceptable new employment. This conflict between the neoclassical and Keynesian theories has had strong influence on government policy. The tendency for government is to curtail and eliminate unemployment through increases in benefits and government jobs, and to encourage the job seeker to both consider new careers and relocation to another city. Involuntary unemployment does not exist in agrarian societies nor is it formally recognized to exist in underdeveloped but urban societies, such as the megacities of Africa and of India/Pakistan. In such societies, a suddenly unemployed person must meet his or her survival needs by getting a new job at any price, becoming an entrepreneur, or joining the underground economy of the hustler.

A direct demand-side solution to unemployment is government-funded employment of the able-bodied poor. According to classical economic theory, markets reach equilibrium where supply equals demand, and everyone who wants to sell at the market price can. Those who do not want to sell at this price do not; in the labor market, this is classical unemployment. Increases in the demand for labor will move the economy along the demand curve, increasing wages and employment. The demand for labor in an economy is derived from the demand for goods and services. If the demand for goods and services in the economy increases, then the demand for labor will increase, increasing employment and wages. Monetary policy and fiscal policy can both be used to increase short-term growth in the economy, increasing the demand for labor and decreasing unemployment.

The labor market is not efficient. Minimum wages and union activity keep wages from falling, which means too many people want to sell their labor at the going price but cannot. Supply-side policies can solve this by making the labor market more flexible. These include removing the minimum wage and reducing the power of unions. Other supply-side policies include education to make workers more attractive to employers. Supply-side reforms also increase long-term growth. This increased supply of goods and services requires more workers, increasing employment. It is argued that supply-side policies, which include cutting taxes on businesses and reducing regulation, create jobs and reduce unemployment.

Economists distinguish between various types of unemployment, including cyclical unemployment, frictional unemployment, structural unemployment, and classical unemployment. Frictional unemployment occurs when a worker moves from one job to another. While he searches for a job he is experiencing frictional unemployment. Classical or real-wage unemployment occurs when real wages for a job are set above the market-clearing level, causing the number of job seekers to exceed the number of vacancies.[139]

Cyclical and structural unemployment are most important to this discussion. Cyclical or Keynesian unemployment, also known as demand-deficient unemployment, occurs when there is not enough aggregate demand in the economy. It gets its name because it varies with the business cycle, but it can also be persistent, as during the Great Depression. This is caused by a business cycle recession and wages not falling to meet the equilibrium level. Cyclical unemployment rises during economic downturns and falls when the economy improves. Keynesians argue that this type of unemployment exists because of inadequate effective aggregate demand. Demand for most goods and services falls and less production is needed and consequently fewer workers are needed. When wages do not fall to meet the equilibrium level, mass unemployment results.[140] Some consider this type of unemployment one type of frictional unemployment in which factors causing the friction are partially caused by some cyclical variables. For example, a surprise decrease in the money supply may shock participants in society. In this case, the number of unemployed workers exceeds the number of job vacancies, so that if even all open jobs were filled, some workers would remain unemployed. This kind of unemployment coincides with unused industrial capacity (unemployed capital goods). Keynesian economists see it as possibly being solved by government deficit spending or by expansionary monetary policy, which aims to increase nongovernmental spending by lowering interest rates.[141]

Structural unemployment is caused by a mismatch between jobs offered by employers and potential workers. This may be due to geographical location, skill variation, and many other factors. Even though the number of vacancies may be equal to the number of the unemployed, the unemployed workers might lack the skills needed for the jobs or be in the wrong part of the country or world to take the jobs offered. If such a mismatch exists, frictional unemployment is likely to be more significant as well. For example, in the late 1990s there was a tech bubble, creating demand for computer specialists. In 2000–2001 this bubble collapsed. A housing bubble soon formed, creating demand for real estate workers, and many computer workers had to retrain to find employment. Another example in developed countries is the present combination of the shortage of nurses with an excess labor supply in information technology. Unemployed programmers cannot easily become nurses because of the need for new specialized training, the willingness to switch into the available jobs, and the legal requirements of such professions.

Structural unemployment is a result of the dynamics of the labor market and the fact that these can never be as flexible as, e.g., financial markets. Workers are left behind because of costs of training and moving (e.g., the cost of selling one's house in a depressed local economy), plus inefficiencies in the labor markets such as discrimination or monopoly power. Structural unemployment is hard to separate empirically from frictional unemployment, except to say that it lasts longer. As with frictional unemployment, simple demand-side stimulus will not work to easily abolish this type of unemployment.

Structural unemployment may also be encouraged to rise by persistent cyclical unemployment: if an economy suffers from long-lasting low aggregate demand, it means that many of the unemployed become disheartened, while their skills (including job-searching skills) become rusty and obsolete. Problems with debt may lead to homelessness and a fall into the vicious cycle of poverty. This means that they may not fit the job vacancies that are created when the economy recovers. The implication is that sustained *high* demand may *lower* structural unemployment. This theory of persistence in structural unemployment has been referred to as an example of path dependence or *hysteresis*.

Much technological unemployment (e.g., due to the replacement of workers by machines) might be counted as structural unemployment. Alternatively, technological unemployment might refer to the way in which steady increases in labor productivity mean that fewer workers are needed to produce the same level of output every year. The fact that aggregate demand can be raised to deal with this problem suggests that this problem is instead one of cyclical unemployment. The demand side must grow sufficiently quickly to absorb not only the growing labor force but also the workers made redundant by increased labor productivity. Otherwise, we see a jobless recovery such as those seen in the United States in both the early 1990s and the early 2000s.

From their actions, it appears that our government leaders see the current economic crisis as a Keynesian equation that can be solved by social policies that are based on assumptions from the Keynesian economics. I argue that the current economic crisis is not cyclical but structural. The unemployment we are seeing is a result of the misalignment of the major social structures of American society. Moreover, the cyclical approach being taken by our leaders in government around monetary and fiscal policies doesn't factor in the affect of a retiring baby boom generation. For example, we may have lost seven million jobs in 2009, but with almost one-third of the population ready to retire over the next decade, that still leaves over seventy million jobs to fill. We don't have the people to fill those jobs.

Though many people care about the number of unemployed, economists typically focus on the unemployment rate. This corrects for the normal increase in the number of people employed due to increases in population and increases in the labor force relative to the population. The unemployment rate is expressed as a percentage and is calculated as follows:

$$\text{Unemployment rate} = \frac{\text{Unemployed workers}}{\text{Total labour force}}$$

I argue that if we include baby boomers who are retired in this formula that the unemployment rate escalates to over 40 percent. From a social standpoint, retirement is not the same as unemployment. As I demonstrate in chapter 10, it is the same from an economic perspective, however. From this vantage point, the retirement of the baby boomers will have a devastating effect on the economy because productivity will bottom out. The American dollar is based on our productivity in terms of the value of goods and services produced in America as measured by Gross Domestic Product or GDP. [142]

THE BABY BOOM GENERATION

The baby boom generation will have a drastic influence on the future generations. This generation could devastate our economy to such a degree that it never recovers. This is not an indictment against baby boomers. This is an explanation of the effects of the demographics of this generation on the standard of living in the United States over the next decade if our leaders continue down the same roads on the same course. At first glance, the explanation may not be obvious to the untrained eye, but the implications are clear.

The end of World War II brought a baby boom to many countries, most notably, the United States of America. There is some disagreement as to the precise beginning and ending dates of the postwar baby boom, but it is most often agreed to begin in the years immediately after the war, ending more than a decade later; birth rates in the United States started to decline in 1957. There are an estimated 77.3 million Americans who were born during this demographic boom in births. Baby boomers are now middle age and entering senior years. In the economy, many are now retiring and leaving the labor force. It is important to distinguish between the demographic boom in births, and the actual generations born during that period. Here, we are focused on demographic boom in births, not generations. The United States Census Bureau defines the demographic birth boom as between 1946 and 1964—almost twenty years or an entire generation.

This cohort shares characteristic like higher rates of participation in higher education than previous generations and an assumption of lifelong prosperity and entitlement developed during their childhood in the 1950s. Boomers grew up at a time of dramatic social change. In the United States, that social change marked the generation with a strong cultural cleavage, between the proponents of social change and the more conservative. Some analysts believe this cleavage has played out politically since the time of the Vietnam War, defining, to some extent, the political landscape and division in the country. Although boomers across the world are said to have come of age at about the same time, the people in the United States were driving over to Woodstock, organizing against the Vietnam War or fighting and dying in the same war. It was a time of discontent and disagreement for many, as American boomers found a new home in Canada and escaped the draft and the Vietnam War.

The baby boomers are at a different place now in 2010. With the year 2012 rapidly approaching, many will start into retirement. As with all human beings, baby boomers must now face their own mortality and the same end of life issues that everyone else must face. As of 1997, it was reported that, as a generation, boomers had tended to avoid discussions and planning for their demise, and avoided much long-term planning. However, beginning at least as early as that year, there has been a growing dialogue on how to manage aging and end-of-life issues as the generation ages. In particular, a number of commentators have argued that baby boomers are in a state of denial regarding their own aging and death, and are leaving an undue economic burden on their children for their retirement and care. Research on memory loss has indicated that the baby boomer generation has been confronted with increasing loss of memory due to the agitated life they lead that requires attention on many different things at a time. Since older generations were not faced with this rapid lifestyle, and younger generations have lived with this society all their lives, it is said that the baby boomer generation was the most damaged one in terms of memory loss due to age.

Most importantly, baby boomers who are ready to retire have a significant need based on their end-of-life issues. These will come in two forms. 1.) Money to support them in their retirement. 2.) Soaring medical costs to cover medical needs that happen to occur most often at the end of a person's life. In 2009, the American Heritage Foundation conducted a study to look at these financial impacts on America in comparison to the bailouts in 2008. In this study, they report that "At nearly a trillion dollars, taxpayer-funded bailouts of failing financial institutions loom as a staggering threat to the free-market system. Even as Congress must protect taxpayers from this risk, it "pales" as to how much Americans would have to hand over to cover retirement promises in Medicare and Social Security." In this study, they report unfunded benefits due to baby boomers of somewhere around 40 trillion dollars. This debt is in addition to the 12 trillion we already owe. [143] We are deep in debt, and the debt keeps climbing. Whatever other assessment may be made, we can be sure that to be debt poor is not a road to prosperity for future generations. The risks to America and future generations are real.

MIDDLE-CLASS AMERICA AND DEBT POOR

If you take the middle class out of America, then you take the backbone out of America. It is the middle class that does all the work in this country. Don't think so? Let all middle class Americans stop working for one day, and this country will come to a grinding halt. Let all middle-class Americans stop working for one month, and then the whole world will stop. It is true.

There is a strange inconsistency in America. The middle class performs all the work, produces the goods and services, drives the economy, pays all the taxes, and yet they control only about 10 percent of the nation's wealth in terms of money. Money, after all, is how we pay for those resources that are necessary for survival—food, shelter, and clothing. How can this be so? Let's examine this strange phenomenon in more detail.

As shown in figure 5, the distribution of the population in the United States largely falls within the middle class income distribution. Although demographers may disagree somewhat on the exact numbers, it is clear that this group makes up the largest proportion of the U.S. population. As show here, about 80 percent of this population falls within this category.

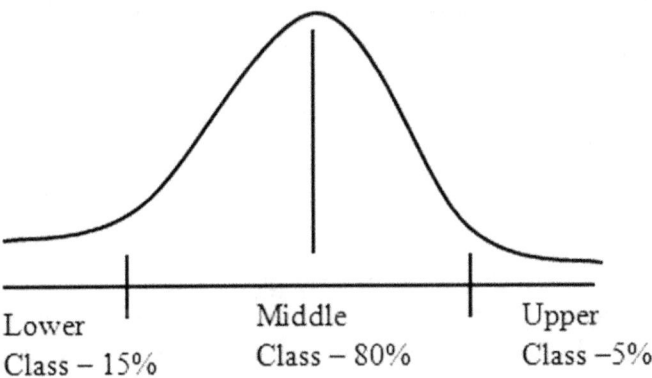

Figure 5: U.S. Population Distribution by Class

As shown in figure 6, the wealth distribution in this country is somewhat different. Here we can see that while only about 5 percent of the population makeup what would be called an upper class, they control about 84 percent of the wealth. This is a strange inconsistency, as it shows that the wealth of the nation resides primarily in the hands of a few.

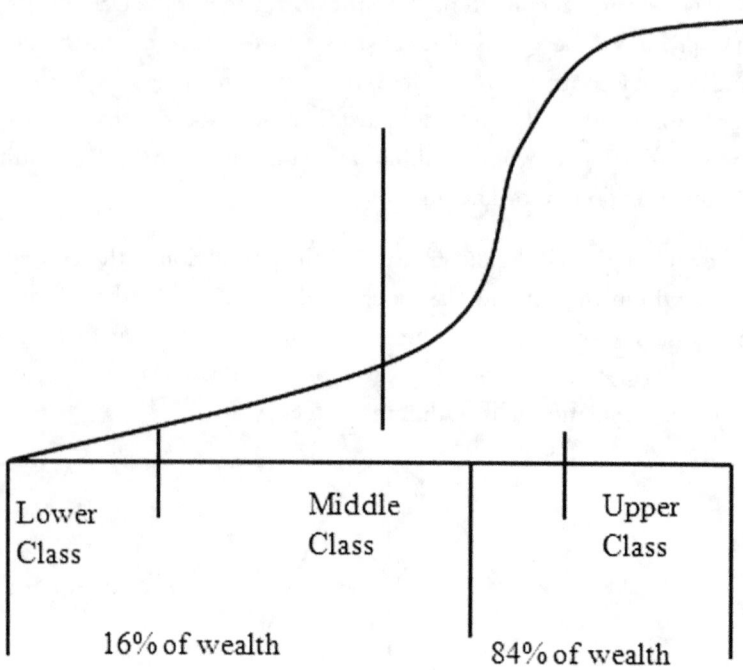

Lower
Class

Middle
Class

Upper
Class

16% of wealth

84% of wealth

Figure 6: U.S. Wealth Distribution by Class

If we apply these same numbers to the baby boom population, this means that most are members of the middle class. A few have accumulated significant amounts of wealth over their lifetimes that will support them in old age. A larger, but still small, number would be classified as lower class. This group of baby boomers has been dependent on government assistance in one form or another most of their lives. Their retirement age will register little significance in terms of overall government entitlement. However, for the vast majority of baby boomers, who fall within the middle class, their retirements will drastically affect the economy in the United States. As pointed out in the previous section, they will expect the social security and Medicare benefits guaranteed to them as part of the social contractual arrangement whereby the government told them that if they paid into the system during their adult working lives, they would be covered in their old age. Their old age is now. Their retirement is now, but the problem is that our government has taken the nation deep into debt. Moreover, the average middle-class American carries significant personal debt. As a baby boomer, this debt load makes early retirement impossible, and therefore, their time in the workforce is likely to be extended. As reported by the Federal Reserve Board in 2004, the average debt of American families is $79,083. With such debt loads, who can think about retirement?

With the downturn in the economy of 2008 and 2009, the impending retirement of baby boomers starting in 2012 and their associated entitlements in social security and Medicare, the reduction of the workforce, high school dropout rates, and finally the mismatch of skills taught in an outdated education system to the needs of an information society and knowledge-based economy, we have the makings of a perfect storm. We could continue down the current road, but the likely outcome would be an even larger welfare state in the United States.

THE EVOLUTION OF THE WELFARE STATE

Until the Great Depression, government interference in the daily lives of the citizens of this country was not tolerated. With economic depression and the conditions that resulted from the depression, it created an environment ripe for changes. Generally, these changes and the government's involvement through social policies and social programs began what today is commonly referred to as *the welfare state*. Although a certain amount of welfare existed before that time period, it was generally left to individuals and communities to provide for those less fortunate in times of need. Self-sufficiency and independence were the watchwords for most citizens, and the idea of taking a handout from anyone, especially the government, wasn't acceptable to good, decent, hard-working folks. The Great Depression changed all of that.

Changed attitudes in reaction to the Great Depression were instrumental in the move to the welfare state in many countries, a harbinger of new times where cradle-to-grave services became a reality after the poverty of the depression. During the Great Depression, it was seen as an alternative *middle way* between communism and capitalism. In the period following the Second World War, many countries in Europe moved from partial or selective provision of social services to relatively comprehensive coverage of the population.

There are two main interpretations of the idea of a welfare state. In the first model the state assumes primary responsibility for the welfare of its citizens. This responsibility in theory ought to be comprehensive because all aspects of welfare are considered and universally applied to citizens as a *right*. Welfare state can also mean the creation of a *social safety net* of minimum standards of varying forms of welfare. The welfare state involves a direct transfer of funds from the public sector to welfare recipients, but indirectly, the private sector is often contributing those funds by redistributionist taxation; the welfare state has been referred to as a type of *mixed economy*. There are two ways of organizing a welfare state. According to the first model the state is primarily concerned with directing the resources to the people most in need. This requires a tight bureaucratic control over the people concerned, with a maximum of interference in their lives to establish who are in need and minimize cheating. The unintended result is that there is a sharp divide between the receivers and the producers of social welfare, and the producers tend to dismiss the whole idea of social welfare because they will not receive anything from it. This model is dominant in the United States. According to the second model, the state distributes welfare with as little bureaucratic interference as possible, to all people who fulfill easily established criteria (e.g., having children, receiving medical treatment, etc). This requires high taxing, of which almost everything is channeled back to the taxpayers with minimum expenses for bureaucratic personnel. The intended—and also largely achieved—result is that there will be a broad support for the system since most people will receive at least something.

Empirical evidence suggests that taxes and transfers considerably reduce poverty in most countries, whose welfare states commonly constitute at least a fifth of GDP. Unsurprisingly, the information shows that welfare states would have higher poverty rates than a nonwelfare state such as the United States before the transfer of wealth; an example would be Sweden that has a 23 percent poverty rate pretransfer while the U.S. has a 21 percent poverty rate pretransfer. Some criticism of welfare states concern the idea that a welfare state makes citizens dependent and less inclined to work. Certain studies indicate there is no association between economic performance and welfare expenditure in developed countries and that there is no evidence for the contention that welfare states impede progressive social development.

Socialists and Marxists criticize welfare state programs as concessions made by the capitalist class in order to divert the working class and middle class away from wanting to pursue a completely new socialist organization of the economy and society. Furthermore, socialists believe it is an attempt to patch up the ineffective capitalist market economy and proves that capitalism does not work effectively. By implementing state or public ownership of the means of production, socialists believe there will be no need for a welfare state.

Another criticism characterizes welfare as theft of property or forced labor (i.e., slavery). This criticism is based on the classical liberal human right to obtain and own property, wherein every human being owns his body and owns the product of his body's labor (i.e., goods, services, land, or money). It follows that the removal of money by any state or government mechanism from one person to another is argued to be theft of the former person's property or a requirement to perform forced labor for the benefit of others, and thus is a violation of his property rights or his liberty, even if the mechanism was legally established by a democratically elected assembly.

A third criticism is that the welfare state allegedly provides its dependents with a similar level of income to the minimum wage. Critics argue that fraud and economic inactivity are apparently quite common now in the United Kingdom and France. Some conservatives in the United Kingdom claim that the welfare state has produced a generation of dependents who, instead of working, rely solely on the state for income and support; even though assistance is only legally available to those unable to work. The welfare state in the United Kingdom was created to provide certain people with a basic level of benefits in order to alleviate poverty, but that as a matter of opinion has been expanded to provide a larger number of people with more money than the country can ideally afford. Some feel that this argument is demonstrably false: the benefits system in the United Kingdom provides individuals with considerably less money than the national minimum wage, although people on welfare often find that they qualify for a variety of benefits, including benefits in-kind, such as accommodation costs that usually make the overall benefits much higher than basic figures show.

Fourth, another criticism of the welfare state is that it results in high taxes. This is usually true, as evidenced by places like Denmark (tax level at 48.9 percent of GDP in 2007) and Sweden (tax level at 48.2 percent of GDP in 2007). Such high taxes do not necessarily mean less income for the nation overall, since the state taxes ideally go directly to the people it is taxed from. These high taxes are argued to result in a major redistribution of that income from the citizens who do not accept welfare to the citizens who do accept welfare.

A fifth criticism of the welfare state is the belief that welfare services provided by the state are more expensive and less efficient than the same services would be if provided by private businesses. In 2000, Professors Louis Kaplow and Steven Shafell published two papers, arguing that any social policy based on such concepts as justice or fairness would result in an economy that is Pareto, a term used to describe efficient situations in which it is impossible to make one person better off without necessarily making someone else worse off, inefficient. Anything that is supplied free at the point of consumption would be subject to artificially high demand, whereas resources would be more properly allocated if provision reflected the cost.

The most extreme criticisms of states and governments are made by anarchists and Libertarian Socialists, who believe that all states and governments are undesirable and/or unnecessary. Most anarchists believe that while social welfare gives a certain level of independency from the market and individual capitalists, it creates dependence to the state, which is the institution that, according to this view, supports and protects capitalism in the first place. Nonetheless, according to Noam Chomsky, "social democrats and anarchists always agreed, fairly generally, on so-called 'welfare state measures'" and "Anarchists propose other measures to deal with these problems, without recourse to state authority." Anarchists believe in stopping welfare programs only if it means abolishing government and capitalism as well.

Welfare provision in the contemporary world tends to be more advanced in countries with stronger, developed economies. Poor countries tend to have limited resources for social services. There is very little correlation between economic performance and welfare expenditure. There are individual exceptions on both sides, but the higher levels of social expenditure in the European Union are not associated with lower growth, lower productivity, or higher unemployment, or with higher growth, higher productivity, or lower unemployment. Likewise, the pursuit of free market policies leads neither to guaranteed prosperity or social collapse.

From this perspective then, it's not social welfare we need to focus on to address the social problems in America. We should focus on the social changes that we are experiencing in America as a result of shifting from one system of production (the industrial society model) to another system of production (the information society model). As I described in chapter 1 and in chapter 2, the macro-level trends and the accompanying social structure changes are where we need to focus our efforts and our social policies. We need to direct attention through new and better social policies that facilitate this time of transition in America. This recognition seems totally lacking by Washington and Wall Street. The political economy in America is formidable. In the remaining chapters, I describe how we need to address this transition, and the changes we need to make as a nation. I am sure that social programs that promote dependence on government do not put America on the path to prosperity in the twenty-first century.

If we apply the power of ten to the population based on the current path of our country, the demographics are likely to include four people who don't have the right skills and knowledge to compete and work in a twenty-first century world, and need public assistance just to meet basic needs for survival; three people who are retired and are dependent on social security and Medicare; one person who is a child and dependent on a public education system that doesn't deliver what it needs to in order to prepare them for the future of the twenty-first century, and two people who are likely government employees who will be responsible for processing the government entitlements of the other eight. This must not be the future welfare state of America.

CHAPTER 9: GLOBALIZATION

It has been said that arguing against globalization is like arguing against the laws of gravity.

Kofi Annan

THE CHANGING MODELS OF GLOBALIZATION

Generally, globalization describes the ongoing process whereby societies and cultures are integrated through a global network of communication and trade. Globalization is usually recognized as being driven by a combination of economic, technological, sociocultural, political, and biological factors. Although economists and social scientists began to widely use the term in the 1960s, it didn't catch on in the mainstream press until the 1980s. When used in an economic context, globalization may be thought of as the removal of barriers between national borders that facilitates the flow of goods, capital, services, and labor.

Scholars disagree on the earliest known forms of globalization.[144] However, most generally agree that globalization in its current form, modern globalization, began to emerge during the twentieth century. It was during this time that we saw World War I, the gold standard crisis, and the Great Depression of the late 1920s and 1930s. Some have argued that globalization was a financial force that created such events. In more modern times, globalization has been accused of being responsible for the deep recession in 2008 and 2009, and currently still in progress in America and around the world. Is it, or is this simply a misinterpretation of the events that coincide with globalization?

Since World War II, globalization has been the result of planning by politicians to break down borders hampering trade to increase prosperity and interdependence thereby decreasing the chance of future war. Their work led to the Bretton Woods conference, which led the world's leaders of that time to create a framework for international commerce and finance that included several key international institutions to oversee the process of globalization.[145] Most notably, these institutions include the International Bank for Reconstruction and Development (the World Bank) and the International Monetary Fund. The World Bank's stated purpose is an international financial institution that provides leveraged loans to developing countries for capital programs as a means of reducing poverty around the world. The International Monetary Fund (IMF) was the second institution created during the Bretton Woods conference. It is the international organization that oversees the global financial system by following macroeconomic policies of member countries (originally 45 now 186 countries as of 2009), in particular those with an influence on exchange rates and the balance of payments. The original objective of IMF was to stabilize exchange rates and facilitate the reconstruction of the world's international payment system. Realize that when the Bretton Woods conference was held was right after World War II, and the countries involved in the war were deep in debt as a result. The two key representing countries at the table during negotiation and formulation of these institutions were the United States and the United Kingdom—the winner, if a winner is appropriate to describe the outcome of World War II. The architect who represented the United Kingdom was John Maynard Keynes.[146]

The World Bank's mission is to assist developing countries and their citizens to achieve development and the reduction of poverty, including the achievement of the Millennium Development Goals, by helping countries develop an environment for investment, jobs, and sustainable growth, thus promoting economic growth through investment and enabling the poor to share in the fruits of economic growth. The World Bank focuses on five key factors that they believe as necessary for economic growth. 1.) They build capacity by strengthening governments and educating officials. 2.) They help implement a legal and judicial system that encourages business and business development, and the protection of individual and property rights through the honoring of contracts. 3.) They assist in the development of a financial system that establishes a strong system capable of supporting financial ventures of all types and sizes. 4.) They support the countries' efforts to combat corruption. 5.) They provide a platform for research on development issues, consulting, and conduct training programs to support participating countries.

Similarly, the role and goals of the International Monetary Fund has also changed from its original charter in 1944. The organization's influence on the global economy has steadily increased as it accumulated more members, which is a reflection of the attainment of political independence by many developing countries, and more recently the collapse of the Soviet bloc. The changing world economy has forced the IMF to adapt to a variety of ways to continue to serve its purposes effectively. The primary mission of the IMF is to provide financial assistance to countries that experience serious financial and economic difficulties. When countries experience such distress, they request loans from IMF, and to get these loans, they are required to make certain reforms that have been dubbed the *Washington Consensus*. These reforms are beneficial to countries with fixed exchange rate policies where fiscal, monetary, and political practices often create the crises themselves. The structural adjustment programs run by IMF are intended to prevent financial crises rather than merely fund recklessness.

Although both the World Bank and IMF report significant positive effects on developing countries, there are many critics of both who portray the role and interference in other countries financial and economic development as detrimental. In the 1990s, the World Bank and IMF forged the Washington Consensus policies, which included deregulation and liberalization of markets, privatization, and the downscaling of government. Though the Washington Consensus was conceived as a policy that would best promote development, it was criticized for ignoring equity, employment, and how reforms like privatization were carried out. Many critics now agree that the Washington Consensus policies placed too much emphasis on GDP and not enough on the permanence of growth or whether growth contributed to living standards. Some analyses have shown that contrary to their stated goals, the World Bank and IMF have increased poverty and been detrimental to the environment, public health, and cultural diversity. Some critics further argue that the World Bank has pursued a neoliberal agenda that has imposed damaging and destructive policies on developing nations. Although controversial, there is also an abundance of criticism that the World Bank and IMF are used as a means to fulfill business and political interests of the main IMF donors, primarily the United States.

I suggest that the World Bank and IMF represent one form of globalization, but it is not the only form. As with all institutions, they take on a certain life of their own, and they act in ways that ensure their survival. The role and reasons that these institutions were created have played out long ago. The ideas and idealism of the men behind their creation are long gone. They too should've been gone long ago but continue to survive, even when their policies and actions aren't helpful. One of the main problems can be found in the fact that the economics that set policies and directions for the institutions are based on the ideas of John Maynard Keynes and others. As I describe in the next chapter a healthy economy cannot be ascertained through the use of GDP. It is also an outdated model of macroeconomics, which came from none other than Dr. Keynes.

There are other models of globalization. One in particular is that globalization is flattening the world and will continue to have an effect on economic development and the world economy. As previously described, globalization is not new to the world of ideas, but the how and who of globalization has changed. In his book *The World is Flat*, Thomas L. Friedman identifies three different periods of globalization that he labels as Globalization 1.0, Globalization 2.0, and Globalization 3.0. Globalization 1.0 (1492–1800) was about brawn, and how much forcefulness a country had in breaking down walls that prevented entry into other countries in different parts of the planet. In this era, countries and governments led the way to global integration.

Globalization 2.0 (1800–2000) had as its driving force of change multinational companies. Spurred by the Industrial Revolution, these companies were searching for new markets and cheaper labor. The first part of this era was driven by ever cheaper transportation costs. The second half similarly was driven by cheaper telecommunication costs. Globalization 2.0 was the birthplace of a mature global economy with the free flow of goods and information across the entire planet. The question most often asked during this period of globalization was where I fit into the global economy, and how to take advantage of the opportunities created by this type of globalization.

Globalization 3.0 (2000–unknown) is different in that it is driven by "the force that gives it unique character is the newfound power for individuals to collaborate and complete globally. And the phenomenon that is enabling, empowering, and enjoining individuals and small groups to go global so easily and so seamlessly is what I call the *flat-world platform*."[147]

Friedman correctly identifies what I outlined in chapter 1 as the three macro level trends that define an information society and a knowledge-based economy that are restated for convenience. These three macro-level trends are: 1.) the decentralization of production processes; 2.) the elimination of the need for time and space management; and 3.) individuals as the new owners of the means of production. These trends can only be supported in America through globalization.

In his description of globalization, Friedman details the convergence of the personal computer, the Internet, and software that allows individuals to begin realize that they had the power to go global as individuals; they began competing not only against people in the same city, state, or nation but all across the world. Global competition and global collaboration was possible for the first time for anyone with a personal computer and an Internet connection. In Globalization 3.0, individuals are empowered for the first time in human history to realize Descartes' law of I think, therefore I am.[148] The real key to the full realization of this type of globalization is only possible through an advanced infrastructure of computers and networks, as well as the social structures that support that type of society. America is not there, but we must get there. We don't need shovel-ready projects in the twenty-first century, we need wireless-ready projects.[149]

Remember, the problems of today that brought about the recession that began in 2008 are the result of structural problems not cyclical issues. Globalization makes the new production system of a twenty-first-century America possible. Social policies that facilitate the structural changes around philosophical, social, political, and economic structures that make up American society make this new system of production practical and doable. Infrastructure that supports that type of society is critical.

BENEFITS OF GLOBALIZATION

Friedman in *The World is Flat* orders a new Dell laptop and decides to follow it along every step of the process through the global supply chain from the time he places the order using the company's 800 number until the laptop is delivered to him.[150] When the order was placed, and e-mail was sent out to the Dell notebook factory in Malaysia, where all the parts were ordered from global suppliers. The production of the notebook involved many people and many companies in many different countries across the world. They were connected by a sophisticated production system that was made possible through computers, networking, global communications, and the Internet.

His description highlights two important facts about the twenty-first century. First, his story demonstrates how advanced technology of the information society has been leveraged to build efficiencies and effectiveness into the production processes of manufacturing resulting in increased productivity in the industrial system of production. Second, this use of information technology and advanced telecommunications makes globalization possible through an advanced infrastructure that results in a finished product that would've taken years to produce in an agricultural society (if possible), months in an industrial society, and only days in an information society. It truly shows the benefits of globalization in establishing a new system of production.

While globalization has many benefits, most people do not view it so positively. If we examine economic globalization specifically, these benefits can be measured in different ways that consists of four main economic flows:

1. Goods and services, e.g., exports plus imports as a proportion of national income or per capita of population;
2. Labor/people, e.g., net migration rates; inward or outward migration flows, weighted by population;

3. Capital, e.g., inward or outward direct investment as a proportion of national income or per head of population; and
4. Technology, e.g., international research and development flows; proportion of populations (and rates of change thereof) using particular inventions (especially *factor-neutral* technological advances such as the telephone, motorcar, and broadband).

Other benefits include the emergence of worldwide production markets and broader access to a range of foreign products for consumers and companies, particularly movement of materials and goods between and within national boundaries. International trade in manufactured goods increased more than 100 times (from $95 billion to $12 trillion) in the fifty years since 1955. The emergence of worldwide financial markets and better access to external financing for borrowers have greatly expanded the financial capabilities. By the early part of the twenty-first century, more than $1.5 trillion in national currencies were traded daily to support the expanded levels of trade and investment. The economic realization of a global common market, based on the freedom of exchange of goods and capital, and the interconnectedness of these markets, however meant that an economic collapse in any one given country could not be contained.

Some use the term *globalization* to mean the creation of a world government that regulates the relationships among governments and guarantees the rights arising from social and economic globalization. Politically, the United States has enjoyed a position of power among the world powers, in part because of its strong and wealthy economy.

There has been a significant increase in information flows between geographically remote locations. Arguably this is a technological change with the advent of fiber-optic communications, satellites, and increased availability of telephone and Internet. Survival in the new global business market calls for improved productivity and increased competition. Due to the market becoming worldwide, companies in various industries have to upgrade their products and use technology skillfully in order to face increased competition. Finally, the technical benefits have resulted in the development of a global information system, global telecommunications infrastructure, and greater data flow, using such technologies as the Internet, communication satellites, submarine fiber-optic cable, and wireless telephones.

Productivity in a knowledge-based economy can only come from a foundation of skills, know-how, and advanced technological infrastructure that support the way people perform their work. When that infrastructure and societal structures don't exist to support the production processes, productivity bottoms. Capacity is the key component. We have to build that capacity. In the twenty-first century of America's political economy, the infrastructure has already been built; we need but to continue to improve and utilize it. Computers, telecommunications, and the Internet represent that type of infrastructure. It provides the medium of exchange of information that supports a knowledge-based economy. This medium of exchange is comparable to the money of a capitalistic economic system.

The problem we are faced with is how to translate this medium of exchange into an economic growth system. Clearly, money represents a physical form that is unnecessary in the digital world of a knowledge-based economy. The digits on a computer system can as easily represent value in a digital form, rather than the physical paper form. How then do we translate a knowledge-based economy into value? How is it monetized?

If ideas are beliefs, and beliefs can be true or false, then clearly we cannot use a standard of measure of value as simply one where we exchange ideas. The Internet in its current form already provides that, but where does the value come from?

If we look at past economic theories of value, we can begin to find some clues. If we examine various economic schools of thought over the past 300 years starting with Adam Smith and *The Wealth of Nations*, then we find various theories that have been proposed as theories of value. The classical economist thought that the value of a commodity was based on the labor required to produce it, and thus created the labor theory of value. This particular theory was again taken up and formed the basis of Karl Marx theorizing, and thereby extension Marxian economics.

The Austrian School of Economics created the subjective theory of value that theorized that the value of a commodity was subjective. The basic proposition here is that for an object to posses value it must be both useful and scarce. The value of a commodity, as based on this theory, is dependent on the ability of an object to satisfy the wants of any given individual. That want is then translated into a price. This theory served to provide the foundation of the marginal utility theory of value. Although not mainstream, this theory further establishes the marginal utility of a good or of a service as the basis of price. The utility of a given good or service would be abandoned in response to a given decrease.

All of these theories provide insight into how price is assigned to a commodity within a capitalistic economic system. In the twenty-first century America, within an information society with a knowledge-based economy, that economic system must be based on knowledge as a commodity and the knowledge theory of value must be firmly established with a common standard of knowledge that must become acceptable in order to establish the actual value of knowledge. It must be monetized in some form, even if that form is represented by only digits in a computer somewhere. I suggest that knowledge as a commodity must encompass all of these in order to have value. It must contain labor, a creation of the human mind; it must have an intrinsic value that can be subjective to the user of that knowledge, and it must be of some marginal utility in the production process.

Knowledge as a commodity must be based on the truth, and not simply a belief. It must be more than an idea or an ideal. If it's not based on truth, then price for the knowledge commodity could be based on a lie. An exchange of the knowledge commodity that is false lacks integrity in the medium of exchange, and it can never survive the test of supporting the economic growth of the American population of the twenty-first century. A knowledge-based economy must be based in truth as an absolute standard, not as a relative standard. It must have a fixed standard of measurement. What is this standard? Who establishes this standard? How do we export it? How do we control it and protect it from would-be thieves?[151]

The only way Americans can return to the productivity levels that will support the consumption levels of the country is through hyperproductivity, and this is possible only by taking advantage of globalization and the benefits it affords us. The population must be able to literally work twenty-four hours a day. How is this possible? What about sleep?

Life and living is more than about just work. Granted, it is. Over the next few years, it will seem that America has returned to its former greatness. This is a false sense of security, as we will be in the eye of the hurricane. It will seem calm, but then the category-five storm will reach landfall as we encounter the backside of the storm. What does this mean?

Productivity in America will drop to an all time low. We will not be in a great depression; we will be in a mega depression. It will be the perfect storm. Why? The reason this storm will be so bad is because of the steps taken by President Bush, and now President Obama, to stave off a depression. In other words, their actions, the policies put into place, and the infusion of cash into the financial system will actually cause the very problem they have been and are trying to prevent. I hope I wrong, but I've looked at all the numbers, and I know that I am not. It all goes back to my previous arguments that the major structures of American society don't align with the macro-level trends of an information society and a knowledge-based economy.

The same problems our government has been trying to fix by infusing enormous amounts of money into our financial system will cause the mega depression of the next decade. It will linger for years. The main reason for this is tied to economics, money, and productivity. For an economic system to be truly healthy, its lifeblood, or medium of exchange (money) must be anchored by something of value. Printing up money out of thin air with nothing of value being produced to anchor it is like pouring gasoline on a fire to put it out. It just doesn't work.

So while the Federal Reserve and our government is busy dumping trillions of dollars of cash into the financial system, it is at the same time devaluing or driving the value down of each and every dollar. What this means to every worker is that your work, your productivity, is worth less and less as represented by the medium of exchange or the American dollar. This further depresses the production system because the dollar cannot sidestep the law of supply and demand.

It's hard to believe, but economic theorists with economic theories that are bankrupt drive our economic policies. Don't believe it? Look around. Some of these theories may have had some significance at a particular point in our history, but now they are outdated, empty, without merit, and bankrupt. America is now around twelve trillion dollars in debt. Does that seem like the theories are working? Most of the national debt we are now faced with has come about in the years of the twenty-first century. By 2020, it is quite conceivable that the national debt will rise to somewhere between thirty-five and fifty trillion dollars.[152] When you consider the reduction in the workforce based on the number of baby boomers set to retire in this time period, it is a mathematical impossibility that our future generations can work and produce enough goods and services (value) to pay for the debt. Desire at that point has absolutely nothing to do with it. The numbers don't compute. This generation (primarily baby boomers) in power now has literally sold their grandchildren, and the rest of the country, into a life of servitude to other countries and foreign powers. We will be slaves in our own country; the land that our forefathers set free will be the one where our children now beg for bread. Speaking on behalf of my generation and my children, please stop—just stop. Won't you please leave something for future generations of Americans?

Capitalism is a system of production. This system is driven by economics and economic theories that are based on theories and models that no longer apply. As I described in chapter 3, we are no longer in the age of industrialism. We need a system of taxation based on consumption. Why is this necessary? Shifting economic models from one based on finite resources of industrialization used in the production process such as coal, oil, gas, etc. to the infinite resources of the human mind would alleviate the current economic growth dilemma. This is connected to production, consumption, style of living, standard of living, and the three macro-level trends currently found in the twenty-first century. This also supports a knowledge-based economy that can achieve virtually unlimited growth.

The United States will never be defeated militarily. With two oceans surrounding us, a population that is armed as well as most militaries in other countries, and an arsenal of nuclear weapons unmatched by any other nation in the world, it's unlikely that anyone on the world would even try. This would be a foolish move. However, economically, it's a different story.

The United States is dangerously close to failing, probably closer than even most leaders realize much less the population. When we were attacked on September 11th, I cried along with everyone else as I watched the planes smash into the buildings on TV. Now that I've had the time to overcome the emotional trauma of the event, I can better make an assessment of the significance of the event. Whatever else may be said of the mastermind of the attack, his strategy was nothing less than brilliant. He didn't attack this country militarily. He attacked two of the foundational pillars that lie at the heart of its power—the economic and political pillars. Look at how divided we are now in this country over the war in Iraq. Consider the economic catastrophe that has befallen us at the end of 2008. A house divided will fall. An economic system that's defunct will falter. We're there! I don't mean to preach doom and gloom. The glass is half full and an optimistic outlook is always the better approach, but we would be remiss to simply ignore the realities of our current situation in America. We're rapidly approaching a critical time for the country. The risks we're facing are many.

RISKS FOR THE TWENTY-FIRST CENTURY U.S. ECONOMY

Wall Street Banks brought on the current financial crisis in the United States that began in the late 2008 with subprime lending and that is the result of both greed and bad decisions where no one wants to take responsibility and be held accountable. This event, while impossible to predict its outcome with accuracy, could've turned out quite differently with social policies that were more conservative in their application that strictly adhered to the rights of individuals while restraining the government intervention to the role outlined by the Constitution.

This crisis represents the worst social policies within the last 100 years. It is an example of laizze-faire economics and the welfare state all rolled into one. People buy homes they can't afford. Bankers make bad loans without strict review. These loans get repackaged and sold as mortgage-backed paper assets for enormous profits in the open market. Both of these assume a future that is uncertain and uncontrollable—therein is the fatal flaw. Downturns in the business cycle put people out of work. Without a job, you can't pay a mortgage, regardless of the interest rate. Adjustable rate mortgages where people assume rates won't go up, or that if they do, that they can refinance at a later date make the same grievous error in decisions—that no one loses their job. The whole thing is a house of cards just waiting for the right wind to blow it over. Well, the wind came. The house fell down. Bad policies, corporate greed, and inaccurate mathematical models with wrong assumptions are all to blame for this financial catastrophe. Republicans and Democrats, lenders and homebuyers, all are responsible, and all must be held accountable.

As weak as the America dollar is right now along with our twelve trillion in debt, it really wouldn't be difficult to throw the knockout punch right now. Here's how simple it is. The Euro has an exchange rate that is roughly double that of the U.S. dollar as shown below in figure 7. The power of the Euro comes from linking together twenty-seven countries. The current efforts at implementing the Lisbon Strategy also contribute to the strength of the Euro.[153] With over 500 million citizens, the European Union combined generates an estimated 30 percent share (US$ 18.4 trillion in 2008) of the nominal gross world product and about 22 percent (US$15.2 trillion in 2008) of the PPP gross world product. The EU has developed a single market through a standardized system of laws that apply in all member states, ensuring the free movement of people, goods, services, and capital

If the European Union could ever unite behind a dynamic leader with a vision to completely implement the Lisbon Strategy, they would catapult so far ahead of the United States that we would never catch up. It wouldn't take much convincing to get the E.U. behind the idea of decoupling the Euro from the American dollar and making it the world standard currency.[154] This would be the first knockout punch. If OPEC set the price of oil based on the Euro instead of the American dollar, then that would be the second knockout punch.[155] We would be down for the final count. If $4.00 a gallon is unbearable, try $10.00 or $12.00. This would drive up the price of everything. When you consider the vast distances driven each workday by millions of Americans as they commute from the suburbs, then the cost becomes prohibitive to all but a few. Suddenly $100 dollars in groceries won't feed a family of four for even a day. Between the inflationary effects of higher price gasoline and the debased currency, these conditions are not only possible, they are probable. America, look out. It will be a challenge just to survive. This might seem impossible, but so did 9/11. It's not as farfetched as our leaders would have us believe. Denying the risk won't make them go away. Wishful thinking can't fix these problems.

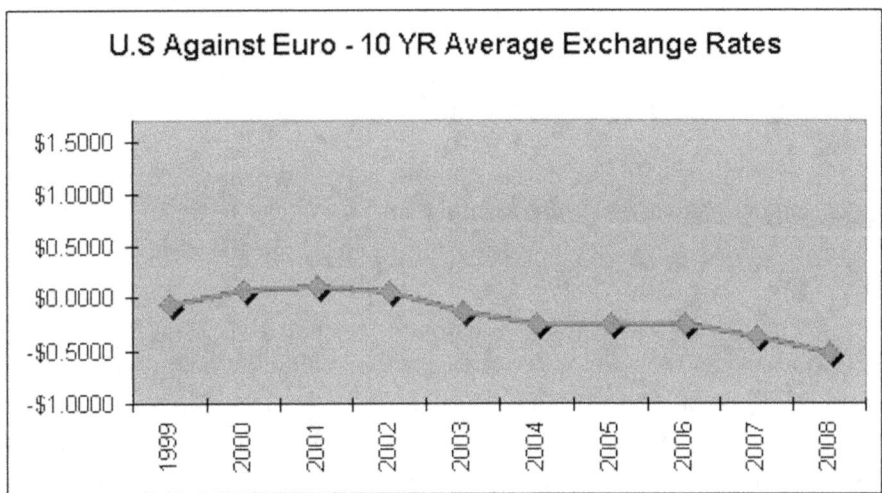

Figure 7: Comparison of U.S. Dollar to E.U. Euro

Middle class America is the force that keeps America moving. It is there in the middle class that all of the work gets done. If you take the middle class out of America, then you take the backbone out of the country. This country can't survive without a growing, thriving middle class.

The middle class is a wide, diverse group of people. It consists of the lawyer, the doctor, and the college professor. It's also the truck driver and the local restaurant owner. It's the beautician, the plumber, and the electrician. Why is this important? If the middle class all agreed to not go to work for one day, America would stop. If they didn't go to work for a week, then the world would stand still. That's the power of the middle class. Very few middle class Americans even recognize that this power exists.

Wealth in the form of capital (money) is also a source of power. When we look at the distribution of wealth in the United States, we see that power is concentrated in the hands of a few. Over the past few decades, wealth has become concentrated to an even greater degree in the hands of a few people. Contrary to Reaganomics and supply-side economics pundits, wealth doesn't automatically trickle down to the masses. When there is great upheaval in an economy as we see today with uncertainty on every corner, rich people get scared too just like poor people. The reason may be different, but the reaction is the same. The consequence of the fear is to not spend more, invest more, and release more of their money so that the rest of us can get a small piece—a trickle. The opposite happens. The water is completely turned off. As wealth is now only in the hands of a few, when they don't spend, the rest suffer. Capital in a capitalistic system when withheld is the same as withholding water from crops in the field. Sooner or later, they will wither and die without water.

If you can, try to imagine two opposing political ideologies whose strategy is to divide the middle class down the center. When this line moves to the left, Republicans win control. When the line moves to the right, Democrats win. That is to say, the party who can articulate an ideology that appeals to more people in the middle class will always be the party in control. What a perfect strategy! They divide the power of the middle class by pretending to represent different interests. It's a magician's trick. If middle-class America ever woke up and recognized how career politicians and the two political parties have manipulated them, then there would be a revolt the next day. Don't misunderstand my point here. A revolution by force is unnecessary; the middle class simply needs to recognize what is going on and unite to form a new political party that represents its interests. Members of the middle class need to demand their rights and take back what is rightfully theirs—life, liberty, and the pursuit of happiness.

The U.S. Constitution guarantees these rights. Unfortunately, special interests have eroded them. By allowing this, liberty in America is restricted because choices are eliminated. Unfortunately, freedom of choice is what makes liberty possible, and without that ability our style of living becomes endangered. As I described in chapter 3, the choices people make are what defines a specific style of living. In an information society with a knowledge-based economy, the restriction of those choices has a direct influence on standard of living.

As the new owners of the means of production in a knowledge-based economy, it is now the middle class that rules. We simply have to take back the power that has been stolen away from us. I must insist that the people be set free again. Let freedom ring throughout America once again, and prosperity will follow; not only prosperity for today, but prosperity for all future generations of Americans. With such prosperity, America can once again lead the world.

CHAPTER 10: THE THREE ES OF PROSPERITY

Power tends to corrupt, and absolute power corrupts absolutely.

Lord Acton

A CHANGE IN COURSE AND DIRECTION

Political parties, and by extension the U.S. government, are in the business of concentrating and centralizing their power. The more power is concentrated, the less power individuals have. They lose their liberty in every sense of the word. A government cannot function when the people of a nation depend on that government to meet all of their needs. In this sense, the relationship is not one of government and citizen; it becomes one of parent and child. A paternalistic government, where everyone is dependent on the government, can never be sustained.[156] Every citizen must become independent and earn his or her own way. Social policies that promote independence of this nation and all of its citizens must be the order of the day.

The reality of the situation we are faced with in the twenty-first century seems to elude almost everyone in America, especially our political leaders. Eventually, the U.S. government will be forced to realize that it cannot support an entire population that is dependent on the government to meet every need. To create value, the population, and that includes everyone, must produce on some level. They must produce something of value. When the people don't work, nothing is produced. When nothing is produced, there is no value. With no value, the monetary system is nothing more than pieces of paper. Total dependency cannot be sustained. This type of dependency will crash the system, and we're almost at that point now. This is the logical conclusion of the welfare state. As I demonstrated in chapter 8, the power of ten can be a negative force that drags the entire nation toward poverty. If everyone is entitled, and everyone is waiting for the government to provide all their needs, then eventually, somewhere, some way, somehow, someone must provide it for them. Since the government produces nothing, it only consumes, sooner or later, the government must demand that someone produce something. Finally, the paternalistic relationship must be turned into a master-slave/serf relationship. The leviathan must eat too, and with no one producing, the monster only gets hungrier.[157]

Government cannot be the solution to all our problems. It is too bureaucratic, too centralized, and too corrupt. We as citizens must be the bearers of our own problems. We must solve them on our own. The real power of change lies in the hands of each individual citizen and the choices he/she makes. In order to do so, government must return the power to the people.

Power cannot be centralized, and the people cannot be denied the power that can only come from true liberty. For this to be denied is to deny the citizens of this country their inalienable rights of life, liberty, and the pursuit of happiness.

Power in the form of wealth is now concentrated in the hands of a few people. We're not talking about a personal wealth of a 1 million dollars or even 10 million dollars. This wealth is defined by trillions of dollars. Millions or even thousands of people don't control this wealth; it is controlled by a very small group of people that are probably no more than 200 people. As such, they use this power to influence politicians and social policies to their advantage. This is how corrupt our government has become. Power is abused at every turn. The government can no longer be trusted to do the right thing and work on behalf of the best interests of the people. It now works on behalf of the few. Power corrupts. Absolute power corrupts absolutely.[158]

This type of corruption leaves the people without a voice. While those in government should be busy implementing social policies that are in the best interests of the nation, they're busy implementing policies that protect special interests in the form of advocacy groups who use various forms of advocacy to influence public opinion and/or policy. These special interests continue to play an important part in the development of political and social systems. Unfortunately, it is all too often to the benefit of a few. Groups vary considerably in size, influence, and motive; some have wide-ranging, long-term social purposes, and others are focused and arise as a response to an immediate issue or concern. Motives for action may be based on a shared political, faith, moral, or commercial position. Groups use varied methods to try to achieve their aims including lobbying, media campaigns, publicity stunts, polls, and research and policy briefings. Some groups are supported by powerful business or political interests and exert considerable influence on the political process, others have few such resources.

These special interest groups have developed into important social, political institutions, or social movements. Some powerful lobby groups have been accused of manipulating the democratic system for narrow commercial gain and in some instances have been found guilty of corruption, fraud, bribery, and other serious crimes. This has become the mode of operation in Washington. In this scenario, the interests of the population go unheard by our political leaders. The type of structural changes we need to make requires power to implement. This power can only come from individual freedom of choice.[159] However, if that freedom is granted through the use of social policies, then those special interests lose their stronghold. In short, the interests of the special interests group become threatened and protectionism begins.[160]

It is clear that we need a course correction in this country to move forward as a nation at this crossroads in U.S. history. That course correction doesn't involve a move to the left or a right turn. It is also clear that our current government, and the two political parties of Democrat and Republican, have no real intentions of accomplishing this feat. We must move forward by aligning the major social structures with the macro-level trends of an information society and a knowledge-based economy. To do so requires that we focus very heavily on three key areas—education, energy, and the economy (3E). In realigning the philosophical, social, political, and economic social structures, we must create social policies that drive efficiency and effectiveness (2E) in these three areas. Thus, we must follow the formula of 2E x 3E or 6E = Productivity, which is a function of work.

If we build efficiencies and effectiveness in education that supports a knowledge-based economy, energy policies that transform people and the United States into energy producers and not just energy consumers, and a growth economy that is based on the knowledge theory of value that rests on the infinite resources of the human mind, then we will see the end of poverty and the beginning of the age of prosperity in America in the twenty-first century. This will require a change in our style of living, but these changes will drastically affect our standard of living. This is the reason that individuals must have complete freedom of choice because it is through our choices that we create our style of living. The power to make the changes we need to make rests in the individual choices of each and every person within the United States. It is "we the people" who have to make the course adjustment.

TWENTY-FIRST CENTURY EDUCATION STRATEGY

Public education is in crisis, and the crisis seems to be worsening with each passing year. The crisis stems from the social, economic, and political forces that are demanding change from an institution inherently designed to resist change. Public education plays a specific role within American society by providing a foundational pillar that transmits culture, norms, and values from one generation to the next. Unfortunately, K-12 public education is not fulfilling this function in its current form. A massive overhaul of the entire structure is required, but best efforts to date are only providing a piecemeal approach that entails little more than band-aids, and it's not enough. Like a child with arms crossed refusing to take the medicine that will make him better, public education is resistant to change in spite of all the evidence insisting that change is a must; America's future depends on it.[161]

In 2002, the No Child Left Behind Act (NCLB) was passed as a major renovation of the Elementary and Secondary Education Act. The act has received mixed reviews across the board. Some say the act places undue burdens on teachers and schools, and should be repealed. Others simply argue the act needs major changes before it can really accomplish its goals. All seem to agree that more money must be spent, although America already spends more than any other first world nation and gets results that are nowhere near number one. Will more money really provide the solution?

Certainly there are problems with the NCLB legislation. As written, it places heavy emphasis on test results and this has lead many teachers to simply teach to the test; this does not provide an education for America's children. On the other hand, teachers and schools are threatened with heavy penalties when student performance is not demonstrated on state-mandated summative tests. What should teachers do when they are given the burdens, but they're not provided with the necessary tools and training required to meet the demands of NCLB? How can teachers deliver education services in the classroom without the resources to do so?

While NCLB is many things, some good and some bad, it certainly is an attempt by society through a legislative process to induce change within public education. Clearly, test results from the children in the education system before the passage of NCLB were unacceptable as a measure of preparedness for living and working in a twenty-first-century information society. Whereas the intent of the legislation may have been to improve student achievement in this regard, the actual implementation and realization of the intent has proven to be difficult and elusive.

Three major problems seem to obstruct the fulfillment of the intent of NCLB. First, NCLB requires major systemic changes within the social fabric of public education. Industrial society's education delivery models do not support this type of change. An information society education delivery model is now required, and that model of delivery must be reflected in the classroom through the learning transaction between the teacher and *each student*. Second, teachers are now required to be not only teachers but also lawyers and doctors. Unfortunately, the diversity in teacher skill sets required for twenty-first century education is increasing, and to make matters worse, teachers have not been given the tools and the training that will make them successful in the classroom in the delivery of education under a twenty-first century information society education model. This would be a complete paradigm shift for education. Third, and perhaps most importantly, the systemic changes required within public education can only occur with changes in attitudes and behaviors of those people within public education. That is to say, the problems within public education can only be solved from within public education. Accordingly, this can only be accomplished through the use of technological systems that provide for the free flow of information as reflected by an information society paradigm. In their current state, most education systems are riddled with design flaws that create major information and data challenges and prevent the free flow of information within the classroom as well as up and down the education enterprise. In short, these technological systems do not align with the needs and problems of a public education social system reflective of an information society paradigm. Education is also not in alignment with the three macro-level trends of an information society and knowledge-based economy.

In the information society with a knowledge-based economy, intellectual ability must become more highly valued commodity. This type of economy can only function if the knowledge base of the people supports it. Knowledge itself stems from intellect and accumulated information stored within a person's brain. As such the process of accumulating knowledge must become more refined and defined.

The scientific method is but one means of accumulating knowledge in the education process. The five senses of sight, taste, smell, hearing, and touch can no longer be the basis of accumulated knowledge. Knowledge, then, in the context of a knowledge-based economy must become rationalized, and this will require people to develop abstract-thinking skills. The philosophy of science and knowledge must become something entirely different. This is the task of the American education system in the twenty-first century. A shift away from pure empiricism to one of rationalization will not be easy, but it is necessary.

This idea is further extended by the decentralization of production processes. Basically a production process such as this no longer requires a face-to-face interaction with individuals. You don't have to know the person who is getting the work done. With this type of decentralized model, it simply is not possible. Therefore, we can no longer rely solely on our senses to complete the tasks of production. From this perspective, work becomes a totally intellectual exercise of the mind. Napoleon Hill wrote in *Think and Grow Rich*, "Thinking is some of the hardest work there is and that's why so few people do it." I wouldn't pretend to judge what is on everyone's mind, but thinking *is* hard work. A knowledge-based economy requires a lot of hard work.

Given the unique role education plays within society—transmitter of culture, values, and norms from one generation to the next—it's not surprising that public education would be the last place to embrace changes that are already reflected by the society at large. For the most part, American society has been transformed into an information society that is connected to a global economy. While a history lesson is not necessary, this transformation has been ongoing since World War II, and some of the greatest and most significant advances came in the last twenty years of the twentieth century. In order for America's citizens to live, work, and play in the twenty-first century information society, American public education must now play catch-up.

Although all is not known and understood about the information society and the global economy of the twenty-first century, there are some unique attributes that can be identified to aid in understanding what an information society paradigm means. An information society can be defined as a "society whose infrastructure is closely defined by *information technology* and characterized by the development of a large *service* sector that is heavily dependent upon *professional and technical* occupations denoted by the increasing *intellectualized nature of work* which can only be performed through *ongoing educational endeavors* where the *knowledge theory of value* gets translated into *information* and treated as *commodity*."[162] Moreover, the American lifestyle within the information society is driven by choices that are available only through economics that are driven by a global economy model. These choices are made based on consumption that is dependent upon an individual's abilities, skills, education level, and personal preferences. It all boils down to a simple question: How do Americans in the twenty-first century make money in an information society that is driven by a highly competitive global economy?" Public education is the answer.

In order for public education to fulfill its mission and obligations to American taxpayers, these same attributes must be infused into education delivery in the classroom. Holdovers from bygone eras can still be found throughout public education. Most notably, summers are still in recess in order to help on family farms that no longer exist as they did in the agricultural society, and bells are still ringing to instill time-management skills required in the industrial society. While others may be apparent, the most obvious and perhaps most difficult to change, holdout from the industrial society paradigm is that of specialization. Public education is stuck in the industrial society paradigm of teaching because teachers and administrators are still plagued by the idea of specialization of skills in a division of work that no longer exists. Public education is still operating as if twenty-first century living requires industrialization skills, when it does not. The problem is not only reflected through the teaching and learning occurring in the classrooms, but it's also evident in the construction of technological systems designed to support teaching and learning. This condition has been aptly described as analog teaching to children that are living in a digital age.[163]

Clearly, new and different skills are required for the next generation of Americans to live and thrive in a twenty-first century information society. These skills must come through public education, but before that can happen, teachers, administrators, and others involved in the education process must also embrace and utilize these same skills. In short, you can't pass along what you don't possess.

Which skills are required for life in the twenty-first century? Although there may be some disagreement about which skills, the Partnership for Twenty-First Century Skills identifies these as including:

- Creativity and Innovation

- Critical Thinking and Problem Solving

- Communications and Collaboration

- Information Literacy

- Media Literacy

- Information, Communication, and Technology Literacy

- Flexibility and Adaptability

- Initiative and Self-Direction

- Social and Cross-Cultural Skills

- Productivity and Accountability

- Leadership and Responsibility[164]

Moreover, new technological systems must be put into place to support an education structure to teach these skills. According to the Partnership for Twenty-First Century Skills, these systems must include a comprehensive framework of:

- Twenty-first Century Standards

- Assessment of Twenty-First Century Skills

- Twenty-first Century Curriculum and Instruction

- Twenty-first Century Professional Development

- Twenty-first Century Learning Environments[165]

Attitudes have changed somewhat in public education, but behaviors are still lagging. Most educators agree that there is a problem in public education, but they lack the knowledge, skills, and tools to change it. The key to aligning attitudes with behaviors is access to information that confirms the facts. The key to change in public education is changing the attitudes and behaviors of people within the institution. Over the past few years, attitudes appear to be changing. Most educators realize there's a problem within education, but they don't know how to fix it; instead, they continue on the same road. Going down the same road and driving the same car will get you to the same destination every time. Public education needs to take a different road and drive a different car in order to reach a different destination with different results.

The important word in information society is information. This is no different for public education, and especially teachers in the classrooms. In order for teachers to effectively deliver education to each student within the class, they must have information at their fingertips that confirms the facts. This information is derived from data. Data may be appropriately described as the digital representation of facts about people, places, and processes. In order for this process to function properly, the facts represented in the data must be high quality, and nowhere is this more critical than in the accountability requirements of NCLB.[166]

Another important attribute of the information society is advanced technology, and thus the term information technology. However, advanced technology does not guarantee access to the information needed to support decision-making. Technology is a tool, and no matter how good the tool, it still requires someone who knows how to use it. Just purchasing technology will not provide teachers and administrators with the information they need to better deliver education services under NCLB.

With the passage of NCLB in 2002, a number of critical issues became obvious as public education began compliance with the legislation. These issues have proven to be major obstacles in solving the problems within education under NCLB, and they are tied directly to data, information, and systems. While there may be others, the major data and information challenges for public education are:

- A lack of systems integration both vertically and horizontally.

- No data standardization across systems.

- Multiple sources of data that result in islands of disconnected and duplicated data.

- Poor data quality resulting from a lack of quality control in the data collection process.

- Inappropriate use of systems not designed to provide information—operational versus analytical questions.

- Limited information availability and sharing of information, especially cross-functional information.

Given these problems, efforts have to be made to design a comprehensive system to provide public education the means to overcome the obstacles, and thereby solve the problems within public education under NCLB. America must do better with public education; America *can* do better with public education. The systems must include a broad-based framework that provides a platform to encompass all essential educational functions, so that educators and administrators can do all that is required to deliver education services to students under NCLB.

The education mission must take the best technologies and build systems that provide solutions to solve K-12 education's data and information challenges, and positively affect the learning experience of all children in the twenty-first century through assessment, achievement, and accountability. The mission is accomplished by doing the following:

- Establish the processes and procedures that facilitate the creation, presentation, and interpretation of information in education.

- Create, standardize, and maintain the vehicle that provides access to and use of information.

- Provide everyone (teachers, parents, administrators, and community leaders) involved in the education of a child with the skills and knowledge that will empower them to effectively utilize information in education.

Information is critical to changing public education in America under NCLB. Teachers in the classroom must deliver education services that will prepare students for life in the twenty-first century information society. For this to happen, educators must not only teach skills, but they must also use those same skills in the classroom.

Systems designed to support education under NCLB must be driven from the top down by policy, but they must be designed and built from the bottom up. Education does not take place within administrative offices at a state or district level; education takes place in the classroom. The teacher teaches and the student learns. For this educational delivery model to work within an information society paradigm, information must drive the process. Therefore, teachers need a system in the classroom that is integrated and cross functional in order to get a complete and accurate picture of what's going on with each student at any given point in time. This type of system must provide a comprehensive integrated view of all functional areas as they relate to the education process in the classroom.

A typical hierarchical organizational view is represented for an education enterprise within a state. Within this type of enterprise, systems are typically designed by using a top down approach that is based on specialization—one system to perform one function. A system to support lesson planning is an example. The problem with this approach is that by the time it gets to the bottom of the hierarchy—the classroom—it forces users to jump from one system to the next just to perform the basic functions necessary for the delivery of education services. The system is too far removed from the people it's designed to serve. Moreover, these types of systems generally only serve to create additional islands of data. Continuing to design systems with this approach under NCLB only propagates the problems identified above.

The system is designed and built from the bottom up. Simply stated, this type of system starts where the action is—education in the classroom. The system is designed to provide an integrated view across multiple functional areas by providing educators with a sophisticated toolset that supports education delivery under an information society paradigm. In short, it is a framework with a broad foundation on which an education enterprise can build on. This approach has a number of vantage points.

1. Tying teachers to the data collection process in the classroom instills quality control processes at the point of collection. In doing so, data collection becomes a by-product of the education process rather than a separate process.
2. Systems integration is accomplished by integrating multiple functional areas into one application. This will result in a consolidation of functions and applications reducing the number of systems and islands of data.
3. Data standardization across systems ceases to be an issue because there is only one system.
4. Information is easily shared within the enterprise and across multiple functional areas getting everyone on the same page about each child's education.

The most significant benefit of using the bottom up approach to designing systems to support education under the information society paradigm is cost. System design, development, and implementation involve huge costs that generally make them prohibitive for many within the education enterprise. Two economic principles must be followed that will serve to drive down costs, thereby making it affordable to all.

First, it embodies the Ford principle of the assembly line. The education system of the twenty-first century must establish an education assembly line that will allow future development to be accomplished within days. It provides a framework that everyone is working from. The development of new modules that support new policy changes could occur almost instantaneously. The cost of production would drop drastically.

A second principle is aptly termed the *Wal-mart principle*. People shop at Wal-mart because of value and convenience—low prices and one-stop shopping. The systems of the twenty-first century education must provide teachers and administrators with value and convenience. All major functions are available in one place—one application. Rather than having to use multiple systems/applications to accomplish education delivery in the classroom, the tasks are reduced to a single function and application. This type of system makes it very convenient for users, and it also provides a great deal of value. The system must allow public education to consolidate functions and applications. This consolidation will free up existing resources in terms of money and people. Personnel who currently have to support multiple applications and multiple functions now only have to support one. This will free time to do other things to support the education process. Additionally, buckets of monies currently allotted to pay and support multiple applications can be reallocated to other needs.

Lowering the cost of ownership for information systems is paramount for the education enterprise to comply with NCLB. Both of these principles will enable public education to control cost and make meeting the demands of NCLB affordable.

Still not convinced? For those who still argue for the top-down approach, this point can be conceded if they agree that the proper organizational view is one where the organizational hierarchy is inversed and the classroom is now at the top of the hierarchy. In fact, this is the proper view of the education enterprise, and it is also consistent with the information society paradigm. In this view, administrative functions become more support functions with a service type of role. As stated previously, the information society is one that is heavily dependent on services. This too should be reflected in the education enterprise by modeling the organizational view in this fashion. Either way, the same is accomplished with emphasis for the delivery of education services being put back into the classroom.

The basic premise behind education is that assessment is what a child does not know, achievement is what a child does know, and accountability is the factors that influence each of these areas. While it sounds simple, the actual implementation is not simple. It involves a comprehensive strategy for teach-ers in the classroom that covers all the major focal points of NCLB. In order to successfully support education delivery in the classroom, teachers must have a closed-loop system that provides them with constant feedback and is designed to support continuous improvement in the education process.

The closed loop system involves the following main elements:

1. High quality data is fed into the system through the core components of the learning transaction in the classroom that includes standards, assessments, instruction, and curriculum.
2. The high quality data representing the facts of the people, places, and processes involved in the learning transaction can then be used to provide meaningful information about those same people, places, and processes through analysis and reporting of the information to key stakeholders and decision makers.
3. Training must be provided to teachers and other decision makers on how to utilize the information in order to make better decisions about the educa-tion process.
4. By improving the quality of the decisions, leadership, strategy, and planning can result to help drive the education process.
5. Focusing resources based on the information directly influences the qual-ity of the learning transaction and improves the education for each student throughout the entire process.
6. The results of the education process are fed back into the data through the learning transaction.

The least well-defined part of the model is around school improvement and adequate yearly progress as defined within NCLB to measure student achieve-ment. The term *school improvement* is misused in this sense because the focus of the accountability model is on student performance and not school perform-ance. When certain targets are not met, it's not the schools that have to improve in their performance. It's the students' performance that has to improve. With the reauthorization of NCLB or some other similar legislation, one of the major changes likely to occur is acceptance of growth-based accountability models. Even if the reauthorization of NCLB includes the ability to use growth models to measure student performance, this still will not address the needs of teachers in the classrooms. That is to say, teachers do not need growth models—they need growth-optimization models. Teachers need to pinpoint deficient areas in learning against standards, so that they can then move resources and implement strategies that address those deficient areas for each child.

While the definition of the growth model cannot be absolutely determined at this time, there are certain things that are knowable about them that also make it easier to project what a growth optimization model might look like. The following facts are currently known about growth models:

1. They are heavily dependent on data and data quality.
2. They measure learning based on standards.
3. They are time dependent, and there must be two points in time that are defined as the beginning point and the ending point.

To create a growth optimization model, one must include not only these facts, but one must also utilize advanced predictive analytics that require historical data that would be available only through a longitudinal data system.

With the increased focus on student performance and growth models under NCLB, it is not surprising to see more education agencies attempting to design systems to support performance management. However, many agencies mistakenly see performance management as an activity that takes place after the fact. Performance management, when utilized as it is meant to be, should provide education agencies with a clear picture of where the education enterprise is at any given point in time in meeting the goals and objectives of the organization and thereby meeting the requirements of NCLB. That is to say, performance management is about monitoring performance across the enterprise each day; when specific areas are not functioning as they should be, then resources can be allocated to address the problem that year before it becomes a statistic reported about last year's performance. It is not about reporting results from last year— performance management is not a report card. Last year's results are history, and therefore cannot be changed.

To accomplish performance management across the enterprise, systems must be designed and integrated so that those who are doing the monitoring can immediately identify problem areas. Once identified, full investigation into the causes of the problem necessitates the use of longitudinal data that covers multiple years of history. In short, a true performance management system must integrate operations data and historical data to provide the tools necessary to accomplish the intent of the system. Both types of data provide the foundation for performance management across the education enterprise. Today's problems can be fixed today; they don't have to become last year's embarrassment.

ENERGY: THE POWER BROKER OF THE TWENTY-FIRST CENTURY

The reengineering of processes that facilitate the redirection of energy and energy resources is what is required for America in the twenty-first century. That America needs energy, and more of it, is obvious. The reasons may not be quite so obvious. As described previously, power is the rate at which work is performed or energy is converted. Energy is a scalar physical quantity that describes the amount of work that can be performed by a force; it is an attribute of objects and systems that is subject to a conservation law. Any form of energy can be transformed into another form, although there are often limits to the efficiency of the conversion from thermal energy to other forms of energy because of the second law of thermodynamics.[167] As an example, when oil is reacted with oxygen, potential energy is released. The concept of force is used to describe an influence that causes an object to undergo acceleration. Inertia is the resistance of any physical object to a change in its state of motion. It is represented numerically by an object's mass. The principle of inertia is one of the fundamental principles of classical physics, which are used to describe the motion of matter and how it is affected by applied forces. To be inert is to be in a state of doing little or nothing. As I stated at the beginning of this book, America has become inert.[168] Why does America need more energy, and how does this apply to the twenty-first century information society and knowledge-based economy?

From its founding until the late 1700s, the United States was largely an agrarian country with abundant forests. During this period, energy consumption overwhelmingly focused on readily available firewood. Rapid industrialization of the economy, urbanization, and the growth of railroads led to increased use of coal, and by 1885, coal had eclipsed wood as the nation's primary energy source. Coal remained the dominant fuel for the next seven decades. By 1950, coal was surpassed in turn by both petroleum and natural gas. While coal consumption today is the highest it has ever been, it is now mostly used to generate electricity. Natural gas, which burns more cleanly and is more easily transportable, has replaced coal as the preferred source of heating in homes, businesses, and industrial furnaces. Although total energy use increased dramatically during this period, by approximately a factor of fifty between 1850 and 2000, energy use per capita increased only by a factor of four.

At the beginning of the twentieth century, petroleum was a minor resource used to manufacture lubricants and fuel for kerosene and oil lamps. One hundred years later it had become the preeminent energy source for the United States and the rest of the world. This rise closely paralleled the emergence of the automobile as a major force in American culture and the economy.[169] While petroleum is also used as a source for plastics and other chemicals, and powers various industrial processes, today two-thirds of oil consumption in the United States is in the form of transportation fuels. Oil's unique qualities for transportation fuels in terms of energy content, cost of production, and speed of refueling have made it difficult to supplant with technological alternatives developed so far.

The United States is the largest energy consumer in terms of total use, using 100 quadrillion BTUs (105 exajoules, or 29 PWh) in 2005. This is three times the consumption by the United States in 1950. The United States ranks seventh in energy consumption per capita after Canada and a number of small countries. The majority of this energy is derived from fossil fuels: in 2005, it was estimated that 40 percent of the nation's energy came from petroleum, 23 percent from coal, and 23 percent from natural gas. Nuclear power supplied 8.4 percent and renewable energy supplied 7.3 percent, which was mainly from hydroelectric dams although other renewable energy sources are included such as wind power, and geothermal and solar energy. Energy consumption has increased at a faster rate than energy production over the last fifty years in the United States when they were roughly equal. This difference is now largely met through imports.

According to the Energy Information Administration's statistics, the per capita energy consumption in the United States has been somewhat consistent from the 1970s until today. The average has been 335.9 million BTUs per person from 1980 to 2006. One explanation for this is that the energy required to produce the increase in U.S. consumption of manufactured equipment, cars, and other goods has been shifted to other countries producing and transporting those goods to the United States with a corresponding shift of greenhouse gases and pollution. In comparison, the world average has increased from 63.7 in 1980 to 72.4 million BTU's per person in 2006.

There have been economic and political problems associated with the country's past dependence on foreign oil supply. America's past consumption of petroleum has resulted in environmental problems as well. U.S. oil consumption is approximately 21 million barrels/day, yet domestic production is only 6 million barrels per day. The cost to import oil is approximately $630 billion dollars a year (at $115/barrel).[170] While it costs oil companies operating in the Arabian Peninsula just one U.S. dollar to extract a barrel of oil, the cost on the world market has varied up to $100/barrel in 2007 dollars. While U.S. oil usage increases by 2 percent per year, the economy has been growing at 3.3 percent per year. The Strategic Petroleum Reserve currently holds about 720 millions of barrels of oil and is near capacity.[171]

During the Carter administration, in response to an energy crisis and hostile Iranian and Soviet Union relations, President Jimmy Carter announced the Carter Doctrine, which declared that any interference with U.S. interests in the Persian Gulf would be considered an attack on U.S. vital interests. This doctrine was expanded by Ronald Reagan. This type of foreign policy around energy sources vital to the United States persists today.

The United States has and continues to get most of its electrical production from conventional thermal power plants. Most of these are coal; however, the 1990s and 2000s have seen a disproportionate increase in natural gas and other kinds of gas powered plants. From 1992 to 2005 some 270,000 megawatt electric (MWe) of new gas-fired plant were built but only 14,000 MWe of new nuclear and coal-fired capacity came on line, mostly coal, with 2,315 MWe of that being nuclear. Nuclear and coal are considerably more capital intensive when compared to gas, and the great shift to gas plant construction is often attributed to deregulation and other political and economic factors. U.S. wind power capacity now exceeds 18,302 MW, which is enough to serve 4.5 million average households. Several solar thermal power stations, including the new 64 MW Nevada Solar One, have also been built. The largest of these solar thermal power stations is the SEGS group of plants in the Mojave Desert, which have a total generating capacity of 354 MW, making the system the largest solar plant of any kind in the world. In 2007, summer demand for electricity was 783 GW and 640 GW for winter. By 2017, North American Electric Reliability Corporation (NERC) projects summer consumption to be 925 GW for summer and 756 GW for winter.

CHAPTER 10: THE THREE ES OF PROSPERITY

Visible or embedded computers are found everywhere in the United States. In 1999 a study conducted by Mark. P. Mills of the Green Earth Society reported that computers consumed 13 percent of the entire U.S. supply. Numerous researchers questioned Mills' methodology, and it was later demonstrated that he was off by an order of magnitude; for example, Lawrence Berkeley Labs concluded that the figure was nearer 3 percent of U.S. electricity use. Although Mills' study was inaccurate, it helped drive the debate to the national level, and in 2006 the U.S. Senate started a study of the energy consumption of server farms.[172] Server farms are typically located with the network switches and/or routers that enable communication between the different parts of the cluster and the users of the cluster. Server farms are increasingly being used instead of or in addition to mainframe computers by large enterprises, although server farms do not as yet reach the same reliability levels as mainframes. Because of the sheer number of computers in large server farms, the failure of individual machines is a common event, and the management of large server farms needs to take this into account, by providing support for redundancy, automatic failover, and rapid reconfiguration of the server cluster. The performance of the very largest server farms (thousands of processors and up) is typically limited by the performance of the data center's cooling systems and the total electricity cost rather than by the performance of the processors. A computer that runs twenty-four/seven consumes (over its lifetime) electricity worth many times its initial purchase cost. For this reason, the critical design parameter for both large and continuous systems tends to be performance per watt, rather than cost of peak performance.

Here's where we get to the heart of the matter. Clearly the energy requirements of the twentieth century were met through the use of petroleum. Much of this was consumed through the production and distribution of products and services. As discussed in the previous paragraph, the primary energy needs for the twenty-first century information society will be around electricity that will be required to support an advanced technological infrastructure of computers, networks, data centers, etc.

As described in chapter 3, American society is in transition from an industrial society to an information society. The completion of this transition and the type of infrastructure that will support it has its own unique demands. Currently, almost half of the electricity supply in the United States is produced using coal fired burners. Coal is abundant in the United States. The sectors that consume the most electricity are residential and commercial sectors. As the electricity demands continue to grow in the twenty-first century, we must find ways through established social policies to redirect energy and energy sources that will support such growth. That is to say, residential and commercial electricity needs must be met by some other energy source. Once that is accomplished, the current residential and commercial dependencies can be reduced and that energy can be redirected to support the substantial electricity needs of the infrastructure of the information society and knowledge-based economy.

At the same time, a comprehensive energy policy for the United States in the twenty-first century must take into account the increased demands for petroleum (oil) that are required in the manufacturing and transportation industries. While manufacturing may increasingly be transferred to other countries, the energy needs to produce the goods and services for consumption have not disappeared. We must also decrease our needs for petroleum. Such changes will not be easy, as they require considerable alterations to structures and organization of our society. These changes can only come from individual choices that are reflected in our style of living. Such changes are directly tied to a healthy U.S. economy and cannot be ignored. If not addressed, they will have dire consequences on our standard of living.

In the twenty-first century, the force that will propel America forward is the work of the individuals as the owners of the means of production in a knowledge-based economy. This force will require energy as individuals contribute to the efficient and effective forces of production of an information society and a knowledge-based economy. This work is mental, not physical, and it requires the tools and technologies that allow individuals to be productive as active participants in the production process. As long as individual Americans allow politics to stand in the way, we will never be able to regain the power we need for a healthy twenty-first century economy. The gravitational pull toward poverty will be too great, and the object called America will continue its downward spiral. As a result, our standard of living as a nation must decline.

THE U.S. ECONOMY IN THE TWENTY-FIRST CENTURY

In chapter 7, I focused more on economics and economic theory as it is related to philosophies, ideas, and social policies that are driven by the politics of such thinkers. That is to say, economists and economic theory do not make an economy. They simply have ideas about what it is that should make an economy healthy; they aren't always right, as we have seen at the end of the first decade of the twenty-first century. My focus here is to describe a healthy economy based on the macro level trends mentioned in chapter 1 and the 2E x 3E or 6E = Productivity as a function of work formula I described in the first section of this chapter.

There are a number of ways to measure economic activity of a nation. The one currently used by the United States is Gross Domestic Product or GDP. GDP is a basic measure of a country's overall economic output. It is the market value of all final goods and services made within the borders of a country in a year. It is often positively correlated with the standard of living. GDP per capita is not a measurement of the standard of living in an economy. However, it is often used as such an indicator, on the rationale that all citizens would benefit from their country's increased economic production. Similarly, GDP per capita is not a measure of personal income. GDP may increase while incomes for the majority of a country's citizens may even decrease or change disproportionately. For example, in the United States from 1990 to 2006 the earnings (adjusted for inflation) of individual workers, in private industry and services, increased by less than 0.5 largely per year while GDP (adjusted for inflation) increased about 3.6 largely per year over the same period. The major advantage of GDP per capita as an indicator of standard of living is that it is measured frequently, widely, and consistently. It is measured frequently in that most countries provide information on GDP on a quarterly basis, which allows a user to spot trends regularly.

The major disadvantage is that it is not, strictly speaking, a measure of standard of living. GDP is intended to be a measure of particular types of economic activity within a particular country. Nothing about the definition of GDP suggests it is necessarily a measure of standard of living. For instance, in an extreme example, a country which exported 100 percent of its production and imported nothing would still have a high GDP but a very poor standard of living. The argument in favor of using GDP is not that it is a good indicator of the standard of living, but that, all other things being equal, the standard of living tends to increase when GDP per capita increases. As such, GDP can be a proxy for the standard of living, rather than a direct measure.

Productivity is a measure of output from a production process, per unit of input. For example, labor productivity is typically measured as a ratio of output per labor hour, an input. Productivity may be conceived of as a metric of the technical or engineering efficiency of production. Production is a process of combining various material inputs (stuff) and immaterial inputs (plans, know-how) in order to make something for consumption (the output). The methods of combining the inputs of production in the process of making output are called technology. Technology can be depicted mathematically by the production function that describes the relation between input and output. The production function can be used as a measure of relative performance when comparing technologies. The production function is a simple description of the mechanism of economic growth. Economic growth is defined as any production increase of a business or nation. It is usually expressed as an annual growth percentage depicting growth of the company output (per entity) or the national product (per nation). Real economic growth (as opposed to inflation) consists of two components. These components are an increase in production input and an increase in productivity.

Politicians and economists judge America's economic health based on the GDP. Production within a country's borders, both domestically and foreign-owned enterprises, counts as part of its GDP. A similar measure Gross National Product (GNP) is almost the same, but GNP is products produced by enterprises owned by a country's citizens. Those produced by noncitizens are not counted. In 1991, the United States switched from using GNP to using GDP as its primary measure of production.

While this aggregate measure of a healthy economy may have been appropriate in the twentieth-century industrial society where the output of goods and services for consumption was the primary objective of the system of production, it no longer applies today. An economy consists of the specific economic system of a country or other area, the labor, capital, and land resources, and the economic agents that socially participate in the production, exchange, distribution, and consumption of goods and services of that area. A given economy is the end result of a process that involves its technological evolution, history, and social organization, as well as its geography, natural resource endowment, and ecology, as main factors. These factors give context, content, and set the conditions and parameters in which an economy functions. The first economist in the true meaning of the word was Adam Smith. He defined the elements of a national economy: products are offered at a natural price generated by the use of competition—supply and demand—and the division of labor. He maintained that the basic motive for free trade is human self-interest. The United States of America became the place where millions of expatriates from all European countries were searching for free economic evolvement. In Europe wild capitalism started to replace the system of mercantilism (today: protectionism) and led to economic growth. The period today is called Industrial Revolution because the system of production and division of labor enabled the mass production of goods. As I pointed out earlier, the production processes of the twenty-first century are decentralized, which means that the mass production of goods no longer takes place in a given country.

After the chaos of two World Wars and the devastating Great Depression, policymakers searched for new ways of controlling the course of the economy. The prevailing view was that held by John Maynard Keynes, who argued for a stronger control of the markets by the state.[173] The theory that the state can alleviate economic problems and instigate economic growth through state manipulation of aggregate demand is called *Keynesianism*. In the late 1950s the economic growth in America and Europe brought up a new form of mass consumption economy.

Labor productivity is the ratio of (the real value of) output to the input of labor. Labor productivity should be interpreted very carefully if measured by hours worked, rather than the number of employees. With an increase in part-time employment, hours worked provides the more accurate measure of efficiency. In particular, it reflects more than just the efficiency or productivity of workers. Labor productivity is the ratio of output to labor input, and output is influenced by many factors that are beyond the workers' influence, including the nature and amount of capital equipment that is available, the introduction of new technologies, and management practices. Productivity growth is a crucial source of growth in living standards. Productivity growth means more value is added in production, and this means more income is available to be distributed. In the most immediate sense, productivity is determined by: 1.) the available technology or know-how for converting resources into outputs desired in an economy, and 2.) the way in which resources are organized in firms and industries to produce goods and services.

This principle can be demonstrated by the following set of numbers. As demonstrated, the sum total output that would be possible from a system of production is shown. In a system of production, one person can only produce what one person can produce. It is possible that one person produced nothing. It is possible that input can be divided. It is also possible that input is additive or multiplicative in the cases where tools and technology is used by the person to increase productivity. Let's take the number four as an example. As shown below, in a production system where individuals are the owners of the means of production, they may choose to not be productive and their output would essentially be zero. It is also possible that the input of four people cancels out or divides the output such that the total net result of productivity is a value of one or 4/4. If the four people involved in the production system extend themselves through the use of technology, tools, etc., then their output can be additive and the output value of four people may be eight or 4 + 4. By the same logic, using technology and tools, individuals may be able to maximize their output. In this way, their maximum output is multiplicative and the maximum value produced is sixteen or 4 x 4. If we add the individual parts to get the total possible output from a system of production of four individuals, then we would have a total output value of twenty-five or 0 + 1 + 8 + 16. This total output value is not possible in a system of production where only four individuals are the owners of the means of production. However, as we see in the illustration of numbers below, if we add another person to the system of production and then maximize their productivity, then we can get the total maximum output of twenty-five or 5 x 5.

This simple list of numbers and basic mathematical operations demonstrate the challenge of developing a healthy economy in the twenty-first century. In a society where individuals are the owners of the means of production, the philosophical, social, political, and economic structures must allow for the maximization of output in the system of production. This currently does not exist. We must build effectiveness and efficiency into the system so individuals are measured based on their output or performance. Such a system would eliminate the need for time and space management, which has its own set of challenges, as time and space are also commodities in America that contain vested interests in maintaining the structures that protect those investments in those commodities.[174] National measures must focus on the intersection of national productivity and consumption as a means of health. If people are consuming but not producing, that is they are not productive, then we cannot achieve prosperity in America in the twenty-first century.

$1 - 1 = 0$ $4 - 4 = 0$ $7 - 7 = 0$

$1 / 1 = 1$ $4 / 4 = 1$ $7 / 7 = 1$

$1 + 1 = 2$ $4 + 4 = 8$ $7 + 7 = 14$

$1 \times 1 = 1$ $4 \times 4 = 16$ $7 \times 7 = 49$

Sum $= 4$ Sum $= 25$ Sum $= 64$

$2 - 2 = 0$ $5 - 5 = 0$ $8 - 8 = 0$

$2 / 2 = 1$ $5 / 5 = 1$ $8 / 8 = 1$

$2 + 2 = 4$ $5 + 5 = 10$ $8 + 8 = 16$

$2 \times 2 = 4$ $5 \times 5 = 25$ $8 \times 8 = 64$

Sum $= 9$ Sum $= 36$ Sum $= 81$

$3 - 3 = 0$ $6 - 6 = 0$ $9 - 9 = 0$

$3 / 3 = 1$ $6 / 6 = 1$ $9 / 9 = 1$

$3 + 3 = 6$ $6 + 6 = 12$ $9 + 9 = 18$

$3 \times 3 = 9$ $6 \times 6 = 36$ $9 \times 9 = 81$

Sum $= 16$ Sum $= 49$ Sum $= 100$

CHAPTER 11: THE FUTURE OF AMERICAN SOCIETY

Strategy without tactics is the slowest route to victory. Tactics without strategy is the noise before defeat.

Sun Tsu

A TWENTY-FIRST CENTURY STRATEGY

I wish I could say that careful analysis shows that America's future is bright. I cannot! America's future is undetermined. It's up to us, the people of this great nation, to make the changes that are required, so that many future generations of Americans can also have a bright tomorrow and enjoy the fruits of prosperity. This absolutely cannot and will not happen based on our current status. It appears that our leaders have no strategy. They certainly are busy executing something, but just like the quote from Sun Tzu, I believe these tactics are nothing but noise, and we are dangerously close to being defeated.

Think of the stress most Americans experience every year starting around January 1st and ending around April 15th. We all have to pay Uncle Sam, but he's not our uncle. Whose uncle is he, and most importantly, why do we have to pay him every year not a little but a lot?

Taxation has been around a very long time in America. If you study our history, this nation was forged in response to excessive taxation by England. The Boston Tea Party and the slogan No Taxation without Representation come to mind. How is it that their taxation warranted a revolution but the current levels of taxation do not? We are taxed heavily and often—not fairly and evenly. We pay taxes on income derived from our work, and we also pay taxes on everything that can be taxed—food, shelter, clothing, etc. Why is this necessary? Where does all that money go? Some is used to support welfare programs. Why does someone I've never even met need so much of my money? No American wants to pay taxes, so why are we forced to do so? As Americans, the Declaration of Independence declared our freedom, but our system of taxation does not provide freedom. If anything, it's a form of slavery.

Most Americans would agree that some level of taxation is necessary, but it is baffling that we pay so much in taxes, and yet the national debt continues to grow. A commonsense approach would be to collect one trillion dollars and to only spend one trillion dollars, but this never happens. Our government seems to know no bounds that require fiscal discipline. This national debt is real, isn't it? Our children can pay for it. They're young, and they have their whole lives to work. We need to only be concerned with today. This is the attitude of our elected officials in Washington and business leaders on Wall Street. Let's live for today and only think of ourselves.

Such a thought process makes a number of assumptions about economics and the future of America that are not based on anything more than wishful thinking.

CHAPTER 11: THE FUTURE OF AMERICAN SOCIETY

It's nice to dream about the American dream, but that ideal is no longer an option for most Americans based on our current situation. A little reality pill could go a long way toward curing what ails this country. What is this ailment?

The trends we're witnessing today aren't new. We've seen it before during the 1920s and the 30s, and again in the 50s and 60s, and again in the 80s and 90s, and again in the first and second decades of the twenty-first century. You would think that we'd get tired of the merry-go-round, but we seem destined to repeat it over and over. The trouble is that we are at a point where we can't afford to repeat it again. We're at a crossroads, and we need to move forward. We need a vision of the future for America in the twenty-first century. Without a vision, the people of this nation will perish.[175] We need leaders with a vision for the country that leads to a twenty-first-century prosperous nation where all can share in that prosperity. Based on the analyses provided throughout this book, the strategy map in figure 8 illustrates that vision.[176]

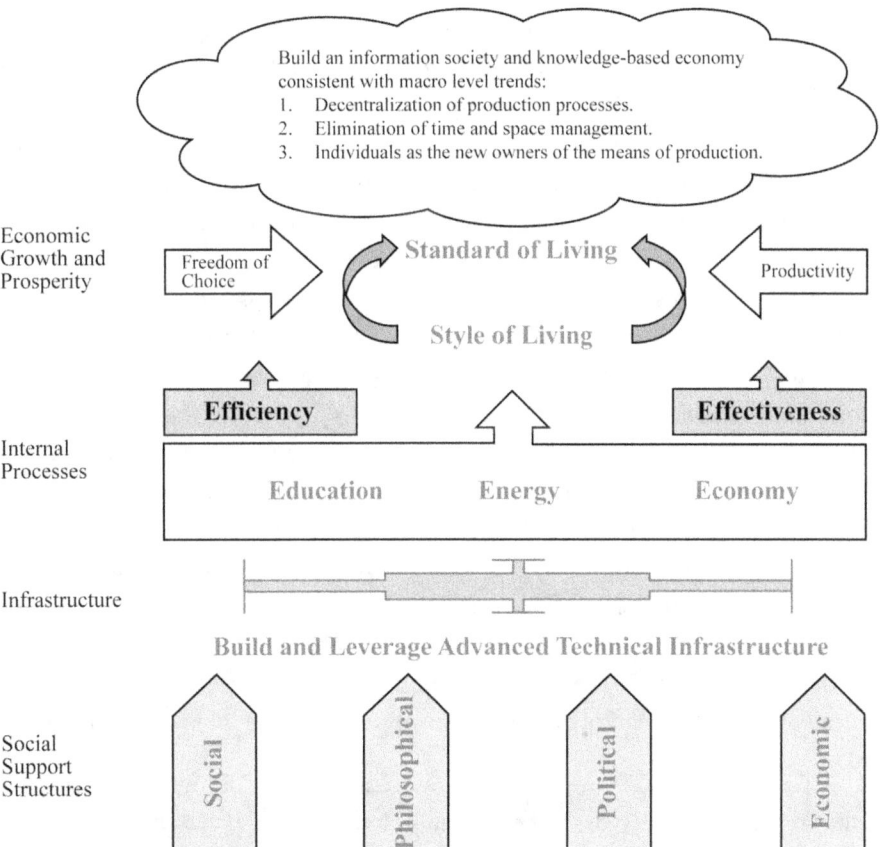

Figure 8: A Twenty-First Century Strategy Map for America

MEASURING PROGRESS OF TWENTY-FIRST CENTURY RECONSTRUCTION

It's not enough to simply establish a vision and a strategy map for America in the twenty-first century. We must measure our progress toward accomplishing the strategy, which means we must put into place a means of measuring the tactical execution of the strategy. As alluded to previously in chapter 2, the object we have created called American society and supported by the existing social, philosophical, political, and economic social structures cannot stop at this crossroads and simply exist within the time-space continuum in its current form. America must move forward. However, in its current form, the object is too heavy, and we lack the power to make the changes that will apply the force that is needed to propel it forward toward prosperity. Unfortunately, the gravitational forces will pull this object downward toward poverty, if we let it.

The changing social structure of the twenty-first century has already proven that we don't have to be in a specific physical location at a specific time. That is to say, when you can pick up your cell phone and call someone today on the other side of the world tomorrow, you know that the constraints of time and space no longer apply. We can leverage social networking to keep track of friends, family, and professional networks all over the world. These same three macro-level trends must be applied to and woven into the very social fabric of social life. That means that such things as urban centers are no longer necessary, if production processes are decentralized and individuals are now the owners of the means of production. It's no longer necessary to get into an automobile and commute into the cities for two plus hours a day. A community-based approach must be implemented that creates jobs, skills, and workforce development and education delivery utilizing this same approach. Social policies around such community-based social structures are necessary, and the types of measures to ensure that this happens would be the percentage of the workforce working from home; the percentage reduction in commute time to work; the percentage of income earned from Internet-based work activities; the percentage of workers engaged in knowledge-based jobs; and the percentage of high school graduates who remain in the local community workforce. Such measures would logically force a redesign of education to support this type of social structure.

A redesign of America's education system must be driven by a changing philosophical system. Work is no longer strictly a physical activity; it's a mental activity. As an information society with a knowledge-based economy, the education system must embrace this type of change by implementing methods of teaching and learning that are more rationalized and rely heavily on abstract thinking skills. Education programs must shift away from a posteriori knowledge transferred that is experiential to a priori knowledge that is transferred independent of experience. We must be able to know that something is true even if we can't rely on the five senses to prove it. All children must be taught to think abstractly and rationally with the ability to apply such knowledge in all aspects of life, especially work. That is to say, they must always be able to know that $2 + 2 = 4$ in every aspect of life and work. This type education model would be a dramatic paradigm shift, but it's absolutely essential for the twenty-first century style of living. Social policies must drive this type of transformational education paradigm shift. The types of measures that must be utilized are the percentage of students who are enrolled in virtual schools, the percentage of teachers engaged in virtual teaching, the percentage of students with electronic book devices, the percentage increase in electronic textbooks, the percentage of postsecondary programs designed for knowledge-based careers, and the percentage of students enrolled in knowledge-based career programs.

The changes in our political system are probably the most difficult. These changes must come from a number of constitutionally based pieces of legislations. The reason such reforms are so difficult is that we need to strip away the power of elected officials and return it into the hands of American citizens. Clearly, no politician from either party will vote for such legislation. The measures of success in changing our political structure must start with the election of at least one new constitutionally based party that represents the interests and voices of middle-class America. This party must be the majority party in control of the House, Senate, and the presidency by 2013. Legislation must be passed that provides citizens the ability to recall any elected official at anytime with a majority vote of all registered voters within that elected official's district. A second piece of legislation must be passed to set term limits of no more than eight years for both the Senate and the House. A third piece of legislation must restrict everyone to the use of public funds of no more than $100,000 per election—no more campaign contributions. The initial measure here is the number of these pieces of legislation that are put into law by 2014. Upon accomplishing this measure, other measures could be used such as the percentage of elected officials with voting scorecards available online, percentage of elected officials who can securely cast votes for legislation online, and percentage of voters who can cast ballots online by 2016.

Similarly, the changes in our economic structure must begin with social policies put into place by the new political party. The first piece of legislation would be the elimination of the current system of taxation that is based on income, and the adoption of a new system based on consumption. The second piece of legislation would require that all government entities have balanced budgets—no more borrowing from future generations. Excluding citizens with current entitlements in Social Security and Medicare, all citizens would receive a lifetime allotment of public funds assistance in the amount of $100,000. A fourth piece of legislation would be the creation of a new governing body that was responsible for the e-commerce regulation of the Internet. The fifth would be to change the role of the Federal Reserve from the lender of last resort to the guarantor of last resort with special, controlled powers to enforce and protect American citizens' economic interests in the virtual world of the Internet. The sixth would be the establishment of new economic policies that eliminated the use of GDP and instituted new measures of economic health based on Gross Domestic Productivity and Gross Domestic Consumption. The measure of success here would be the number of these new policies instituted by 2014.

These changes to the major social structures of American society would provide the foundational pillars that would support America in the twenty-first century. With these accomplished, then we could focus on the other objectives of the strategy map and start to execute those as well.

We must continue to build and leverage an advanced technical infrastructure that can support the mass of the American population in the twenty-first century. Although some of these are already measured, we must continue to do so to ensure that everyone has equal access to the technology. The type of measures that we need here are the percentage of American who have high-speed access to the Internet; the percentage of wireless access towers per square mile; the percentage of Americans who have wireless access; and the percentage of children with access to the Internet within their homes. With an increase in reliance on technology and an advanced technical infrastructure, we would have even greater needs for electricity. Our current internal processes around education, energy, and the economy cannot meet this need.

I've already talked about the need for a new education model that will support the social and philosophical structures around a community-based approach, so I won't repeat it here. The major thrust of social policies must be around energy for the twenty-first century. If we institute a community-based social and philosophical approach, we would also decrease the need for oil and gas because millions of people would no longer have to commute such distances to work. However, the technical infrastructure that would be required would increase the need for electricity. One major area of change that must be measure is the percentage of homes using solar power, and the percentage of businesses using solar power. Our goal should be to transform 100 million American home to run off of solar power by 2020. By doing this, we can transform every American family into energy producers and not just energy consumers. Such changes would have a dramatic direct impact on our economy, as it would allow us to move from a consumer only society to a producer society. The excess electric and oil and gas energy could be redirected to meet our needs around the technical infrastructure of a twenty-first century society.

These changes would have a dire effect on the organization of America society. It would be different. It would be a different style of living. However, with such changes, this new style of living would allow us to direct more power to the productivity of work activities that would then result in a drastic rise in everyone's standard of living. It is only through the increases freedom of choice brought about through social, philosophical, political, and economic systemic changes that we can achieve economic growth and prosperity for all in the twenty-first century. The final measure would be the percentage of American citizens living above absolute poverty line, and the percentage of Americans with incomes 100 percent above the absolute poverty line. Our objectives here are to increase both of these, of course.

FINAL THOUGHTS

The gravitational pull will be toward poverty seems very strong in America. We must through our own force of will chart a new course. If we don't make the changes and start to execute a new strategy, then just like the apple that falls from the tree, we will hit the ground very hard. It's unnecessary. We must stop politics as usual. We need the power to move forward quickly; this need seems to totally elude our current political and economic leaders, as well as many American citizens.

If the people who collectively represent the baby boom generation don't get out of the way and let my generation do what we need to do, then the next generation, their grandchildren, will hate them and curse their names because they'll be forced to become nothing more than serfs in a country set free by our forefathers and destined to beg for bread in the streets of despair and lack.

Poverty in America will freely reign. We must defeat this monster in order to revel in the glory of prosperity for the next generation and generations to come.

Speaking to my father to tell him it's time to retire isn't an easy thing. From his perspective, I'm still just a child. What do I know? I couldn't possible have any worthwhile ideas. Speaking on behalf of my generation, it's okay to turn over the reins of power. We're all grown up now, and you can trust us to do the right things. Let us take what we've learned and begin to build a new America that will usher in prosperity for future generations. It is a new day. We're not being disrespectful, but it's time. We need fresh, new ideas that can move America forward in the twenty-first century and sustain the country for many generations to come.

America the beautiful, land of the free, and the home of the brave—oh, how I love her. She is still the greatest nation on planet Earth. She is a shinning beacon of hope on a hillside. Let us not hide her light under a bucket. I live and breathe to restore her to her greatness. GOD BLESS AMERICA, please.

NOTES

(Endnotes)

1. A belief is a psychological state of mind in which an individual holds a premise or proposition to be true. A set of beliefs may be more appropriately defined as a philosophy or an ideology. Fundamental to the arguments I make in chapter 4, is the fact that beliefs can be either true or false.

2. I'm referring to the financial meltdown that began under the Bush administration in 2008 with many large banks going under, massive infusions of cash from the Treasury Department and the Federal Reserve, and culminated in a large bailout of Wall Street banks.

3. This is also known as the Year 2000 bug or simply Y2K. The problem stemmed from programming computers with two digit years instead of four digit years, that is, 99 instead of 1999. When the millennium changed to the twenty-first century, it was feared that major systems would break down and stop working correctly on January 1, 2000. This fueled major investments in fixing the problem and helped to create the dot-com bubble, which officially burst on March 10, 2000.

4. This excerpt is from George W. Bush's State of the Union Address delivered on January 29, 2002. It was over a year before the actual invasion of Iraq.

5. I must admit that I subscribe to the just war doctrine espoused by St. Thomas Aquinas and embraced by the Catholic Church. Wars are sometimes necessary, and this fact can't be ignored. However, I believe that they must be for defense only, and therefore the reasons for waging war on another country must completely justify military action. With the just war doctrine, the first criteria that has to be satisfied is that a country must establish the right to go to war. The evidence and reasoning used by the Bush Administration to justify the Iraq Invasion in 2003 don't satisfy this criterion.

vi. On January 26, 1998, the Neoconservatives sent a letter to President Bill Clinton urging him to invade Iraq and remove Saddam Hussein from power, thereby removing the threat of weapons of mass destruction. Some of the key people listed as signatories were John Bolton, Donald Rumsfeld, Paul

Wolfowitz, Richard Perle, Elliot Abrams, and Richard L. Armitage—all were key people in the Bush Administration.

7. The original Social Security Act was signed into law in 1935 by Franklin Delano Roosevelt as part of his New Deal. Poverty rate among senior citizens was around 50 percent at that time.

8. Medicare was added to the Social Security Act in 1965 by Lyndon B. Johnson as part of his Great Society program. It was during this time that Social Security was changed to withdraw funds from the independent trust fund and put it into the general fund for additional congressional revenue. As is true of all politicians, they just couldn't resist tapping into that big pot of money. The government uses extra Social Security funds just like any other tax revenue—they spend it. They justify this by issuing IOUs that will be paid in the future through the collection of taxes. What a scam! See John, 2004.

9. If the history of man on planet Earth is one that is defined by different stages of development, this time period must be the age of accountability. This includes the U.S. government and the politicians we elect to office.

10. The Great Depression is considered the great economic depression of the twentieth century. Generally, it started around 1929 with the stock market crash and ended around 1942 with America's entry into World War II. Unemployment in the United States rose to 25 percent during the Great Depression.

11. On Monday December 1, 2008, the National Bureau of Economic Research declared what everyone else knew—the United States was in a recession at the end of 2007. It took a year for the government to acknowledge what main street already knew. See "It's Official," MSNBC.com, 2008.

12. Parillo, Stimson, and Stimson, 1996, 5.

13. Microsoft Encarta Online Encyclopedia, 2008. This article on poverty was reviewed by Dr. Thomas J. Corbett, assistant professor, School of Social Work, and associate director, Institute for Research on Poverty, University of Wisconsin-Madison.

14. Ibid.

15. Unemployment in the United States is reported by the U.S. Bureau of Labor Statistics. As of October, 2009, the Bureau reported unemployment at 10.2 percent.

16. It certainly is not an exclusive characteristic of the Democrat Party to put large-scale social programs into place. However, most of the ones that seem to persist over time and push us toward socialism always come from this party.

17. I subscribe to the idea that money is a medium of exchange only. (See Marx, 1906).

18. It certainly would make no sense to make an unqualified statement that everyone must work. Children, the elderly, those ill, etc. may not be in a position to work. However, everyone that can work must work.

19. Natural law or the law of nature is a theory that posits the existence of a law whose content is set by nature and that therefore has validity everywhere. The phrase *natural law* is opposed to the positive law (which is manmade) of a given political community, society, or nation-state, and thus can function as a standard by which to criticize that law. Natural law theories have exercised a profound influence on the development of English common law, and have featured greatly in the philosophies of Thomas Aquinas, Thomas Hobbes, Hugo Grotius, and John Locke. Because of the intersection between natural law and natural rights, it has been cited as a component in United States Declaration of Independence and the Constitution of the United States. These are discussed in more detail in chapter 5.

20. This is based on the Pauli Exclusion Principle formulated by Wolfgang Pauli in 1925. It is one of the most important principles in physics because all particles that make up ordinary matter—electrons, protons, and neutrons—are subject to it. It is the characteristic property of matter to occupy space that makes it stable.

21. Immanuel Kant was an influential eighteenth-century philosopher whose ideas were used in the theory of knowledge. He believed that people use time and space to define human experience. He also thought that the principle of causality could not be applied outside of experience. This, for example, prevented metaphysics from answering such questions as whether the world always existed or if it had a cause. This prevents science from accumulating

knowledge, because all sciences are controlled by the laws of the mind. I will argue in chapter 4 that this is incorrect if we consider math a science.

22. For the purpose of this book, *social change* is defined as the change in a social structure including the nature, the social institutions, the social behavior, or the social relations of a society. *Social structure* is a common use term in sociology to describe a political, social, economic, or philosophical system. It was first used by Alex de Tocqueville in *Democracy in America*, and then by many social thinkers such as Karl Max, Herbert Spencer, Max Weber, Ferdinand Tonnies, and Emile Durkheim.

23. I will discuss in more detail in chapter 3 how this principle applies to American society during a time of transition. That is to say, we can use the transition of American society during the 20s and 30s as a baseline of reference to know the future state of America based on our current state in the transition from an industrial society to an information society.

24. It's very important to understand this philosophical concept of determinism, because it goes directly to understanding beliefs and America's belief systems in terms of philosophy. As discussed in chapter 4, our philosophical system is built around two main concepts—determinism and free will.

25. I am arguing that since American society is a deterministic, dynamic system that we can know the current and future state of the system if we can determine its initial condition.

26. A thermodynamic system is one major example.

27. Gleick, 1988.

28. Lorenz, 1996.

29. Caplow, 1991.

30. Caplow, 1991, 11.

31. Caplow maintains that Emile Durkheim provides the most sophisticated account of this type of transition in "The Division of Labor in Society" (See page 12).

32. Leading and lagging indicator as used to measure performance based on Norton and Kaplan's Balanced Scorecard. I suggest here that this type of

idea will become more important in achieving higher levels of productivity in human organizations and human work efforts, as we begin to more fully understand what it means for individuals to be the new owners of the means of production in the twenty-first century.

33. As I will discuss more thoroughly in chapter 3, America has seen these types of technological advances with the advent of computing technologies and the Internet. It is this technology that makes the three macro-level trends possible as I have outlined them in chapter 1 on page 24. With these types of technologies, we have new choices to make. These choices translate into a style of living that defines an information society and a knowledge-based economy. As I will demonstrate in chapter 7, this style of living is the only way we can maintain our standard of living in the United States.

34. See both Volti, 1992, 21-22 and Atkinson, 2004, 180. Both authors use the case of the Luddites to make their points of resistance to change; especially when that change threatens jobs.

35. For illustration purposes, I assume fifty weeks of work per year with two weeks off for vacation time.

36. It would be great to put a date on just when the shovel was first invented. The truth is that no one really knows. How magnificent it must have been to stop digging with your hands and to start digging with a shovel. Simple by today's standards of technological wonders, at one time is was a monumental breakthrough.

37. The Space Shuttle is part of the Space Transportation Program operated by NASA. The first operational flights were in 1982.

38. To bring about a different and better understanding of social change, I use chaos theory in this chapter and apply it to the human system we call American society.

39. See description in chapter 3 where I describe the transition from an agricultural society to an industrial society and then from and industrial society to an information society.

40. Henry Ford and the Ford Motor Company is credited with creating the first assembly line in manufacturing between 1908 and 1915, which resulted in

the mass production of the Ford Model T at an affordable price for the average American.

41. Belief systems are more fully discussed in chapter 4.

42. Schumpeter, 1976.

43. Schumpeter, 1976, 82.

44. Schumpeter, 1976, 83.

45. I first saw this quote in Atkinson, 2004. It was written by Nicoli Machiavelli in 1515 in *The Prince*.

46. As I argue in chapters 4-6, freedom of choice is fundamental to the unalienable rights guaranteed by the Declaration of Independence and the U.S. Constitution. When these rights are restricted, it threatens the very liberty that defines Americans as free citizens. In our current political situation, those in power use their power to force their will on the rest of the people, thereby restricting our freedom of choice. This is not, and never has been, the classical liberalism envisioned by the founding fathers when they constructed the U.S. Constitution.

47. The division of labor was perfected during industrialization because it was there that the complexity of the work effort required a greater degree of specialization to accomplish the goal, work product, or final output of the system.

48. This is the first indicator that new technology and new ways of doing things had been applied to the old system of production—in this case, it was the basis of agricultural society as a means of subsistence for a vast majority of Americans. Once the nature of work changed and few people were needed, other forms of work had to be devised such as in the case of industrialization. This transition was slow, occurring over many years.

49. Bell, 1999.

50. For example, we couldn't be where we are today without the first mainframe computer invented by IBM in 1955. The pc revolution began in 1981, the Microsoft windows operating system was introduced in 1990, and ARAPANET became operational in 1983. The Internet became publicly avail-

able around 1993 with the creation of a browser called Mosaic; cell phones widely introduced in the early 1990s.

51. See chapter 10 where I discuss education as one of the major areas of concern to be addressed by our government and new social policies to build a new education system.

52. See U.S. Department of Commerce, 1999 and U.S. Department of Commerce, 2002.

53. Max Weber's theory of lifestyle or style of living is fundamental to the execution of a twenty-first century strategy that will lead the nation toward prosperity.

54. If such theoretical propositions are true, it is impossible to ignore the relationship of style of living to poverty and standard of living.

55. See discussion in chapter 4 around beliefs and belief systems as they are related to philosophical systems.

56. In the Bible, Jesus spoke of the parable of sower and the seeds. Matthew 13:3-9 (KJV) reads:

And he spake many things unto them in parables, saying, Behold, a sower went forth to sow; And when he sowed, some seeds fell by the way side, and the fowls came and devoured them up: Some fell upon stony places, where they had not much earth: and forthwith they sprung up, because they had no deepness of earth: And when the sun was up, they were scorched; and because they had no root, they withered away. And some fell among thorns; and the thorns sprung up, and choked them: But other fell into good ground, and brought forth fruit, some a hundredfold, some sixtyfold, some thirtyfold.

57. See note 21 on Immanuel Kant. As I state there, humans use time and space to define reality.

58. I subscribe to the creation story that is a part of Judeo-Christian belief system. I know that there is a God who created everything. I think that evolution is certainly a valid observation of science as made by Charles Darwin— it describes change, and living organisms do change. This whole book is

about the evolution of American society, after all. I just can't subscribe to the notion that man evolved from apes.

59. See Adler, 1978; Adler writes in his book on Aristotle (384–322 B.C.) that no idea he presents is less than 2,400 years old. I specifically single out Aristotle in this chapter because so many of the ideas that are America and American society are a result of the influence of Aristotle and his writing on other people.

60. The Bible in its current form didn't take place all at once. The canonization of the Bible took place during the third and fourth centuries AD. This would've been 700 to 800 years after Aristotle lived.

61. Saint Thomas Aquinas was an Italian priest in the Roman Catholic Church who lived in the thirteenth century. He was a philosopher and theologian whose influence can be seen in the areas of Western ethics, natural law, and political theory. He acted as a modifier and a vehicle of Aristotelian philosophy with the thought of Augustine in his most important work Summa Theologica.

62. Adler, 1978, 187.

63. It is here that we must tackle some of the most difficult questions because this is where Greek philosophy meets theology and the questions of God as a creator and man as his creation. Such questions are fundamental to this chapter and this book because the human condition and issues of poverty and prosperity are directly tied to work and systems of production. Work as a means of subsistence from this perspective is a curse God put on humans when he kicked Adam and Eve out of the Garden of Eden for disobeying him. If true, everyone must work.

64. See Descartes, *Meditations on First Philosophy*. He was a French philosopher, mathematician, and physicist (1596–1650). During his life he had a profound influence on philosophy and mathematics as the creator of the Cartesian coordinate system and the father of analytical geometry.

65. The mind-body dichotomy is the view that *mental* phenomena are, in some respects, *nonphysical* (distinct from the body). In a religious sense, it refers to the separation of body and soul.

66. In chapter 3 of Exodus in response to Moses inquiry, God describes himself as "I am."

67. I take the position that God never endowed human beings with free will as described by Greek philosophy where a human being can act and do without restraint according to his innate will. I argue that God did not give Adam and Eve free will; he gave them freedom of choice. While a fine distinction, perhaps, it nonetheless is distinctly different. The freedom of choice view presumes that actions, that is the choices we make, have consequences. Free will to be truly free would not have consequences associated with actions.

68. The point I wish to make here is that I am not trying to present and argue points of theology per se. However, theology is a major contributor to the American belief system, and therefore issues such as God and whether he exists can't be ignored when addressing the need to change our philosophical system.

69. Almost all the signers of the Declaration of Independence were professing Christians.

70. Weberin *The Protestant Ethic and the Spirit of Capitalism*.

71. I argue that a human being is different from every other living thing because we are not animals. We are beings. To be a human being is a state of being that is expressed through Rene Descartes' law of "I think, therefore I am." This state of being is what gives us the creative ability to transform ideas into real things or objects. We create.

72. Division of labor or economic specialization is the specialization of cooperative labor in specific, circumscribed tasks and roles, intended to increase the productivity of labor. Historically the growth of a more and more complex division of labor is closely associated with the growth of total output and trade, the rise of capitalism, and of the complexity of industrialization processes.

73. As I discuss in chapter 6 on government and political parties, the best way for America to move forward is through a third political party. It would be a good strategy for that party to represent the middle class interests, which could be articulated in language that serves the Independents and significant proportions of both the Democrat and Republican parties. The Democrats and Republicans now focus their political strategies by dividing the voting populace down an imaginary line called the center. The center right is considered Republican. The center left is considered Democrat.

This line moves generally based on particular issues at the time of elections, especially economics. I contend that a party representing the broad middle class would be successful in helping the country to move forward, instead of left or right as the two current parties would prefer.

74. See Adler, 1978, 167.

75. See Mills, 2000, 350. Here he describes that Washington relaxed with the Voltaire's 'letters' and Locke's "On Human Understanding." He wasn't the only one reading the popular ideas of the day. Thomas Jefferson, the drafter of the Declaration also read and was influenced by these ideas, especially those of John Locke. Mills writes that "in the higher political, economic, and military circles, the briefing and the memorandum seem to have pretty well replaced not only the serious book, but the newspaper as well."

76. Independence Hall Association, 2010.

77. See Habermas, Theory and Practice, 1973, 88.

78. Locke, 2007, section 6.

79. The State of Nature of man is governed by the Laws of Nature established by their Creator.

80. At the close of the Constitutional Convention, Benjamin Franklin was asked by an anxious bystander, what form of government had been formed. He responded, "A republic if you can keep it."

81. See chapter 6 for a discussion of how political parties use public opinion to push political agendas.

82. I use the terms Creator and God interchangeably.

83. See chapter 6, where I discuss the history of political parties in the United States.

84. Originally, political economy meant the study of the conditions under which production and consumption within limited parameters was organized in the nation-states. It involved the examination of an economy that was made possible by political structures generally supported by established legal means through social policies.

85. See Mills, 2000, 338.

86. *The Prince* is a political treatise written by Niccolo Machiavelli in 1513.

87. See Hayek F.A., *The Road to Serfdom*.

88. See Habermas, *Theory and Practice*, 1973, 77-78.

89. Atkinson, 2004, 203.

90. The dangers of centralized planning by government are explained well by Fredrick A. Hayek in his book *The Road to Serfdom*. There's little more I can say to do justice to this great work.

91. The basic idea I used here comes from the Cato Institute Web site in the About Cato section of the site. It was accessed on 04/10/2009.

92. Ibid.

93. It's impossible to know the exact debt level by 2020. It really depends on how much is spent beyond tax revenues collected. In the twenty-first century, America's debt has grown from about four trillion in 2000, when George W. Bush took office to about twelve trillion currently. Congress just increased the debt level again to over fourteen trillion. With entitlements that are due to baby boomers over the next decade, thirty-five to fifty trillion isn't an unrealistic expectation.

94. I'm simply referring to the Troubled Asset and Relief Program (TARP) funds allocated in 2008 through the Emergency Economic Stabilization Act of 2008.

95. Changed attitudes in reaction to the Great Depression were instrumental in the move to the welfare state in many countries, a harbinger of new times where cradle-to-grave services became a reality after the poverty of the depression. During the Great Depression, it was seen as an alternative middle way between communism and capitalism. The party responsible for such social programs is the Democrat Party. As baby boomers retire over the next decade, they will expect to receive the entitlements based on the fact that they will have paid into this system their entire adult working lives. The money to pay them these entitlements in the form of Social Security and Medicare doesn't exist, and it can't exist based on the current system.

96. "I believe that banking institutions are more dangerous to our liberties than standing armies. If the American people ever allow private banks to control

the issue of their money, first by inflation and then by deflation, the banks and corporations that will grow up around them, will deprive the people of their property until their children will wake up homeless on the continent their fathers conquered. The issuing power should be taken from the banks and restored to the people, to whom it properly belongs." Thomas Jefferson in a 1802 letter to Albert Gallatin, the secretary of the treasury.

97. See Hobbes, 1985. A leviathan is a sea monster. Thomas Hobbes titled his book after the creature in describing the structure of society and legitimate government; the book is regarded as one of the earliest and most influential examples of social contract theory.

98. See Heilbroner, *The Wordly Philosophers: The Lives, Times, and Ideas of the Great Economic Thinkers*, 1999, 14.

99. Ibid., 38.

100. Smith, 2003.

101. Ricardo, 2004.

102. David Ricardo lived from 1772 until 1823. His influential work *Principles of Political Economy and Taxation* was published in 1817. Karl Marx lived from 1818 until 1883, and his influential work *Capital: A Critique of Political Economy* wasn't published until 1867. I use this to illustrate here how ideas are transmitted from one generation to the next, from one person to another.

103. See Heilbroner, T*he Wordly Philosophers: The Lives, Times, and Ideas of the Great Economic Thinkers*, 166.

104. Socialism refers to the various theories of economic organization advocating common or direct worker ownership and administration of the means of production and allocation of resources, and a society characterized by equal access to resources for all individuals with a method of compensation based on the amount of labor expended. Most socialists share the view that capitalism unfairly concentrates power and wealth among a small segment of society that controls capital and derives its wealth through exploitation, creates an unequal society, does not provide equal opportunities for everyone to maximize their potential, and does not utilize technology and resources to their maximum potential nor in the interests of the public.

NOTES

105. See chapter 6, 124-125.

106. See Heilbroner, *The Wordly Philosophers: The Lives, Times, and Ideas of the Great Economic Thinkers*, 1999, 248-249.

107. See Keynes, 1997. John Maynard Keynes is the father of Keynesian economics, which argues that private sector decisions sometimes lead to inefficient macroeconomic outcomes and therefore advocates active policy responses by the public sector, including monetary policy actions by the central bank and fiscal policy actions by the government to stabilize output over the business cycle.

108. Macroeconomics is a branch of economics that deals with the performance, structure, and behavior of the economy of the entire community, a nation, a region, or the entire world.

109. Microeconomics is a branch of economics that studies how households and firms make decisions to allocate limited resources, typically in markets where goods or services are being bought and sold. Microeconomics examines how these decisions and behaviors affect the supply and demand for goods and services, which determines prices, and how prices, in turn, determine the supply and demand of goods and services

110. Socialism is the economic system. Communism is the political system.

111. The Austrian school is a school of economic thought that emphasizes the spontaneous organizing power of the price mechanism or price system. Austrians hold that the complexity of human behavior makes mathematical modeling of the evolving market extremely difficult and advocate a *laissez faire* approach to the economy. Austrian school economists advocate the strict enforcement of voluntary contractual agreements between economic agents, and hold that commercial transactions should be subject to the smallest possible imposition of forces they consider to be coercive (in particular the smallest possible amount of government intervention).

112. Friedrich August von Hayek (8 May 1899–23 March 1992), was an Austrian-born economist and philosopher known for his defense of classical liberalism and free-market capitalism against socialist and collectivist thought.

113. See Heilbroner, *The Wordly Philosophers: The Lives, Times, and Ideas of the Great Economic Thinkers*, 1999, 291-292.

114. I didn't think I could do this description of Dr. Schumpeter's work justice, so I greatly relied on Heilbroner's *The Wordly Philosophers: The Lives, Times, and Ideas of the Great Economic Thinkers*, See 293-295.

115. See Mills, 2000, 346.

116. See the McKinley Tariff and the Dingley Tariff as examples.

117. Weber, 2006.

118. Krugman, 2009.

119. Supply and demand is an economic model of price determination. In a competitive market, price will function to equalize the quantity demanded by consumers, and the quantity supplied by producers, resulting in an economic equilibrium of price and quantity.

120. The factors of production are productive inputs that are resources used to produce goods and services. They facilitate production; however, they don't become part of the product. Earlier economists of the nineteenth century thought of factors of production as land or other natural resources that came from nature, human labor, and capital goods such as tools and equipment. More recent theories have also added entrepreneurship and human capital.

121. Many people equate the profit motive as simply a politically correct way of say that business owners are greedy. Certainly greed may be a factor, but to a pragmatic business owner the purpose behind the business is to make money. Without it, you don't stay in business for very long. When businesses close, jobs are lost.

122. Alan Greenspan was listed by *Time* magazine as number three on a list twenty-five top people to blame for the financial crisis of 2008. See *Time*, Inc., 2010.

123. See CBS News, 2009.

124. See Heilbroner, *The Wordly Philosophers: The Lives, Times, and Ideas of the Great Economic Thinkers*, 1999. This is where I originally saw this quoted.

125. The government spending as a part of the stimulus plan put into place by President Obama and the Democrats in 2009 is a classic example of Keynesian economics.

126. I'm referring to the infrastructure projects created by FDR during the 1930s, the interstate highway system for example. This type of infrastructure made the mass production and mass consumption society of the 40s, 50s, and beyond of the baby boomer generation possible.

127. See Keynes, 1997, 89-91 where he defines the propensity to consume as a functional relationship between consumption and level of income in relation to the intersection of aggregate demand and aggregate supply resulting in the volume of employment within a community.

128. The gold standard is a monetary system in which the standard economic unit of account is a fixed weight of gold. After the Second World War, a system similar to a gold standard was established by the Bretton Woods Agreements. Under this system, many countries fixed their exchange rates relative to the U.S. dollar. The United States promised to fix the price of gold at $35 per ounce. Implicitly, then, all currencies pegged to the dollar also had a fixed value in terms of gold. Under the regime of the French president Charles de Gaulle up to 1970, France reduced its dollar reserves, trading them for gold from the U.S. government, thereby reducing U.S. economic influence abroad. This, along with the fiscal strain of federal expenditures for the Vietnam War, led President Richard Nixon to end the direct convertibility of the dollar to gold in 1971, resulting in the system's breakdown, commonly known as the *Nixon Shock*.

129. Admittedly this is not my own thought. I have borrowed it but can't find its original author. I first read it in Heilbroner, *The Wordly Philosophers: The Lives, Times, and Ideas of the Great Economic Thinkers*, 1999.

130. I discuss this new model of education in more detail in chapter 10. Suffice it to say here, that the current model doesn't work. The number of high school dropouts and the unemployment rate demonstrate the how and why it doesn't work in the information society and knowledge-based economy.

131. I can't remember the exact details of the study. What was striking however was the proportion of ten-year-olds who didn't have the basic skills for a twenty-first-century society.

132. These numbers are proven out by the dropout rate every year. More details are presented in the next section.

133. These are the retirees known as the baby boomers. At somewhere around eighty million, this represents about one-third of the American population. As I argue in a latter section, they may be in retirement, but in an economic system of production, they are essentially unemployed and unproductive.

134. As I have alluded to in chapter 2, poverty level is important, because it directly influences the standard of living in the United States.

135. See Bridgeland, Dilulio, and Morison, 2006, 1.

136. The percentage reported in the report was 47 percent. Almost half of the people who dropped out reported that the classes were not interesting. In short, the students weren't being challenged.

137. See Alliance for Education, 2009, 1.

138. This is one of many costs reported in Alliance for Education, 2009. See complete report for other reasons. The point to be made here is that education does have an economic impact.

139. Austrian economist such as Frederick A. Hayek argues that unemployment stems from government intervention in the economy and the more the government intervenes the worse it gets.

140. It is important to understand that Keynesian economics and this type of thinking about unemployment is what many monetary and fiscal policies were based on during the 1930s under FDR and during the Great Depression. Social policies of that time period followed these ideas about the economy and the role of government in the economy. With this recession and the election of President Barack Obama in 2008, there has been a revival of interest in Keynesian economics. To address the current economic crisis, it appears that the play books from the 1930s that included President Roosevelt's policies as well as Keynes economic theories have been reinstated. I argue this is the wrong approach for 2010. It's a different time. See remaining 3 chapters of the book for more details.

141. See America in 2010—enough said.

142. See chapter 10 in the section on the economy of the twenty-first century where I discuss the effects of GDP based on the current macro level trends identified in chapter 1.

143. See www.heritage.org for this and many other useful analyses on how the retirement of baby boomers will impact the American economy in this next decade.

144. Andre Gunder Frank has argued that globalization existed in the third millennium B.C. between Sumer and Indus Valley Civilization. Another example in during the Hellenistic Age when commercialized urban centers were focused on Greek culture influenced a wide range that stretched from India to Spain with such cities as Alexandria and Athens. Other examples can be found between the Roman Empire and other empires of that period, during the Islamic Golden Age, the Mongol Empire, The Age of Discovery that included the discovery of the Americas in 1492, and the nineteenth century imperialism where industrialization began to reach its heights of production and allowed the creation of cheap products that were readily available to masses of populations who demanded such commodities.

145. The Bretton Woods conference led to the creation of a system of monetary management established the rules for commercial and financial relations among the world's major industrial states in the mid–twentieth century. The Bretton Woods system was the first example of a fully negotiated monetary order intended to govern monetary relations among independent nation-states. Preparing to rebuild the international economic system as World War II was still raging, 730 delegates from all forty-four Allied nations gathered at the Mount Washington Hotel in Bretton Woods, New Hampshire, United States, for the United Nations Monetary and Financial Conference. The delegates deliberated on and signed the Bretton Woods Agreements during the first three weeks of July 1944. Setting up a system of rules, institutions, and procedures to regulate the international monetary system, the planners at Bretton Woods established the International Monetary Fund (IMF) and the International Bank for Reconstruction and Development (IBRD), which today is part of the World Bank Group. These organizations became operational in 1945 after a sufficient number of countries had ratified the agreement. The chief features of the Bretton Woods system were an obligation for each country to adopt a monetary policy that maintained the exchange rate of its currency within a fixed value—plus or minus one percent—in terms of gold and the ability of the IMF to bridge temporary imbalances of payments. Then, on August 15, 1971 the United States unilaterally terminated convertibility of the dollar to gold. This action created the situation whereby the United States dollar became the sole backing of currencies and a reserve

currency for the member states. In the face of increasing financial strain, the system collapsed in 1971.

146. It is important to recognize that in the early formulation of these institutions that the ideas of John Maynard Keynes played a role in their development. This is the same man who created Keynesian economics, the basic underlying theories that supported these institutions and their development. Although they have changed somewhat over the last almost 100 years, they still persist today. Most people think of these institutions as representing globalization.

147. See Friedman T. L., 2007, 9-10.

148. See chapter 4 and also Descartes,:1993.

149. Falling back to the playbooks of the 1930s, President Obama and the Democrats pushed through a one trillion dollar stimulus bill in 2009. Unfortunately, the primary focus of this investment in America was on what he called "shovel-ready projects." The twenty-first century is the same time or place, and what we need as a country is a renewed effort to develop the infrastructure of computers and communications networks, such as wireless access to the Internet from anywhere within the United States. This should be free. Education should include free course on how to use the Internet to find jobs. Computers should be passed out to every child enrolled in public education. This is a stimulus for America in the twenty-first century.

150. See Friedman T. L., 2007, 580-588 for a complete description of this process.

151. Although the exact amount of total dollar cost of theft over the Internet using identity theft and other scams, it has been estimated to be well over $100 billion.

152. See chapter 8 in section where I talk about the entitlements due to baby boomers over the next decade as they enter into retirement and are dependent on social security and Medicare.

153. The Lisbon Strategy was an action and development plan for the European Union (EU) between 2000 and 2010. Its aim was to make the EU "the most dynamic and competitive knowledge-based economy in the world capable of sustainable economic growth with more and better jobs and greater social

cohesion, and respect for the environment by 2010." The Lisbon Strategy is intended to deal with the low productivity and stagnation of economic growth in the European Union, through the formulation of various policy initiatives to be taken by all EU member states. It was set out by the European Council in Lisbon in March 2000 and by 2010 most of its goals were not achieved. This should be viewed as a temporary setback, in my opinion.

154. See White, 2009 from the Associated Press dated March 25, 2009, where "the head of the European Union slammed President Barack Obama's plan to spend nearly $2 trillion to push U.S. economy out of recession as 'the road to hell'" that EU governments must avoid.

155. See Karrar-Lewsley and Said, 2009, in the *Wall Street Journal* report that indicated that OPEC was denying that they were in secret talks to replace U.S. dollar with a basket of currencies to price oil.

156. See chapter 8 in the section on the Welfare State.

157. See Hobbes, 1985. I use the reference here to simply illustrate that an out-of-control government that depends on taxation of income, which comes from work, will eventually find itself without the means to sustain itself. This seems like the logical conclusion based on the current path we are on in the United States.

158. This is a quotation by John Emerich Edward Dalberg Acton, first Baron Acton (1834–1902). The historian and moralist, known simply as Lord Acton, expressed this opinion in a letter to Bishop Mandell Creighton in 1887: "Power tends to corrupt, and absolute power corrupts absolutely. Great men are almost always bad men."

159. See Starr, 2007. I would point out that Dr. Starr uses the term *liberalism*, and as a result most would equate this to mean socialism, however, liberalism is not socialism. It is only through liberalism that we can truly come to realize what it means to have freedom in the United States. Liberalism is freedom of choice, and it is this freedom of choice that guarantees liberty. Our power as individuals comes when we have complete freedom of choice.

160. Heads of the G20 at their recent London summit pledged to abstain from imposing any trade protectionist measures. Although they were reiterating what they had already committed to, last November in Washington, seventeen of these twenty countries were reported by the World Bank as having

imposed trade restrictive measures since then. In its report, the World Bank says most of the world's major economies are resorting to protectionist measures as the global economic slowdown begins to bite. There is a growing fear that protectionism will slowly sneak in and grow in the wake of the crisis.

161. America's education system needs a total transformation in order to prepare students for work in the twenty-first century. The institution is stuck in the twentieth-century way of delivering education, and this just doesn't work. As I noted in chapter 8, students are bored. Teachers are still trying to teach using traditional methods that just don't apply to a twenty-first century style of living.

162. See Bell, 1999 and Griffin, 2009.

163. See Kirsch, Braun, Yamamota, and Sum, 2007.

164. See Partnership for Twenty-First Century Skills, 2007.

165. Ibid. They provide an excellent framework for a new education model that fits with twenty-first century education model.

166. The digitization of facts that involve the people, places, and processes involved in education can only provide the needed information to for the effective delivery of educational services by leveraging high quality data.

167. The second law of thermodynamics is an expression of the universal principle of entropy, stating that the entropy of an isolated system which is not in equilibrium will tend to increase over time.

168. I am not trying to provide readers with a course in physics here. I doubt that I could do an adequate job on this subject. I am simply trying to illustrate that American society is a system, and as such it must comply with the same universal laws that all systems must comply with—human creations cannot violate these laws. If we wish to understand the *Inert America* condition, and more importantly how to change it, then we must realize how these concepts apply to American society, at least on a basic level of understanding.

169. This is referring to the invention of the Ford Model T, which was produced from 1908 until 1927, but this age of invention of transportation also in-

cluded the airplane. Orville and Wilbur Wright conducted their first successful flight in 1903.

170.   See the article CBS News, 2009. The $115 is high, but the price of oil has been as high as $150 dollars a barrel. In the report conducted by *60 Minutes* on January 11, 2009, entitled "Did Speculation Fuel Oil Price Swings?" a detailed analysis is provided of how and why the price per barrel rose so high in such a short time frame. The result was average gas prices in America of around $4.00 dollars a gallon. Such a drastic rise in gasoline forces everything else to rise — housing prices, food prices, etc. This makes it increasingly difficult for the average American to meet needs of food, shelter, and clothing.

171.   The Strategic Petroleum Reserve (SPR) is an emergency fuel store of oil maintained by the United States Department of Energy. The U.S. SPR is the largest emergency supply in the world with the current capacity to hold up to 727 million barrels.

172.   A server farm or server cluster, also called a data center, is a collection of computer servers usually maintained by an enterprise to accomplish server needs far beyond the capability of one machine.

173.   See Keynes, 1997 and my discussion in chapter 7.

174.   See Logon and Molotch, 1987 for an excellent description of time and place as a commodity. They focus this on urban places, which in my mind are all but eliminated based on the three macro level trends I identify in chapter 1.

175.   See Proverbs 29:18.

176.   See Norton and Kaplan's work on the Balanced Scorecard to understand the necessity of and role of a strategy map.

BIBLIOGRAPHY

Able, Thomas. "Measuring Health Lifestyles in a Comparative Analysis: Theoretical Issues and Empriical Findings." *Social Science and Medicine*, 1991: 899-908.

Adler, Mortimer J. *Aristotle for Everybody: Difficult Thought Made Easy.* New York: Macmillan Publishing Co., Inc., 1978.

Afifi, A.A., and Virginia Clark. *Computer-Aided Multivariate Analysis.* New York: Van Nostrand Reinhold Company, 1990.

Alamaki, Ari. *Technological Reasoning as a Human Side of Technological Innovation.* University of Turku, 2001.

Alcorn, Paul A. *Social Issues in Technology: A Format for Investigation.* Upper Saddle River Prentice Hall, 1997.

Aldrich, John H., and Forrest D. Nelson. *Linear Probability, Logit and Probit Models.* Beverly Hills: Sage Publications, 1984.

Alien, Mike. "Obama to impose tough bailout rules." *Yahoo! News.* January 27, 2009. http://news.yahoo.com (accessed April 7, 2009).

Alliance for Education. *High School Dropouts in America.* Washington, D.C.: Alliance for Education, 2009.

Archer, Margaret S. "Theory, Culture and Post-Industrial Society." *Theory, Culture, and Society*, 7 1990: 97-119.

Arthur, Brian W. "Is the Information Revolution Dead." *Business 2.0*, March 2002: 65-72.

Associated Press. "Financial Meltdown Summit Featured Lavis Dinner Menu, $300 Bottles of Wine." *FoxNews.com.* November 15, 2008. http://www.foxnews.com (accessed April 6, 2009).

Atkinson, Robert D. *The Past and Future of America's Economy: Long Waves of Innovation that Power Cycles of Growth.* Cheltenham and Northhampton: Edward Elgar Publishing Limited, 2004.

Augstums, Ieva M., and Jeannie Aversa. "Fed 'extremely uncomfortable' about bailouts." *Yahoo! News.* April 3, 2009. http://news.yahoo.com (accessed April 6, 2009).

Aversa, Jeanine. "Economy moving in reverse faster than predicted." *Yahoo! Finance.* February 27, 2009. http://finance.yahoo.com (accessed April 7, 2009).

Aversa, Jeannine. "Economy's new plunge is worst in quarter-century." *Yahoo! Finance.* January 30, 2009. http://finance.yahoo.com (accessed April 7, 2009).

Baer, Doug, Edward Grabb, and William A. Johnston. "The Values of Canadians and Americans: A Critical Analysis and Reassessment." *Social Forces*, 1990: 693-713.

Bartos, Otomar. "Postmodernism, Postindustrialism, and the Future." *The Sociological Quarterly*, 1996: 307-325.

Baudrillard, Jean. *SelectedWritings.* Stanford: Stanford University Press, 1988.

Bauman, Zygmunt. *Imitations of Postmodernity.* London: Sage Publications, 1992.

Beck, Anatole. "The Knowledge Business." *Social Policy*, 2000: 42-49.

Bell, Daniel. *The Coming of Post-Industrial Society: A Venture in Social Forecasting.* U.S.A.: Basic Books, 1973:1999.

Bell-Rose, Stephanie, and Thomas W. Payzant. "The Case for Entrepreneurship Education." *EducationWeek.* August 11, 2008. http://www.edweek.org (accessed April 6, 2009).

Beniger, James R. "The Control Revolution." In *Technology and the Future*, by A. Teich. New York: St. Martin's Press, 1993.

Benjamin, Matthew, and Christine Harper. "Goldman, JPMorgan Won't Feel Effects of Executive-Salary Caps." *Bloomberg.* February 5, 2009. www.bloomberg.com (accessed April 7, 2009).

BIBLIOGRAPHY

Berger, Peter L., and Thomas Luckmann. *The Social Construction of Reality.* New York: Doubleday, 1966.

Berry, John M. "Fed Not in It to Back a 'Strong Dollar' Policy." *Bloomberg.* http://www.bloomberg.com (accessed April 6, 2009).

Bijker, Wiebe, Thomas P. Hughes, and Trevor Pinch. *The Social Contruction of Technological Systems: New Directions in the Sociology and History of Technology.* Cambridge: The MIT Press, 1997.

Bohrnstedt, George. "Measurement." In *Handbook of Survey Research*, by P. Rossi, J. Wright and A. Anderson. Orlando: Academic Press, Inc., 1983.

Bourdieu, Pierre. *Distinction.* Cambridge: Harvard University Press, 1984.

Boyd, Monica, Ann Mulvihill, and John Myles. "Gender, Power, and Postindustrialization." *Canadian Review of Sociology and Anthropology*, 1991: 407-436.

Bridgeland, John M., John J., Jr. Dilulio, and Karen Burke Morison. *The Silent Epidemic: Perspectives on High School Dropouts.* Washington, D.C.: Civic Enterprises, LLC, 2006.

Brown, David L., and John B. Cromatie. "The Nature of Rurality in Post Industrial Society." 2002.

Burkett, Ingrid. "Beyond the "Information Rich and Poor": Futures Understanding of Inequality in Globalising Informational Economies." *Futures*, 2000: 679-694.

Burns, Scott. "Is America about to go broke?" *MSN.com.* http://articles.moneycentral.msn.com (accessed May 17, 2009).

BusinessWeek. "GOP to Detroit: Drop dead." *MSN Money.* November 17, 2008. http://articles.moneycentral.msn.com (accessed April 2006, 2009).

Callicinos, Alex. *Against Postmodernism.* New York: St. Matin's Press, 1990.

Calmes, Jack. "Obama Asks Bush to Provide Help for Automakers." *The New York Times.* November 11, 2008. http://www.nytimes.com (accessed April 6, 2009).

Caplow, Theodore. *American Social Trends.* U.S.A.: Harcourt Brace Jovanovich, Inc., 1991.

Castells, Manuel. "Toward a Sociology of the Networked Society." *Symposia*, 1995: 693-699.

Castells, Manule. *The Rise of the Networked Society.* Cambridge: Blackwell Publishers, Inc., 1996.

CBS News. "Did Speculation Fuel Oil Price Swings?" *CBS News.* January 11, 2009. http://www.cbsnews.com (accessed April 6, 2009).

Christie, Les. "Boomers: 30% underwater." *CNNMoney.com.* February 26, 2009. http://cnnmoney.printthis.clickability.com (accessed April 7, 2009).

Christoffersen, John. "Protesters visit AIG officials' lavish Conn. homes." *Yahoo! News.* March 21, 2009. http://news.yahoo.com (accessed April 7, 2009).

CNNMoney.com. "World Bank: Economy worst since Depression." *CNNMoney. com.* March 9, 2009. http://cnnmoney.printthis.clickability.com (accessed April 7, 2009).

Cockerham, William C. *Medical Sociology.* Upper Saddle River: Prentice Hall, 1998.

Cockerham, William C., Alfred Rutten, and Thomas Abel. "Conceptualizing Contemporary Health Lifestyles: Moving Beyond Weber." *Sociological Quarterly*, 1997: 321-342.

Cosgrove-Mather, Bootie. "Baby Boomers In Denial Over Aging." *CBC News.* March 5, 2004. http://www.cbsnews.com (accessed April 6, 2009).

Cox, Harold G. "Roles for the Aged Individuals in Post-Industrial Societies." *International Journal of Aging and Human Development*, 1990: 55-62.

Crutsinger, Martin. "Paulson Laments Errors Which Created Crisis." *ABC News.* 2009. http://abcnews.go.com (accessed April 6, 2009).

Cummings, Jeanine. "Obama losing stimulus message war." *Yahoo! News.* February 5, 2009. http://news.yahoo.com (accessed April 7, 2009).

Dahl, Melissa. "Retirement dreams give way to despair, anger." *MSNBC.com.* November 20, 2008. http://msnbc.com (accessed April 6, 2009).

Dahrendorf, Ralf. *Life Chances.* Chicago: University of Chicago Press, 1979.

BIBLIOGRAPHY

De Tocqueville, Alexis. *Democracy in America*. England: Penguin Books, 1835:2003.

Dedman, Bill. "Banks suffer 149 percent rise in bad loans." *MSNBC.com*. March 17, 2009. http://www.msnbc.msn.com (accessed April 7, 2009).

Denzin, Norman K. *Images of Postmodern Society*. London: Sage Publications, 1991.

Descartes, Rene. *Meditations on First Philosophy*. U.S.A.: Hackett Publishing Company, Inc., 1641:1993.

Desmond, Maurna. "Lines Grow at U.S. Unemployment Offices." *Forbes*. November 20, 2008. http://www.forbes.com (accessed April 6, 2009).

—. "States Try, and Fail, To Halt Spike In Foreclosures." *Forbes*. January 15, 2009. http://www.forbes.com (accessed April 6, 2009).

Doggett, Tom. "U.S. government workers in oil industry sex and drug scandal." *Reuters*. September 11, 2008. http://www.reuters.com (accessed April 6, 2009).

Drucker, Peter. *Post-Capitalist Society*. New York: Harper Business, 1993.

Elster, John. *Explaining Technical Change*. Cabridge: Cabridge University Press, 1983.

Featherstone, Mike. *Consumer Culture and Postmodernism*. Newbury Park: Sage Publications, 1991.

Fincham, Robin. "From "Post-Industrialism" to "Information Society": Comment on Lyon." *Sociology*, 1987: 463-466.

Forester, Tom. *The Information Technology Revolution*. Cambridge: The MIT Press, 1985.

Frankel, Boris. *The Post-industrial Utopians*. Cambridge: Polity Press, 1987.

Friedman, Milton. *Capitalism and Freedom*. U.S.A.: The University of Chicago Press, Fortieth Anniversary Edition, 2002.

Friedman, Milton, and Anna Jacobson Schwartz. *The Great Contraction 1929-1933*. Princeton: Princeton University Press, 1963:2008.

Friedman, Thomas L. *The World is Flat*. New York: Picador, 2007.

Gatto, John Taylor. *Dumbing us Down: The Hidden Curriculum of Compulsory Schooling*. Gabriola Island: New Society Publishers, 1992:2008.

Gerth, H.H., and C. Wright Mills. *From Max Weber: Essays in Sociology*. New York: Oxford University Press, 1946.

Gibson, Donald E. "Post-Industrialism: Prosperity or Decline?" *Sociological Focus*, 1992: 147-163.

Giddens, Anthony. *Modernity and Self-Identity*. Cambridge: Polity Press, 1991.

—. *Sociology*. London: Polity Press, 1997.

—. *The Constitution of Society: Outline of the Theory of Structuration*. Cambridge: Polity Press, 1984.

Giddens, Anthony. "The Multinational Corporation as an Interorganizational Network." *Academy of Management Review*, 1990: 603-625.

Gleick, James. *Chaos: Making a New Science*. New York: Penguin, 1988.

Goldman, David. "Stimulus 101: What's in the Bills." *CNNMoney.com*. January 27, 2009. http://finance.yahoo.com (accessed April 6, 2009).

—. "Where AIG's new bailout ranks." *CNNMoney.com*. November 10, 2008. http://cnnmoney.printthis.clickability.com (accessed April 6, 2009).

Gorondi, Pablo. "Oil retreats below $52 as stock markets turn red." *Yahoo! News*. 2009. http://news.yahoo.com (accessed April 6, 2009).

Gorz, Andre. *Farewell to the Working Class*. London: Pluto, 1980.

Gouldner, Alvin. *The Rice of the Intellectuals and the Future of the New Class*. London: Macmillan, 1979.

Griffin, Gary W. *Beyond Post-industrialism: An Examination of Livestyle in the Information Society*. VDM Verlag, 2009.

Griffiths, Peter. "UK G20 protest to demand global economic reforms." *Reuters*. March 25, 2009. http://www.reuters.com (accessed April 7, 2009).

Gringrich, Newt. *To Renew America*. New York: Harper Collins Publishers, Inc., 1995.

Guile, David. "Education and the Economy: Rethinking the Question of Learning for the "Knowledge" Era." *Futures*, 2001: 469-482.

Habermas, Jurgen. *Knowledge and Human Interests.* Boston: Beacon Press, 1971.

—. *Theory and Practice.* Boston: Beacon Press, 1963:1973.

Hannaway, Jane. "Education's Best-kept Secret." *Urban Insitute.* July 13, 2007. http://www.urban.org (accessed April 6, 2009).

Hayashi, M. Yujiro. *The "Civilisation of Culture" and "Culturisation of Civilisation".* NPO Society, 2002.

Hayek, Frederick A. *The Road to Serfdom.* Routledge: The University of Chicago Press, 1944:2007.

Hayek, Friedrich A. "The Intellectuals and Socialism." *Ludwig von Mises Institute.* August 8, 2008. http://mises.org (accessed April 6, 2009).

Hazelrigg, Lawrence E., and Lopreato Joseph. *Class, Conflict, and Mobility: Theories and Studies of Class Structure.* San Francisco: Chandler Publishing Co., 1972.

Heilbroner, Robert L. *An Inquiry into the Human Prospect.* New York: WW Norton, 1980.

—. *The Wordly Philosophers: The Lives, Times, and Ideas of the Great Economic Thinkers.* New York: Touchstone, 1999.

Hobbes, Thomas. *Leviathan.* England: Penguin Books, 1651:1985.

Hume, David. *An Enquire Concerning Human Understanding.* Stilwell: Digireads. com Publishing, 1748:2005.

Independence Hall Association. *The Declaration of Independence.* 2010. http://www.ushistory.org (accessed February 7, 2010).

Jansen, Sue Curry. "Gender and the Information Society." *Journal of Communication*, 1989: 196-215.

John, David C. "Misleading the Public: How the Social Security Trust Fund Really Works." *The Heritage Foundation.* September 2, 2004. http://www.heritage.org (accessed January 3, 2010).

Kahn, Herman. *The Coming Boom*. New York: Touchstone Books, Simon and Schuster, 1982.

Karl, Jonathan, Z. Byron Wolf, Kate Barrett, and Michael S James. "Senate Bails on Auto Bailout: What Next?" *ABC News*. December 12, 2008. http://abcnews.go.com (accessed April 6, 2009).

Karoub, Jeff. "Workers say Obama treate autos worse than Wall Street." *The Associated Press*. March 31, 2009. http://www.ap.com (accessed April 7, 2009).

Karrar-Lewsley, Tahani, and Summer Said. "3rd UPDATE: Arab Gulf Officials Deny Plan To Ditch USD Oil Trade." *The Wall Street Journal*. October 6, 2009. http://online.wsj.com (accessed October 6, 2009).

Kellye, Maryellen R. "New Process Technology, Job Design, and Work Organization." *American Sociological Review*, 1990: 191-209.

Keynes, John Maynard. *The General Theory of Employment, Interest, and Money*. Amherst: Prometheus Books, 1936:1997.

Kirsch, Irwin, Henry Braun, Kentaro Yamamota, and Andrew Sum. *America's Perfect Storm: Three Forces Changing Our Nation's Future*. Pinceton: ETS, 2007.

Kiviat, Barbara. "How to Understand a Trillion-Dollar Deficit." *Time*. January 11, 2009. http://www.time.com (accessed April 6, 2009).

Klein, Rick. "As Obama Seeks Republican Votes, Worry on His Left." *ABC News*. February 3, 2009. http://abcnews.go.com (accessed April 7, 2009).

Knoller, Mark. "Bush Administration Adds $4 Trillion to National Debt." *CBS News*. September 29, 2008. http://www.cbsnews.com (accessed April 6, 2009).

Krisher, Tom. "GM, Chrysler race deadlines to hold off bankruptcy." *Yahoo! News*. April 1, 2009. http://news.yahoo.com (accessed April 6, 2009).

Krugman, Paul. "How Did Economists Get It So Wrong?" *The New York Times*. September 6, 2009. http://www.nytimes.com (accessed September 9, 2009).

Kumar, Krishman. *The Rise of Modern Society*. Oxford: Basil Blackwell, 1988.

Laffer, Arthur B. "Obama Should Forget About Energy Independence." *The Wall Street Journal*. December 17, 2009. http://online.wsj.com (accessed April 7, 2009).

——. "The Age of Prosperity Is Over." *The Wall Street Journal*. October 27, 2008. http://online.wsj.com (accessed April 7, 2009).

Landler, Mark. "New Terrain for Panel Bailout." *The New York Times*. November 4, 2008. http://www.nytimes.com (accessed April 6, 2009).

Lanman, Scott, and Dawn Kopecki. "Fed Commits $800 Billion More to Unfreeze Lending (Update5)." *Bloomberg.com*. November 25, 2008. http://www.bloomberg.com (accessed April 6, 2009).

Lash, Scott, and John Ury. *Economies of Signs and Space*. London: Sage Publications, 1994.

Laslo, Ervin. *The Systems View of the World*. U.S.A.: Hampton Press, Inc., 1996:1999.

Lenski, Gerhard. *Power and Privilege*. New York: McGraw-Hill, 1966.

Locke, John. *Two Treatises of Government*. U.S.A.: Filiquarian Publishing, LLC, 1689:2007.

Logon, John R., and Harvey L. Molotch. *Urban Fortunes: The Poltical Economy of Place*. Berkeley and Los Angeles: University of California Press, 1987.

Lorenz, Edward. *The Essence of Chaos*. U.S.A.: The University of Washington Press, 1996.

Louv, Richard. "For aging boomers, denial is destiny." *SignOnSanDiego.com*. June 13, 2006. http://signonsandiego.printthis.clickability.com (accessed April 6, 2009).

Luhmann, Niklas. *Social Systems*. U.S.A.: Stanford University Press, 1995.

Lyon, David. "From 'Post-Industrialism' to 'Information Society': A New Social Transformation." *Sociology*, 1986: 577-588.

——. *The Information Society*. New York: Basil Blackwell, Inc., 1988.

Machiavelli, Niccolo. *The Prince*. New York: Bantam Dell, 1513:2003.

Machulp, Fritz. *The Production and Distribution of Knowledge in the United States*. Princeton: Princeton University Press, 1972.

Makridakis, Spyros. "The Forthcoming Information Revolution." *Futures*, 1995: 799-821.

Mantell, Ruth. "U.S. PPI rises for second straight month; energy gains." *Market-Watch*. March 17, 2009. http://www.marketwatch.com (accessed April 7, 2009).

Markman, Jon. "It's a great time to be afraid." *MSN*. October 8, 2008. http://www.articles.moneycentral.msn.com (accessed April 6, 2009).

—. "It's solar power's time to shine." *MSN*. June 5, 2008. http://articles.moneycentral.msn.com (accessed April 6, 2009).

—. "Too late to avoid a depression?" *MSN Money*. February 5, 2009. http://articles.moneycentral.msn.com (accessed April 7, 2009).

Martin, William. *The Global Information Society*. England: Aslib Grower, 1995.

Marx, Karl. *Capital: A Critique of Political Economy*. U.S.A.: Random House, 1867:1906.

Marx, Karl, and Friedrich Engels. *The Communist Manifesto*. England: Penguin Classics, 1848:2002.

Mason, Joseph R. *The Economic Contribution of Increased Offshore Oil Exploration and Production to Regional and National Economies*. Washington: American Energy Alliance, 2009.

Masuda, Yoneji. *The Information Society as Post-Industrial Society*. Bethesda: World Future Society, 1980.

McDermott, John. "Technology: The Opiate of the Intellectuals." In *Technology and the Future*, by A. Teich. New York: St. Martin's Press, 1969:1993.

McDonald, Joe. "China 'worried' about US Treasury holdings." *Yahoo! News*. March 13, 2009. http://news.yahoo.com (accessed April 7, 2009).

McElvaine, Robert S. "Great Depression in the United States." *MSN Encarta*. http://encarta.msn.com (accessed April 6, 2009).

Mesthene, Emmanuel G. "The Role of Technology in Society." In *Technology and the Future*, by A. Teich. Newbury Park: Sage Publications, 1969:1993.

BIBLIOGRAPHY

Microsoft Encart Online Encyclopedia. "Microeconomics." *MSN Encarta.* 2008. http://encarta.msn.com (accessed April 6, 2009).

Microsoft Encarta Online Encyclopedia. "Macroeconomics." *MSN Encarta.* 2008. http://encart.msn.com (accessed April 6, 2009).

—. "Poverty." *MSN Encarta.* 2008. http://encart.msn.com (accessed April 6, 2009).

Mike, F-W. "Postindustrialism." *Education Otherwise Magazine.*

Mill, John Stuart. *The Principles of Political Economy.* New York: Promethus Books, 1848:2004.

Mills, C. Wright. *The Power Elite.* New York: Oxford University Press, 1956:2000.

Mises, Ludwig von. *Nation, State, and Economy: Contributions to the Politics and History of our Time.* U.S.A.: Liberty Fund, Inc., 1983.

Mitchell, Daniel J. "Mislead." *Cato Insititute.* October 1, 2008. http://www.cato.org (accessed April 6, 2009).

Morin, Richard. *America's Four Middle Classes.* Washington: Pew Research Center, 2008.

Moscrip, Lara. "Jobless claims spike to 26-year high." *CNNMoney.com.* February 26, 2009. http://cnnmoney.printthis.clickability.com (accessed April 7, 2009).

MSNBC.com . "It's official: U.S. is in a recession." *MSNBC.com.* December 1, 2008. http://www.msnbc.msn.com (accessed 1 3, 2010).

MSNBC.com. "Boomers face stark choices in bleak economy." *MSNBC.com.* April 2, 2009. http://www.msnbc.msn.com (accessed April 7, 2009).

MSNBC.com News Services. "Obama warns economy likely to get worse." *MSNBC.com.* November 24, 2008. http://www.msnbc.msn.com (accessed April 6, 2009).

—. "Obama, Brown predict G-20 deal for recession." *MSNBC.com.* April 1, 2009. http://www.msnbc.msn.com (accessed April 7, 2009).

—. "Obama: G-20 summit a 'turning point'." *MSNBC.com.* April 2, 2009. http://www.msnbc.msn.com (accessed April 7, 2009).

Mutikani, Lucia. "U.S. workers on jobless benefits hit record high." *Yahoo! News.* March 19, 2009. http://news.yahoo.com (accessed April 7, 2009).

Nam, Charles B., and Mary G. Powers. "Variations in Socioeconomic Structure by Race, Residence, and the Life Cycle." *American Sociological Review,* 1965: 97-103.

Nelson, Joel I. *Post-Industrial Capitalism: Exploring Economic Inequality in America.* Thousand Oaks: Sage Publications, 1995.

Nelson, Joel I., and David Cooperman. "Out of Utopia: The Paradox of Postindustrialization." *The Sociological Quarterly,* 1998: 583-596.

Neuger, James G., and Simon Kennedy. "American Gangster's Wad of Euros Signals U.S. Decline (Update1)." *Bloomberg.com.* http://www.bloomberg.com (accessed April 6, 2009).

Nora, Simon, and Alain Minc. *The Computerization of Society: A Report to the President of France.* Cambridge: The MIT Press, 1980.

Nutting, Rex. "Private sector cuts 742,000 jobs in March ADP says." *The Wall Street Journal.* April 1, 2009. http://www.marketwatch.com (accessed April 7, 2009).

Obama, Barack. *The Audacity of Hope.* U.S.A.: Three Rivers Press, 2006.

Parillo, Vincent N., John Stimson, and Ardyth Stimson. *Contemporary Social Problems.* Needham Heights: Allyn & Bacon, 1996.

Partnership for 21st Century Skills. *Framework for 21st Century Learning.* Tucson: Partnership for 21st Century Skills, 2007.

Partnership for 21st Century Skills. *Statement of Principles: 21st Century Skills and the Reauthorization of NCLB/ESEA.* Tucson: Partnership for 21st Century Skills, 2007.

Paul, Ron. "Commentary: GOP should ask why U.S. is on the wrong track." *CNN.com.* 2008. http://cnn.site.printthis.clickability.com (accessed April 6, 2009).

—. *The Revolution: A Manifesto.* U.S.A.: Grand Central Publishing, 2008.

BIBLIOGRAPHY

Pepitone, Julianne, Larissa Padden, and Lara Moscrip. "Why Can't We Split the Money Among Taxpayers." *CNNMoney.com*. February 3, 2009. http://finance.yahoo.com (accessed April 7, 2009).

Pitt, David. "Economy dampens hope of a comfortable retirement." *Yahoo! News*. http://news.yahoo.com (accessed April 14, 2009).

Plato, and G.M.A. translated by Grube. *Republic*. U.S.A.: Hackett Publishing Compan, Inc., 1992.

Porat, Marc U., and M. Rubin. *The Information Economy: Definition and Measurement*. Washington: U.S. Department of Commerce, 1977.

Rabinbach, Anson. *The End of the Utopias fo Labor*. Princeton: Princeton University Press, 2003.

Read, Madlen. "Investors Give $700B Rescue Plan Cool Reception." *ABC News*. 2009. http://abcnews.go.com (accessed April 6, 2009).

Reuters. "Estimated U.S. Taxpayer Cost for Bailout Jumps." *FoxBusiness.com*. April 6, 2009. http://www.foxbusiness.com (accessed April 6, 2009).

Reynolds, Alan. "The Hoover Analogy Flunks." *Cato Institute*. September 29, 2008. http://www.cato.org (accessed April 6, 2009).

Ricardo, David. *The Principles of Poltical Economy and Taxation*. Mineola: Dover Publications, Inc., 1817:2004.

Riedl, Brian M. "$700 billion bailout? You ain't seen nothin'." *The Heritage Foundation*. September 29, 2008. http://author.heritage.org (accessed April 6, 2009).

Rothschild, Joan. "A Feminist Perspective on Technology and the Future." *Women's Studies International Quarterly*, 1981: 65-74.

Rousseau, Jean-Jacques. *The Social Contract*. U.S.A: BN Publishing, 1762:2007.

Sabar, Ariel. "Economy is top priority for Obama, McCain, and voters." *The Christian Science Monitor*. June 10, 2008. http://www.csmonitor.com (accessed April 6, 2009).

Sainz, Adam. "Foreclosure Rates up 25 Percent Year-Over-Year." *ABC News*. 2009. http://abcnews.go.com (accessed April 6, 2009).

Sawa, Takamitsu. "Technology Key in Postindustrial Society." *The Japan Times*. 1996.

Scherer, Ron. "The job market's big slump." *The Christian Science Monitor*. June 09, 2008. http://www.csmonitor.com (accessed April 6, 2009).

Schoen, John W. "Deflation poses new economic threat." *MSNBC.com*. November 21, 2008. http://www.msnbc.msn.com (accessed April 6, 2009).

—. "Downturn squeezes state budgets." *MSNBC.com*. October 30, 2008. http://www.msnbc.msn.com (accessed April 6, 2009).

—. "Is this another Great Depression?" *MSNBC.com*. January 22, 2009. http://www.msnbc.msn.com (accessed April 6, 2009).

Schumpeter, Joseph A. *Capitalism, Socialism, and Democracy*. New York: Harper Perennial, 1942:1976.

Silver-Greenberg, Jessica. "Next meltdown: Credit-card debt." *The Economic Times*. October 14, 2008. http://economictimes.indiatimes.com (accessed April 6, 2009).

Smart, Barry. *Modern Conditions: Postmodern Controversies*. London: Routledge, 1992.

—. *Postmodernity*. London: Routledge, 1993.

Smith, Adam. *The Wealth of Nations*. New York: Random House, Inc., 1776:2003.

Sowell, Thomas. *Applied Economics: Thinking Beyond Stage One*. New York: Basic Books, 2004.

Sporer, Zeljka. *Controversies of Globalisation*. University of South Australia, 2001.

Squires, Gregory D. *Capital and Communities in Black and White*. U.S.A.: State University of New York Press, Albany, 1994.

Starr, Paul. *Freedom's Power: The History and Promise of Liberalism*. U.S.A.: Basic Books, 2007.

Stiglitz, Joseph E. *Globalization and Its Discontents*. New York: WW Norton and Company, 2002.

Swint, Brian, and Fergal O'Brien. "EU Sees Euro Area in Deepest Slump in 10-Year History (Update3)." *Bloomberg*. January 19, 2009. http://www.bloomberg.com (accessed April 6, 2009).

Tahmincioglu, Eve. "Gen Xers get with double whammy." *MSNBC.com*. March 11, 2009. http://www.msnbc.msn.com (accessed April 7, 2009).

Teich, Albert H. *Technology and the Future*. New York: St. Martin's Press, 1993.

The Associate Press. "Bush signs bill providing extra jobless benefits." *MSNBC.com*. November 21, 2008. http://msnbc.com (accessed April 6, 2009).

——. "Fed chief: U.S. suffering ' severe contraction'." *MSNBC.com*. February 24, 2009. http://www.msnbc.msn.com (accessed April 7, 2009).

——. "Geithner, Bernanke seek broad new powers." *MSNBC.com*. March 24, 2009. http://www.msnbc.msn.com (accessed April 7, 2009).

——. "Government plans bold financial rescue." *MSNBC.com*. September 19, 2008. http://www.msnbc.msn.com (accessed April 6, 2009).

The Associated Press. "American debt nightmare ends easy credit era." *MSNBC.com*. 2008. http://www.msnbc.msn.com (accessed April 6, 2009).

——. "Bailout shifts again; floodgates could open." *MSNBC.com*. December 19, 2008. http://www.msnbc.msn.com (accessed April 6, 2009).

——. "Dismal December sales add to retailer woes." *MSNBC.com*. January 8, 2009. http://www.msnbc.msn.com (accessed April 6, 2009).

——. "Jobless rate jumps 7.2 percent in Dec." *MSNBC.com*. January 9, 2009. http://www.msnbc.msn.com (accessed April 6, 2009).

——. "Jobless rate soars to 8.5 percent in March." *MSNBC.com*. April 3, 2009. http://www.msnbc.msn.com (accessed April 7, 2009).

——. "Obama, Dems look to revamp bailout." *MSNBC.com*. January 9, 2009. http://www.msnbc.msn.com (accessed April 6, 2009).

——. "Report predicts U.S. decline, Russa rise." *MSNBC.com*. November 21, 2008. http://www.msnbc.msn.com (accessed April 6, 2009).

——. "Treasury unveils plan to buy troubled assets." *MSNBC.com*. March 23, 2009. http://www.msnbc.msn.com (accessed April 7, 2009).

——. "U.S. moves to thaw credit for consumers." *MSNBC.com*. November 25, 2008. http://www.msnbc.msn.com (accessed April 6, 2009).

—. "With Obama, many say bye-bye to boomers." *MSNBC.com*. January 11, 2009. http://www.msnbc.msn.com (accessed April 6, 2009).

The International Bank for Reconciliation. *Beyond Economic Growth: Meeting the Challenges of Global Development*. Washington, 2000.

Thrush, Glenn, and Patrick O'Conner. "At Dem retreat, a partisan love fest." *Yahoo! News*. February 5, 2009. http://news.yahoo.com (accessed April 7, 2009).

Time, Inc. *25 People to Blame for the Financial Crisis*. 2010. http://www.time.com (accessed February 21, 2010).

Touraine, Alan. *The Post Industrial Society*. London: Wildwood House, 1969.

Trippi, Joe. *The Revolution will not be Televised: Democracy, the Internet, and the Overthrow of Everything*. New York: Harper Collins Publishers, Inc., 2004.

TSC Staff. "Citigroup to Slash 10,000 Jobs: Report(Update)." *TheStreet.com*. November 14, 2008. http://www.thestreet.com (accessed April 6, 2009).

Turner, Bryan S. *Status*. London: Open University Press, 1988.

U.S. Bureau of Labor Statistics. *Labor Force Statistics from the Current Population Survey*. January 3, 2010. http://data.bls.gov (accessed January 3, 2010).

U.S. Department of Commerce. *A Nation Online: How Americans are Expanding Their Use of the Internet*. Washington: U.S. Department of Commerce, 2002.

U.S. Department of Commerce. *Falling Through the Net: Defining the Digital Divide*. Washington: U.S. Department of Commerce, 1999.

U.S. Department of Commerce. *Falling Through the Net: Toward Digital Inclusion*. Washington: U.S. Department of Commerce, 2000.

USA Today. "U.S. budget deficit hits record $438 billion for year." *USATODAY.com*. http://usatoday.printthis.clickability.com (accessed April 6, 2009).

Vaughn, Martin. "President Takes Aim at Foreign Profits." *The Wall Street Journal*. February 26, 2009. http://online.wsj.com (accessed April 7, 2009).

Volti, Rudi. *Society and Technological Change*. New York: St. Martin's Press, Inc., 1992.

BIBLIOGRAPHY

Waters, Malcolm. *Daniel Bell.* London: Routledge, 1996.

——. *Modern Sociological Theory.* London: Sage Publications, 1994.

Weber, Max. *The Protestant Ethic and the Sprit of Capitalism.* London and New York: Routledge Classics, 1930:2006.

Webster, Frank. *Theories of the Information Society.* London: Routledge, 1995.

Webster, Frank. "What Information Society." *The Information Society,* 1994: 1-23.

Weir, Keith. "Pressure on G7 after muted response to rate cuts." *Reuters.* October 9, 2008. http://www.reuters.com (accessed April 6, 2009).

Wheatley, Margaret J. *Leadership and the New Science: Learning About Organization from an Orderly Universe.* San Francisco: Berritt-Koehler Publisher, 1992.

White, Aoife. "EU presidency: US stimulus is 'the road to hell'." *Comcast.net.* March 25, 2009. http://www.comcast.net (accessed April 7, 2009).

Whoriskey, Peter, and Amit R. Paley. "Treasury Hires Lead Contractor for Rescue." *The Washington Post.* October 15, 2008. http://www.washingtonpost.com (accessed April 6, 2009).

Wiggin, Addison. *The Demise of the Dollar...* Holboken: John Wiley & Sons, Inc., 2005.

Wright, Erik Olin, and Bill Martin. "The Transformation of Amreican Class Structure 1960-1980." *American Journal of Sociology,* 1987: 1-29.

Wrong, Dennis. "The Influence of Sociological Ideas on American Culture." In *Sociology in America,* by Herbert J. Gans, 19-20. Newbury Park: Sage Publications, 1990.

Wutkowski, Karey. "Treasury may capitalize banks by end October: source." *Reuters.* October 8, 2008. http://www.reuters.com (accessed April 6, 2009).

——. "Treasury to unveil bank resue bid soon." *Yahoo! News.* March 21, 2009. http://news.yahoo.com (accessed April 7, 2009).

INDEX

Note: This index does not include names or titles appearing in the Notes.